Signage
and
Wayfinding
Design

Signage and Wayfinding Design

A Complete Guide to Creating Environmental Graphic Design Systems

Chris Calori

Foreword by Ivan Chermayeff

John Wiley & Sons, Inc.

Published by John Wiley & Sons, Inc., Hoboken, New Jersey
Published simultaneously in Canada

For general information about our other products and services, please contact our Customer Care Department within the United States at (800) 762-2974, outside the United States at (317) 572-3993 or fax (317) 572-4002.

Wiley also publishes its books in a variety of electronic formats. Some content that appears in print may not be available in electronic books. For more information about Wiley products, visit our web site at www.wiley.com.

Library of Congress Cataloging-in-Publication Data:
Calori, Chris.
    Signage and wayfinding design / by Chris Calori.
        p.   cm.
    Includes bibliographical references and index.
    ISBN: 978-0-471-74891-5 (cloth)
    1. Computer graphics. 2. Communication in design. 3. Graphic arts. I. Title.
    T385.C351 2007
    729—dc22

                                                            2006022536

Printed in the United States of America

10 9 8 7 6 5 4 3 2

To Dave Vanden-Eynden

Contents

4

5

6

Foreword

Regarding wayfinding, it might be noted that after you get there, in an ideal world, there would be very little that needs to be told about where to go, because on arriving at an unfamiliar destination the next directions would be self-evident. Within the best architecture, finding one's way around should hopefully require a relatively minimal effort and, at least, little signage.

If some sign is needed at all, it should be one of confirmation, to make a visitor comfortable with the path taken. It is far better to say too little than too much. To quote Mies: "Less is more."

Signage either adds some degree of quality to the environment in which it finds itself or it takes something away, diminishing the experience by being distracting to a visitor. If a message is there and is unnecessary, that's a serious distraction that should be avoided.

If a message is too big or too visually loud, if it overwhelms and negates other things such as the feeling of architectural materials, the play of light, reflections, the texture of surfaces, transparency, distant views, and a myriad of other environmental elements, including the presence and contribution of art or even the presence of other people, then the message is not quite right.

Too small a message or a direction misplaced by being too low or too high when its meaning must be instantly grasped and acted upon, doesn't help those who are insecure or hesitant and in need of help.

The best signage is in the right place at the right time, considers the viewer, and is neither overly repetitive nor demanding.

In fact, the best signage seems to take on an air of invisibility. It's there, but is taken in and taken for granted.

Of course, the opportunity exists for signage to add considerably to the excellence of any built environment, adding, by careful attention to details, color, compatible materials, and most importantly good typography that is easy to read and has character, often to reinforce the style and standards of the place, institution, or company which stands behind it.

Chermayeff & Geismar's iconic placemaking sign that has engaged and delighted millions of people passing by 9 West 57th Street in New York City since 1972, and will continue to do so for years to come.

The meticulous specification of all the elements going into the making of signage to meet the reality of each situation, to stay in balance, finding the best point between the most basic adequacy at one extreme and the performance of refined and sophisticated excellence in design terms at the other end of the spectrum, is what Calori & Vanden-Eynden consistently deliver time and time again.

Ivan Chermayeff
Chermayeff & Geismar

 # Acknowledgments

Many thanks to all the wonderful people who contributed their encouragement and support to the writing of this book. It wouldn't have happened without them, and I truly appreciate their contributions. My gratitude goes out to:

David Vanden-Eynden, who shares my passion for life, love, and design—for keeping his cool, his sense of humor, his distance, and for keeping the office running when my pursuit of this book sucked up my time and attention like a black hole.

All the employees of Calori & Vanden-Eynden (C&VE)—current and former—who have shared our dedication to design excellence and have contributed their prodigious skills and talents to each and every one of our projects.

All of C&VE's clients over the years, who have believed in us and provided us with so many wonderful opportunities to create innovative design solutions for them.

Ivan Chermayeff—who, along with Tom Geismar, taught me so much about design during my employ with them—for so generously writing the foreword to this book.

My professors at The Ohio State University's Department of Industrial, Interior, and Visual Communication Design, who instilled me with a systematic, methodological approach to design during my undergraduate studies, and then helped me lay the groundwork for this book in my graduate studies.

Clark Conkling, voluntary manuscript reviewer and copy editor, who provided insightful comments from a layperson's perspective.

Barbara Spiller, whose unending interest and enthusiasm kept me going.

My dearly departed mother, father, and grandparents. I will never forget your faith in me. Special thanks to my grandfather Kinsey.

My great aunt Virginia Anderson (85 years young!), salt of the earth, and my brother, Kevin Calori, for their interest and encouragement.

Ann Makowski, Director of Membership & Communications at the Society for Environmental Graphic Design (SEGD) and Managing Editor of *SEGDdesign* magazine, who has to be the world's most helpful and efficient person.

Hakmee Kim, design intern from the Fashion Institute of Technology, where I used to teach, who applied her considerable talents and energy to developing this book's illustrations and page layout guidelines.

C&VE office managers Pam Nugent and Chloe Aftel, who lent their enthusiasm and organizational skills to a seemingly insurmountable task.

Research intern Michelle Ellis, who applied her energy to organization and outreach to this book's contributors.

Margaret Cummins and Leslie Anglin, my indefatigable editors at Wiley, who helped me wrestle this book into shape, along with all the members of the Wiley support team assigned to this book. Special thanks to Diane McNulty at Wiley.

Olga Da Silva, the clean machine, who has been with us from almost the start, for her encouragement.

Our esteemed colleagues in the EGD field, who so generously shared images of their work to help illustrate and enrich this book:

AGS
Ashworth Environmental Design
Beauchamp Group
Beck & Graboski Design Office
Biesek Design
C&G Partners, LLC
Chermayeff & Geismar Studio LLC
Cloud Gehshan Associates
Gamble Design LLC
Tom Graboski & Associates, Inc. Design
Huie Design, Inc.
Jack Hulme Design Consultants, LLC
Hunt Design Associates
Infinite Scale Design Group
Joel Katz Design Associates
Kate Keating Associates, Inc.
Kolar Design, Inc.
Kuhlmann Leavitt, Inc.
Lebowitz|Gould|Design, Inc.
Lorenc + Yoo Design
Mayer/Reed
The Office of Michael Manwaring
Carol Naughton + Associates, Inc.
Debra Nichols Design
Poulin + Morris
Roll, Barresi & Associates, Inc.
Selbert Perkins Design Collaborative

Sussman/Prejza & Company, Inc.
Thinking Caps
Tracy Turner Design Inc.
WPA, Inc.
Whitehouse & Company
Lance Wyman Ltd.

Our esteemed design colleagues and other professionals who have so generously contributed their written perspectives to augment the content of this book in furtherance of the EGD knowledge base:

Mark Andreasson
Craig Berger
Ken Ethridge
Phil Garvey
Wayne Hunt
Nadav Malin
Don Meeker
Bob Trescott

All of you have helped make this happen, and I thank all of you from the bottom of my heart.

 **Introduction**

Conversation with a New York City cabbie:

Cabbie: "Whaddaya do?"

Reply: "I'm a designer."

Cabbie: "Oh yeah, designer. So you're in fashion design, right?"

Reply: "No. I design signs."

Cabbie: "Whaddaya mean, you design signs?"

Reply: "I design signs. I mean, when you have to drive fares to LaGuardia, how do you know where to drop them off?"

Cabbie: "I follow the signs. Wait, you mean someone designs those things? Never woulda figured that someone designed signs."

Reply: "Well, God didn't put them here."

Cabbie: "People really do that, huh? I mean, design signs?"

Reply: "Yep."

Environmental graphic design, or EGD, being a relatively new hybrid of the design field, is relatively long on practice but short on theory and formalized methodology. This is natural, given that most of us practitioners have forged ahead on the fly, learning by doing, especially since no programs granting an EGD degree currently exist in the United States.

This book aims to fill this knowledge gap by putting forth what I believe is the first formal methodology for solving signage and wayfinding problems: the Signage Pyramid model. The book also discusses the design process in some detail, and it has a broad scope of other information— including the insights of distinguished EGD professionals on selected topics—that I hope will be valuable to anyone involved in EG design.

The world of EGD has become so large, so established, and so knowledgeable that I've left many things out of this book. Some of these omissions are intentional and others are not, so I encourage readers to make their own leaps and apply what's in here to their own projects, keeping in mind that every project is different. You, the readers who were kind or curious enough to purchase this book, are part of the picture, so I invite you to get engaged and get what you can out of this book.

This book is here for gleaning, for discussing, for advancing our field and improving it—for clients, sign fabricators, and ourselves as designers. I hope to inspire more people to enter our field—either as practitioners or as partners—and to promote a greater understanding of what we do and how it touches and improves everyone's lives.

The dialogue will continue, we will all progress—and we will come to realize that signs cannot only offer incredible charm and sensory delight, but also become a beacon of reassurance and safety when we are lost.

A blend of graphic design, architecture, industrial design, and the other design professions, EGD, with its unique set of skills, helps us read the world. You are what you see. And, yes, *people* design signage.

Signage
and
Wayfinding
Design

1 **What Is Environmental Graphic Design?**

What a long, strange trip it's been.
—*The Grateful Dead*

Long before paper was invented, humans made marks on objects, such as cave walls, in their surrounding environment. The intent of making these marks, or signs, was to communicate information visually. Because of their communication intent, these marks were imbued with meaning and became a shared language among the people who made and understood them. As such, environmental graphic design, or EGD, which can be defined as the graphic communication of information in the built environment, is one of the world's oldest professions.

And you thought something else was.

Since the invention of paper and the electronic television or computer screen, most people think of graphic communication as taking place primarily in those two media. But just like those cave people making their meaningful marks on environmental objects, in the present era an enormous amount of information is communicated on signs and other objects located in the built environment.

The contemporary incarnation of EGD is a relatively new, cross-disciplinary field that has gained recognition and importance over the past 30 years. Sure, signs existed prior to that point, but they tended to pop up in an ad

1.1

1.2

hoc, unplanned, almost reactionary manner—in other words, pretty much as an afterthought. As cities grew and mobility increased, making the built environment more complex, people's need for information to better understand, navigate, and use their surroundings also grew. Thus, the need for proactive, systematically planned, visually unified signage and wayfinding programs emerged.

If you don't think EGD is important, ask yourself: Could you understand how to use a large international airport or an urban rail transit system if there were no signs at all, or if the signs were a disparate mishmash of messages, graphics, and physical forms? The answer is most definitely no! As such, contemporary signage and wayfinding programs give a singular, unified voice to an environment or a site within it.

To underscore the relative youth of EGD as a field, consider that the terms *environmental graphics*, *signage*, and *wayfinding* were barely in use 30 years ago. In fact, the word *signage*, whose origins are attributed to Canadian designer Paul Arthur, didn't even appear in U.S. dictionaries until the 1980s. Nevertheless, in the 1970s, a group of designers found themselves designing graphics for a coordinated group of signs rather than for print. And because they often worked in architectural offices, and their design work related to architectural spaces, what they were doing was often referred to as *architectural graphics* or *architectural signing*.

These architectural graphic designers realized that there were significant differences between their design and print design—most notably that architectural graphics encompassed the planning and communication of information on three-dimensional (3D) objects in the built environment, which is far more complex than designing a two-dimensional printed piece,

1.1 Before the dawn of civilization, environmental graphics communicated information.

1.2 Environmental graphics from ancient Rome.

1.3 Ad hoc signage in Greece.

1.4 Unplanned signage in a public building's elevator lobby.

1.3

1.4

The Society for Environmental Graphic Design

SEGD is an international nonprofit educational organization providing resources for design specialists in the field of environmental graphic design; architecture; and landscape, interior, and industrial design. SEGD members are leading designers of directional and attraction sign systems, destination graphics, identity programs, exhibits, and themed environments.

Society for Environmental Graphic Design, 1000 Vermont Ave., Suite 400, Washington, DC 20005, 202.638.5555, www.segd.org

such as a poster, book, or brochure. As these architectural graphic designers discovered each other and the commonalties of their professional interests, they joined together to form the Society of Environmental Graphic Designers, now the Society for Environmental Graphic Design (SEGD).

With the birth of the SEGD, the term *environmental graphics* replaced *architectural graphics,* for two reasons. First, *architectural* was viewed as too limiting, in that this form of graphic design is often geared toward nonarchitectural open spaces, such as roadways, cities, theme parks, and so on—that is, the larger sphere of the built environment. Second, the term *architectural graphics* could be confused with the drawings architects create to document their building designs.

The SEGD has since grown to become the premier professional organization for all designers who practice EGD. And *signage* is now in the dictionary.

The Spectrum of EGD Activity

We've established that contemporary EGD activity involves the development of a systematic, informational-cohesive, and visually unified graphic communication system for a given site within the built environment. Such sites can range from a single building to a complex of buildings to a city or to a transportation network connecting multiple sites on a regional or national scope—all of which have complex communication needs. EGD can respond to those environmental communication needs in three distinct but often overlapping arenas. These have been identified by one of my colleagues, Wayne Hunt, as:

- *Signage and wayfinding*, which orients people to a site and helps them navigate it.

- *Interpretation*, which tells a story about a site.

- *Placemaking*, which creates a distinctive image for a site.

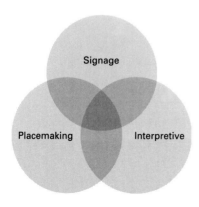

1.5 The three components of EGD and how they can overlap.

Although this book focuses on signage and wayfinding design, these three communication facets of EGD and their interaction warrant a bit more exploration.

Signage and Wayfinding

Signage and wayfinding are most commonly expressed in unified sign programs that informationally and visually knit together a site. Examples of signage and wayfinding programs are in the color plates and in Figures 1.7 through 1.9, as well as throughout other chapters in this book. In the sense that well-designed sign programs serve to visually unify a site, signage can perform a placemaking role by creating a unique identity and sense of place, thereby effectively creating a brand image in environmental form. In addition to wayfinding and placemaking roles, signage programs can also communicate other kinds of information, such as warning, operational, and interpretive information, as examined further in Chapter 4, "The Information Content System."

Although the terms *signage* and *wayfinding* are often used interchangeably, it's very important to keep in mind this important distinction: Typically, the primary objective of a signage program is to help people find their way through an environment, whereas effective wayfinding solutions often require more than signage alone. Clear, well-defined pathways and other visual cues, such as prominent landmarks, all aid wayfinding, as do printed maps, human guides, and, more recently, portable GPS systems.

A key objective in wayfinding is to enable each person to form a mental map of a site or environment, so the clearer the physical layout of a site, the clearer those mental maps will be. In other words, even the most carefully conceived sign program can't solve all the problems of navigating

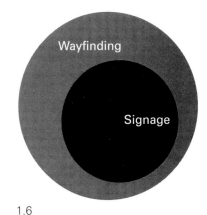

1.6

1.6 Signage plays an important role within the broader realm of wayfinding cues.

1.7 Directional and identification signage at Philadelphia's bustling main train station.

1.7

1.8

1.9

1.8 An identification sign in a series developed for this greater Philadelphia township.

1.9 A directional sign with an interpretive panel on the right at the Illinois Institute of Technology (IIT) campus in Chicago.

a site that contains confusing, circuitous pathways. In such cases, the sign program is like using a Band-Aid to patch together a rather large wound: It's some help, but not a panacea. Think about it: How many times have you blamed the signs when you're having difficulty navigating a complicated highway interchange? In many such cases, the signs themselves aren't the problem; they can only do so much to guide you through what *is* the underlying problem: a badly laid-out interchange.

Wayfinding is an active process, requiring mental engagement and attention to the environment one is trying to navigate. That is why the navigator is just as important as the driver in a sports car rally. The fact is, however, that many people are better at understanding information given to them verbally and so would rather ask someone how to go from point A to point B than to follow the signs or read a map. Signage and other visual wayfinding cues can, however, help even these people navigate their environment when there's no one around to ask.

Interpretative

Interpretative information tells a story about the meaning of a concept or theme (e.g., democracy or science), an object (e.g., the Constitution or an aircraft), a site (e.g., an automobile manufacturing plant or a national park), an event (e.g., Gettysburg or the Jamestown flood), a historical figure (e.g., Franklin Delano Roosevelt or Martin Luther King), a corporation and its products, and so on. Interpretive information is most often expressed in the form of *exhibitry*, which can be composed of a site itself, physical artifacts, audiovisual (A/V) and interactive media, static images and

1.10

1.11

graphics, casework, and more. Interpretive exhibits can be temporary or permanent or exterior or interior. Exhibits can serve a placemaking role in that they often become destinations unto themselves. Interpretive information intersects with signage, in that interpretive information in the form of text and images can also be displayed in signage programs.

1.10 Interpretive information is often communicated in exhibits, such as this exhibit on collegiate sports at Brigham Young University (BYU) Legacy Hall in Provo, Utah.

1.11 Interpretive signage help define the historic Civil War site, Fort Negley, in Nashville, Tennessee.

1.12 Interpretive and orientation panels on a kiosk unit in Bellingham, Washington.

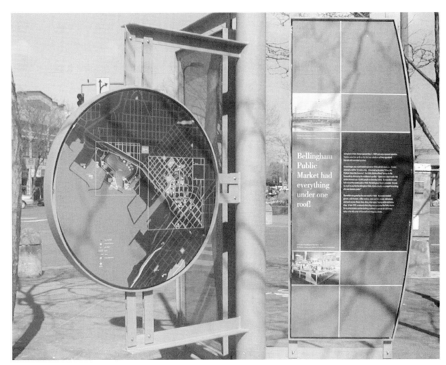

1.12

1.13

1.14

1.13 Placemaking at the entrance to Williams Gateway Airport in Mesa, Arizona, with sculptural flight elements.

1.14 Banners are effective thematic placemaking elements at the Port of Los Angeles.

1.15 A kiosk provides orientation and interpretive information at the same time it creates a sense of place for New York City's Chinatown district.

Placemaking

Placemaking creates a distinctive image for a site, and can be expressed in several ways. As already discussed, signage and interpretive exhibits can create a sense of place, as can gateways, portals, gathering points, and landmarks. What separates placemaking, in the EGD sense, from other forms of placemaking is the explicit communication of information.

1.15

Without this explicit communication intent, placemaking becomes an exercise of architecture, interior design, sculpture, and so on. This is not to discount that EG designers may team with any of those disciplines in order to create placemaking objects, which are often monumental—typically in scale, but sometimes also in quantity.

New York's Grand Central Terminal or an exquisitely designed restaurant interior may convey a wonderful sense of place but they are not placemaking in the EGD sense, because their inherent purpose is not to communicate information. Times Square, on the other hand, derives its entire sense of place from the sheer concentration of signage surrounding it. And because the intent of all that signage is to communicate, Times Square does represent placemaking in an EGD sense.

The Importance of EGD Today

As explained, the difference between EGD and other types of design is the explicit purpose of EGD to communicate meaningful information via words, symbols, diagrams, and images. Because of this express communication function, EGD plays a key—and increasingly recognized— role in how people use and experience the built environment.

Furthermore, the signage and wayfinding aspect of EGD is being recognized more often as a key contributor to a sense of well-being, safety, and security in unfamiliar and often high-stress environments, such as airports, hospitals, and cities. Additionally, EGD is gaining importance for its capability to create a sense of place for a given site and for its power to reinforce a brand image.

Once considered a necessary evil—or worse, an afterthought—a growing number of people in the design, construction, development, and policy arenas have gained an appreciation of signage and EGD's role in humanizing and demystifying the complexities of the built environment. They have found that well-designed signage and environmental graphic programs not only fulfill their communication function of informing, directing, and identifying but also serve to enhance the aesthetic and psychological qualities of an environment.

Certainly, EG designers are often part of the consultant team assembled by architects for a building design or renovation project, but signage and EG design has finally come into its own, as well. Cities and universities are engaging EG designers, sans architects, to create signage and other EG design programs. Real estate managers are engaging EG designers, sans architects, to spruce up the image of a building or facility. Even general contractors and construction managers are including signage as a line item in their procurement budgets. All this has happened, in part, because people have recognized that signage and EG design have a unique branding power.

1.16a

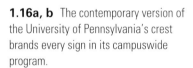

1.16b

1.17

1.18

1.16a, b The contemporary version of the University of Pennsylvania's crest brands every sign in its campuswide program.

1.17 Freedom Trail signage harmonizes with Boston's historical sites.

1.18 Signage at the Jacob Javits Federal Building in Lower Manhattan integrates and harmonizes with contemporary architectural details.

1.19   1.20

Signage and EGD on the Brand Bandwagon

Signage and EGD programs have the power to build brand images in three-dimensional, environmental form. This can take place through *harmony* or *imposition* strategies.

Using the harmony strategy, the visual characteristics of a sign program can reflect and reinforce the visual characteristics of a site's design or architecture to create a seamless, totally integrated identity. The harmony approach works well when the signage program is being designed for an environment with a high level of visual unity, be it an existing site or, more commonly, a new development or major renovation, when design details can be coordinated among all the design professionals involved in the project.

Using the imposition approach, signage can create or impose a unique, singular identity on a site—an identity that's completely independent of the site's visual characteristics. This approach works well for existing sites that have disparate visual elements, such as cities, college campuses, and transportation networks, that can be linked together by the metabranding of the signage program.

Whether a signage program brands by harmony or imposition, signage provides needed information to people using it, engendering feelings of goodwill and security. And since signage programs provide information that people actively seek, signage links this sought-after information directly to the brand. There is no doubt that good signage builds good relations with any given audience.

1.19 The metabrand image of the Amtrak Acela signage links diverse station architecture from Boston to Washington, DC.

1.20 The 1984 Los Angeles Olympics signage linked a wide array of remote venues by imposing a strong brand image distinctive of the city's spirit.

1.21 Signage for an AIGA conference imposes the event's theme onto the venue.

1.21

You Can't Learn This in College

EGD projects are typically complex, with many problems and subproblems, which cross the boundaries of various design disciplines. Accordingly, EGD is a cross-disciplinary specialty field that combines aspects of the graphic design, architecture, and industrial and interior design professions. Currently, there are no known comprehensive EGD degree-granting programs in the United States, although certain design programs do offer students exposure to EGD in a specific course. These courses either may be exclusively dedicated to EGD or incorporate EGD within a broader course of study, such as a corporate identity design course.

Due to the lack of a comprehensive EGD educational program, and because of the cross-disciplinary nature of the field, the only way EGD practitioners can fill gaps in their knowledge base is by learning in the workplace. For example, a graphic designer must learn about three-dimensional forms and materials, working in scale, interpreting architectural drawings, and basic drafting. An architect must learn about graphic communication purposes and techniques, two-dimensional design principles, and graphic application techniques. This book aims to fill in those gaps for both aspiring and current practitioners, including students.

This book is also for clients who procure EGD services, including architects, landscape architects, urban designers, planners, public administrators, transportation officials, real estate developers, general contractors, and facility and construction managers. Design professionals, policymakers, developers, and managers who engage the services of environmental graphic designers will gain an understanding of EGD processes and methodologies, leading to a more effective working relationship with EG designers.

What's Ahead in This Book

This book will take you, the reader, into the wonderful world of EG design, with the focus on signage and wayfinding design. Think of it as a guidebook, which leads you first into the design process as it relates to EG design,

1.22 The spectrum of design disciplines and their products.

City Planning / Urban Design	Landscape Architecture	Architecture	Interior Design	Industrial Design	Graphic Design
Cities, Towns, Campuses	Planned Open Spaces, Parks	Buildings	Interior Spaces	Objects for Living & Work	Objects that Communicate

Macro ⟶ ➤ **Micro**

then reveals what I call the Signage Pyramid methodology, which I developed in graduate school. This methodology divides signage into three interrelated focus areas or components: the Information Content System, the Graphic System, and the Hardware System. This divide-and-conquer strategy makes it easier to solve the complex problems and subproblems posed in the design of a comprehensive signage program. Along the way, you'll also find lots of tips, and a relatively small dose of opinion.

Ultimately, this book is about the design process and methodology that leads to the end product of a built, functioning signage program. Unfortunately, the book could not be printed in full color throughout, but I've made the best use of the 32-page color insert to showcase the built products of the process; in contrast, the black-and-white figures focus on aspects of the process itself. All the photos throughout the book, color and black-and-white, represent the work of my office, as well as that of several leading EGD consulting firms in the United States.

As you read, keep in mind that every signage and wayfinding project is different—different sites, different sizes, different clients, different everything! So the generalized, idealized process and methodology presented in this book won't directly mirror the process for each and every signage project an EG designer or client has encountered or will encounter. But though signage and wayfinding design is complex, it's not rocket science. There are few hard-and-fast rules, and there are many ways to approach many of the items discussed in this book. There's also a multitude of signage and wayfinding issues and technicalities that this book doesn't address. In sum, I recommend you use this as a big-picture book, then adapt what you learn to your own projects.

2 The Design Process

Design is a creative problem-solving process.

The design of signage and wayfinding programs is part of a broader design discipline that has come to be known as environmental graphic design, or EGD. As defined in Chapter 1, EGD activity is concerned with the graphic communication of information in the built environment, which is just about anything built by human intent, be it a single building, such as a hotel or stadium; an assemblage of buildings, such as a city or campus; a planned open space such as a park or historical site; or a transportation network, such as a subway or rail system.

While the primary communication goal of signage and wayfinding design is to help people navigate the built environment, EGD encompasses two other important communication functions, placemaking and interpretation, and signage design often intersects with these other EGD activities, as discussed and illustrated in Chapter 1. And though this book focuses on the signage aspect of EGD, the terms *signage design* and *EGD* are used interchangeably. EGD exists in a broader design universe and is, in fact, the ultimate hybrid—or, if you're less charitable, mongrel—of design. EGD is the ultimate multidisciplinary design discipline, where graphic design, architecture, industrial design, interior design, landscape architecture, city planning, and urban design all converge. And common to all of these design disciplines, including EGD, is the design process.

All design activity is a problem-solving process. All design activity is also creative, but unlike fine art, it takes place under real-world constraints. Designers focus their creative talents on solving problems for their clients. We, as designers, have a unique gift to give: life to our clients' ideas, which we make tangible and real. It's a heady responsibility, one we must undertake with diligence and good stewardship. We must consider all things possible to the extent possible. Moreover, we must extend our best effort to employ our creative talents, skills, and knowledge in making the world a better place.

Designers, including EG designers, typically do not directly produce the objects of their design/creative activity. Unlike painters who put their creative compositions on canvas with their own hands, designers rely on other parties to produce the objects they design. There's the architect, who designs a building but relies on a contractor to build it; the industrial designer, who designs a consumer product but relies on a manufacturing facility to produce it; or the graphic designer, who designs a book but relies on a printing facility to print and bind it. The EG designer relies on a sign fabricator to build and install a signage program.

A key role of the designer emerges in the preceding examples, that of an *intermediary*, between the client and the producer, and between the design problem and the embodiment or realization of the design solution. In this role, the basic process any design professional utilizes becomes evident. It is to:

1. Assess the client's problem.
2. Apply creative skills.
3. Synthesize a solution.
4. Communicate the solution to the producer.
5. Oversee production of the solution.
6. Evaluate effectiveness of the finished product.

The universal design process is evolutionary, with the design solution unfolding in a series of steps, from general to more specific. And while the steps or phases of the design process typically progress from one to the next in a somewhat systematic, linear order, they may at times overlap, repeat or feed back into each other. Ultimately, however, the end goal is to progress from the first phase to the last. And every effective designer on the planet employs essentially this type of systematic process to arrive at design solutions, whether he or she is consciously aware of it or not.

The Client Is Part of the Process

When a client engages any designer, including EG designers, a partnership is formed, with both clients and designers performing various roles. The designer's role is to make a diligent, earnest effort to solve the client's problem. The client's role is to provide adequate information, feedback, and guidance in a timely manner. And to pay the designer's invoices on time.

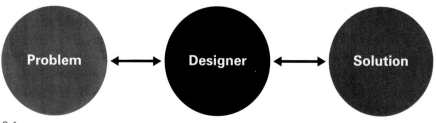

2.1

2.1 The designer's role as mediator between the design problem and the design solution.

Most successful projects are the result of an active working relationship grounded in mutual trust between client and designer.

Message to designers: The client is part of the process, so don't ignore the client's needs and constraints.

Message to clients: You're a part of the process, so don't think the designer can magically solve the problem without your active involvement.

Effective design solutions require client input and engagement. Passivity on the client's part doesn't work. If both clients and designers remember that they have a partnership—and all that this relationship entails—a successful outcome is likely to result.

The Design Process Applied to EGD

The basic design process can be effectively tailored to EGD scenarios, maximizing the efficiency of EGD activity. Because so many EGD projects are coupled with architectural design projects, the design phases of the EGD process model outlined in this chapter are analogous to those used in the architectural profession. This process model is also a useful framework for outlining design services to be performed on a project in fee proposals to prospective clients. Additionally, it's useful for educating clients about the evolutionary process from which design solutions emerge and become implemented. The design process model, which includes predesign, design, and postdesign phases, is shown in Figure 2.2.

Each EGD phase, described in sequence in this chapter, has several tasks associated with it. Keep in mind that though these phases are presented as distinct and in linear order, they often overlap and feed back into each other, as noted previously. Also be aware that while the client's involvement is mentioned primarily at project milestones, the designer typically maintains ongoing contact with the client throughout all the phases.

Coordinating Timing of the EGD Process

2.2 The phases of the design process include predesign, design, and postdesign activity.

If a signage project is independent of any larger design and construction project, the design process timetable can be set fairly easily. If, however, a

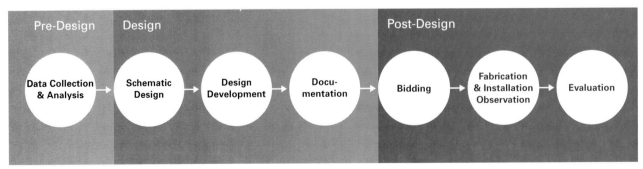

2.2

signage project is part of a new construction, project timing of the EGD process with that of the overall project becomes critical. Often, EG designers are brought into a project too late, but they can also be brought in too early, such as before floor plans are frozen or locked—that is, while the plans are still in a state of flux and sign locations cannot be pinned down. Ideally, the signage design process should lag the architectural design process by one or two phases.

While on the subject of time, note that signage projects are typically of much longer duration than typical graphic design projects for print or web media. It is not uncommon for a signage project to take months or years to complete—although the EG designer may not be working continuously on the project during that time frame—so EGD is definitely not for those who seek instant gratification in their work.

Throughout this chapter the design process is illustrated with photos that trace the development of the Amtrak Acela signage program at my office, from the data collection and analysis phase through to the fabrication/installation observation phase. The end product of the design process for the Acela project—the built signage program—is depicted in the color insert section of this book, as are the built products of the design process for many other U.S. EGD consulting firms.

My office designed the Acela signage program for the advent of the first high speed rail service in the United States, servicing Amtrak stations on the 440-mile-long Northeast Corridor route from Boston to Washington, DC. We designed the Acela sign program with an imposition strategy, as described in Chapter 1, to create a strong, unique brand image derived from a sleek "airfoil" shape to link together the diverse array of station sizes and architectural styles along the route. The Amtrak Acela signage program has received awards from the *Industrial Designers Society of America (IDSA)/Business Week* magazine (Gold IDEA Award), The American Institute of Graphic Arts (AIGA), and the Society for Environmental Graphic Design (SEGD), and it has been published in numerous U.S. and international books and periodicals.

Phase 1: Data Collection and Analysis (Predesign)

Also known by terms such as preschematic, research, and others, this is a very important predesign planning phase that's often neglected in the designer's eagerness to get the creative juices going. But remember that design doesn't happen in a vacuum! You have a client who has engaged your services to solve a signage problem, and that client and that problem come with a whole range of parameters and constraints that you need to know about before you put pencil to paper or mouse to mousepad and begin to synthesize an effective design solution.

2.3 Data collection and analysis phase: Information was gathered on the sleek, new, high-speed Acela train sets and service.

2.3

Put simply, phase 1 is the information-gathering and analysis phase, the discovery or learning phase. During this period, EG designers collect as much information as they can on the fledgling project and then make sense of it. An appropriate description of the designer's role in phase 1 is that of a sponge, absorbing and assimilating as much about the project as possible, then filtering that information into a plan of action.

At first, phase 1 is focused on divergence, when the designer reaches out and plucks as much information about the project as possible with little regard to its ultimate usefulness. At this stage, it's important to be open-minded and nonjudgmental about the data being gathered. As more is

2.4 Data collection and analysis phase: To learn about station conditions and determine the kinds of signs and information content needed, every station scheduled to offer Acela service along the Northeast Corridor, from Boston to Washington, DC, was extensively surveyed and photographed.

2.4

learned about the project, phase 1 activity becomes more convergent. Now the designer analyzes and distills the information to draw conclusions and set goals for the subsequent design-oriented phases.

Subjects for up-front research can vary widely from project to project, but some basics for signage programs include, in no particular order:

- Time and budget constraints
- Image and branding goals
- Formal and thematic context(s) of the site(s)
- User profiles
- Physical characteristics of the site itself
- Circulation pathways and decision points
- Applicable codes affecting signage
- Decision making and client contact protocols
- Whether the client hates the color blue

No doubt both you and your client will be impatient to get to the really fun, pretty-picture phases of design, but it's important to keep in mind that the careful planning of phase 1 sets the stage for more focused, viable solutions in the subsequent design phases. Remember to find out what you're jumping into before you jump in! Remember, too, that while the big research push occurs at the beginning of a project, data collection and analysis often continues throughout a project.

Phase 1 Goals and Results

The primary goal of the data collection and analysis phase is to gain a comprehensive understanding of the project at hand and to verify that your understanding meshes with that of the client. Phase 1 results in conclusions drawn from the data collection and analysis activity, as well as a plan for moving the project forward. Various diagrams and lists may be generated, as well as sketches, photo surveys, and other records. These may be informal working tools just for the design team's use, or they may be formalized for presentation to the client in a written report or visual presentation. In either case, the phase 1 results should be reviewed and discussed with the client.

Phase 2: Schematic Design

Once the predesign project research and planning phase is completed, the EG designer should have a good grasp of what the project entails, and a focused design effort can begin. The schematic design phase is the initial design phase and is undoubtedly the most creative, exciting phase, for it's when the informational and visual foundations of the signage program are laid. Initially, schematic design activity is divergent and exploratory, with the goal of generating as many ideas, concepts and approaches to the

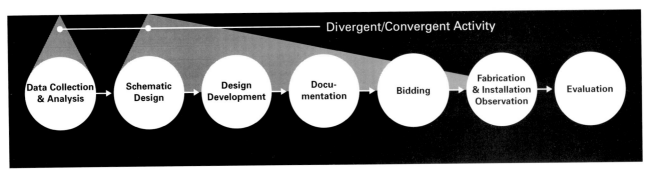

Divergent/Convergent Activity

Data Collection & Analysis → Schematic Design → Design Development → Documentation → Bidding → Fabrication & Installation Observation → Evaluation

2.5

2.5 The design process involves divergent and convergent activity. Divergent activity focuses on gathering as much information or generating as many ideas as possible, whereas convergent activity focuses on selection, refinement, and conclusion.

design problem as possible, and then becomes convergent as these various schemes are evaluated and selected. Overall, subsequent project phases continue to be convergent as the selected design solution is refined and finalized. This divergent-convergent aspect of the design process is illustrated in Figure 2.5.

The visual aspects of a sign program are deeply influenced by its informational aspects, so it's important to start phase 2 with exploration of the program's information content system. Briefly, this includes determining the locations and communication functions of key signs in the program, as well as generating approaches to sign message nomenclature and hierarchy. In this process, the designer begins to formulate the building blocks—such as communication functions, message vocabularies, mounting conditions, and viewing distances—that are expressed in the visual aspects of the sign program. This activity will provide the designer

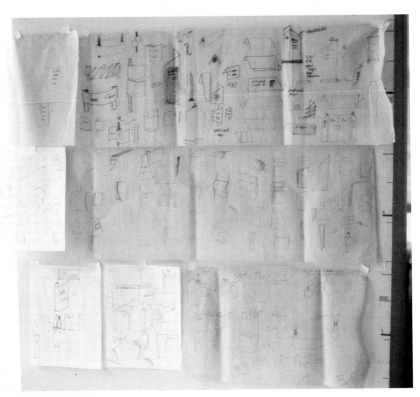

2.6 Schematic design phase: At an early pinup session, many concepts evoke speed with curved forms.

2.6

with an inventory of key signs that represent the range of signs the program will encompass. This key sign inventory then becomes the focus of the visual concepts generated in schematic design. (Chapter 4 has a more detailed discussion on developing the sign information content system, an activity that's often referred to as *programming*.)

While it's essential to address the sign program's informational aspect early on in the schematic design phase, most designers focus their creative energies during this phase on the sign program's visual aspects: the graphics and hardware. The creative juices and wild concepts should flow freely during the early stages of this phase—no holds barred. This is the divergent, ideation portion of phase 2, where the goal is to generate as many rough visual concepts as possible, where every little inkling of an idea is explored and no idea is negated/judged until later. The key word here is *rough;* schematic design should not delve too deeply into detail.

A tip for improving concept generation at the beginning of phase 2 is to never fall in love with your first—or any—idea. If you do, you run the risk of investing too much of your time, effort, and ego into a so-so concept when other, absolutely brilliant ones could be out there just waiting for your

2.7 Schematic design phase: Informal presentation of initial concepts for client input. The client's input was to continue exploring more concepts.

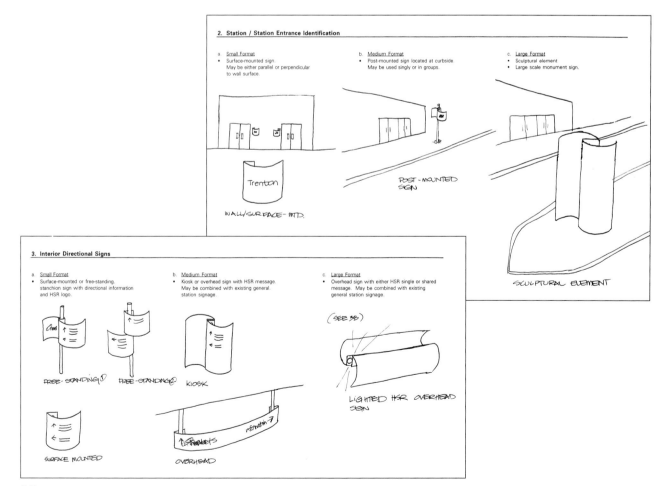

discovery. And when you invest too much of yourself into one concept, and detail it to death too early, you become reluctant to give it up, thereby blinding yourself to potentially exceptional concepts.

Another tip: It may take a while for ideas to emerge. The creative mind often needs what is often referred to as an incubation period to formulate concepts and ideas subconsciously. When this is enabled, often a great idea will just pop out—sometimes at seemingly odd moments, such as in the shower or at the grocery store, in what's known as the "eureka" or "ah-ha" phenomenon. So be aware that creative ideas can take some time to emerge, although a deadline has a wonderful way of focusing the mind.

More brains generate more ideas, so it's often productive to gather as many designers as possible within the EGD firm to participate in the ideation stages of phase 2, even if some of those designers may not be assigned for the duration of the project. Collaborative brainstorming and word association techniques can stimulate the flow of design concepts, as can pencil-and-paper sketching, versus computer rendering, as the computer interface is still not as simple and direct as hand-sketching. Some EGD offices, in fact, don't permit computer use in ideation, in part because computer use tends to foster endless minutely detailed variations on a possibly mundane idea rather than exploration of many, truly novel ideas.

Pinup sessions, too, are very useful for comparing and cross-fertilizing ideas and concepts. The concept sketches generated by the EGD team are

2.8 Schematic design phase: More concepts are generated and displayed at other pinup sessions. An airfoil concept (circled in the lower right of this figure), connoting sleekness and speed, emerges and is selected as the core solution with the "right fit" for the problem.

2.8

pinned up on the wall and discussed among the team, with each designer articulating the thinking behind his or her various ideas. These pinup sessions can be both convergent and divergent. Some concepts will be rejected, but even rejected concepts can stimulate entirely new directions, so plan on at least two pinup sessions to get the ideas out. And check your ego at the door.

As phase 2 progresses, it becomes convergent, as concepts for the sign program's visual aspects are weighed and selected to form clear design directions to finesse for presentation to the client. As with ideation, concept selection should be a team effort, with each concept thoroughly debated, defended, and discussed in relation to how well it points to a solution to the client's problem. The key phrase here is "pointing to a solution." Remember that the design process is evolutionary, that schematic design is an early phase of that process, and that the various problems and subproblems of the sign program will be solved as the process unfolds in subsequent design phases. Think of phase 2 as skimming the surface of the solution and you won't run the risk of becoming too invested too early in what may be a wrong solution. This is not the phase for working out the details.

The culmination of phase 2 is a presentation to the client of the EG designer's schematic design activity. This is typically the first time the client is presented with the visual fruits of the designer's creative labors, so it's a major project milestone that either sets the tone for the rest of the project or sends the designer back to the drawing board to seek other design directions. If the designer has conducted thorough research, however, the need for revisiting other design solutions is minimized. Another strategy is to fly some preliminary concepts by the client on an informal basis to test the waters—to gain input that you're on the right track before investing in an elaborate schematic design presentation.

Many EG designers present up to three schematic design directions, explain the merits of each, and then gently guide the client toward the selection of one concept. Some designers present just one design concept and advocate forcefully for its adoption, which minimizes the risk of the client creating a "camel," that is, an awkward combination of two fundamentally different concepts. The drawbacks to the single-idea approach are that the client may: (1) reject the concept outright, and/or (2) feel that the designer is being too dictatorial by not presenting enough options. Indeed, the designer should have discovered in phase 1 whether the client wants multiple options.

The key to presentation of multiple concepts, however, is to not overwhelm the client with too many options, or with any option the designer doesn't believe to be viable. In other words, don't show the client a direction you don't believe in because that may very well be the concept

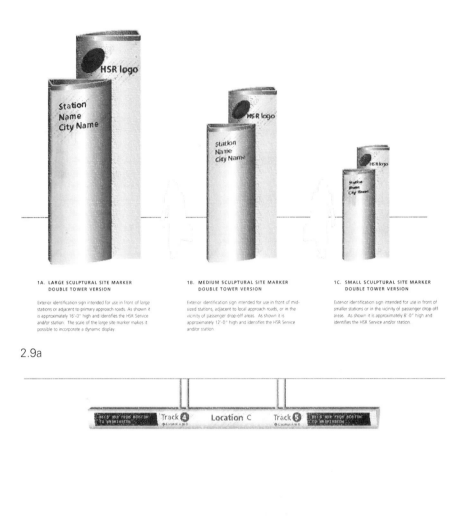

2.9a

1A. LARGE SCULPTURAL SITE MARKER
DOUBLE TOWER VERSION

Exterior identification sign intended for use in front of large stations or adjacent to primary approach roads. As shown it is approximately 16'-0" high and identifies the HSR Service and/or station. The scale of the large site marker makes it possible to incorporate a dynamic display.

1B. MEDIUM SCULPTURAL SITE MARKER
DOUBLE TOWER VERSION

Exterior identification sign intended for use in front of mid-sized stations, adjacent to local approach roads, or in the vicinity of passenger drop-off areas. As shown it is approximately 12'-0" high and identifies the HSR Service and/or station.

1C. SMALL SCULPTURAL SITE MARKER
DOUBLE TOWER VERSION

Exterior identification sign intended for use in front of smaller stations or in the vicinity of passenger drop-off areas. As shown it is approximately 8'-0" high and identifies the HSR Service and/or station.

7C. LARGE PLATFORM SIGN WITH DOUBLE
DYNAMIC DISPLAYS

These sign items are located on HSR platforms and are used to define that portion of the platform occupied by the HSR train set. The double-sided sign span the platform and identify HSR tracks and track location. The length of the sign is determined by the platform width. The dynamic displays would provide information about train arrivals and departures and train destinations. The dynamic displays could also provide real-time information regarding delays or service interruptions.

2.9b

2.9a, b Schematic design phase: Early configuration concepts of the airfoil shape, in freestanding and suspended forms, for client review and input.

the client selects, and you'll be doomed to struggling with it for the duration of the project.

Phase 2 Goals and Results

The primary goal of the schematic design phase is to generate and present informational approaches and visual concepts for client review, selection, and approval in order to proceed to subsequent design phases. Another goal is to obtain client input and feedback that may affect the basic informational or design directions of the sign program.

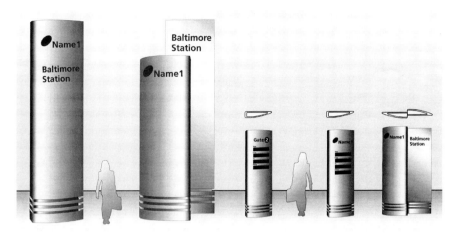

2.10a

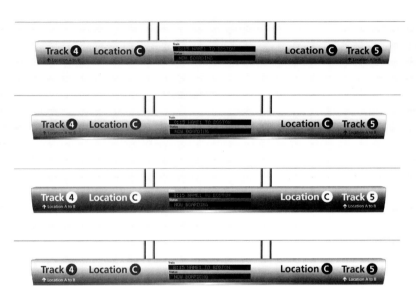

2.10b

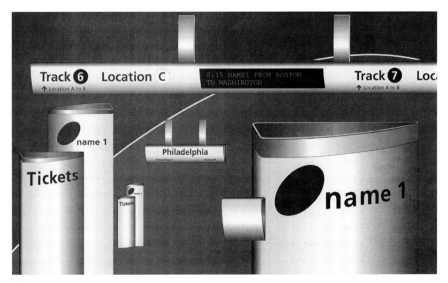

2.10c

2.10a, b, c Schematic design phase: Continuing configuration, size, and color studies of the airfoil concepts for client feedback.

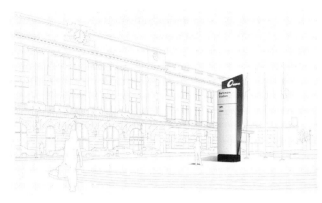

2.11a

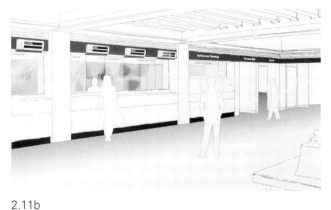

2.11b

2.11c

2.11d

2.11a–d Schematic design phase: Schematic design presentation images show evolution of the airfoil concept into its essentially final form in the various program sign types. The sign types are presented in the order a departing passenger would experience them: from station entrance to ticketing to gate areas to platforms.

Phase 2 results in presentation materials that convey the schematic design concepts and approaches to the client. Depending on the size and nature of the project and client, these presentation materials typically consist of presentation boards and/or an A/V presentation, often accompanied by a booklet summarizing the presentation. A basic content checklist for the phase 2 presentation includes the items listed here. Of course, the EG designer can supplement or omit these basic content items as appropriate to a given project.

- Overview of project context, including survey(s) of existing conditions, if available
- Key sign locations in plan view
- Approaches to sign message nomenclature and hierarchy
- Evocative or metaphorical references, typically images
- Typeface and symbol options
- Material and color palette options
- Basic elevations of key signs, including scale references such as people, cars, and trees, and so on
- Perspective montages of signs in their environmental context, using artist's renderings or photos of the actual site as underlying images
- Basic study models of sign forms and shapes

Persuasion is certainly part of the design process, as is the ability to articulate and present your concepts effectively, sometimes in formalized situations before large audiences. Whatever the context, successful presentations are visually compelling and verbally engaging, and clearly speak to the client's design problem.

In an ideal world, the schematic design presentation is a huge success and the client makes an immediate—or at least prompt—decision to select and approve one of the presented directions. So on to the next design phase, but not until you have clear client input and approval to proceed, especially because some clients take more time than others to reach decisions. And keep in mind that, occasionally, the designer must point to the project time schedule and gently prod the client to make a decision.

Phase 3: Design Development

Approval has now been granted to proceed further onto the design process, and the design development (DD) phase begins. Whereas the initial stages of schematic design (SD) are divergent, seeking many ideas, DD continues the convergence of the later SD stages, to focus more deeply on the selected schematic design direction. Phase 2 just skims the surface of the design solution; it is during DD that the solution is fleshed out, filled in, modified, and refined. The methods for documenting and tracking various project elements are also solidified in phase 3.

As in phase 2, it's important to tackle the sign information content system in the early stages of design development. During phase 3, a complete inventory of all the signs in the program must be developed, meaning that each and every sign must be located, messaged, typed, and assigned a unique identifying/tracking code. This sign inventory process is essential because the EG designer cannot meaningfully proceed with design of the visual aspects of the program until all the particulars of its parts are known. In other words, the designer must know the physical conditions, such as width or height constraints, as well as the specific message content of each sign before it can be designed. Human factors such as viewing angle and distance, as well as code-mandated factors such as typographic sizes, also affect how each sign is designed, as described in more detail in Chapters 4, 5, and 6.

Comprehensive sign programs are composed of hundreds, even thousands, of sign units, so it's inefficient from both design and manufacturing standpoints to design each and every one of them individually. Therefore, after sign locations and messages are established for the information content system, the designer can begin to look for commonalities among the various signs to group them into standardized *sign types*. The objective of *sign typing* is to reduce and simplify the sign program into the fewest number of groups that share common features standardized for each type, while still fulfilling the communication function of the sign program.

2.12 Design development phase: Full-size layout allows study of message content arrangement and size of graphics for viewing distance and angle.

In a simple example of sign typing, assume the EG designer has located and messaged ceiling-hung, freestanding, and wall-mounted plaques within the project environment, and that they all have message content of varying length and importance. The first obvious common characteristic by which certain signs can be grouped together is mounting method; for example, Sign Type A is a ceiling-hung sign, Sign Type B is a freestanding sign, and so on. Then when message length and importance is considered, sign types can be further differentiated; for example, Sign Type A1 is a large ceiling-hung sign to hold message content of the largest quantity or highest importance, Sign Type A2 is a small ceiling-hung sign to hold message content of lesser quantity or importance. Many other factors can also affect the development of sign types, such as low ceiling clearances requiring the use of a smaller ceiling-hung sign type at certain locations, or narrow corridors that limit a sign type's width.

When signs are typed accordingly, the designer gains efficiency and visual unity by designing the sign type, which can cover a large quantity of sign messages and units, rather than designing each individual sign as a unique, stand-alone object. And sign typing improves manufacturing efficiency because, for example, several units of the same size and shape can be cut, formed, and assembled more quickly than if the same quantity of units were all of different sizes and shapes. If you think of sign typing as designing for limited mass production, the usefulness of typing becomes clear. And, from a design point of view, visual order is enhanced, with fewer sizes and shapes of signs in the project environment.

The best way to track and manage sign types is by keeping a list that defines the characteristics and size of each type. Pinning down sign types is, however, a balancing act, as sign types typically evolve and mutate as

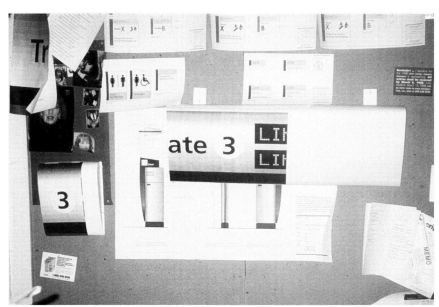

2.13 Design development phase: Various sign types in scaled drawings and full-size study models built in-house are pinned up for comparison and refinement to unify the Acela sign family.

2.13

Amtrak High Speed Rail Station Improvements
Preliminary Sign Type List

Sign Family	Sign Type	Description
A Site Pylons	A1 Site Pylon	Exterior, Free-Standing, Base Service, Small, Internally Illuminated
	A2 Site Pylon	Exterior, Free-Standing, Base Service, Medium, Internally Illuminated
	A3 Site Pylon	Exterior, Free-Standing, Base Service, Large, Internally Illuminated
	A4 Site Pylon	Exterior, Free-Standing, HSR-Enhanced Service, Small, Internally Illuminated
	A5 Site Pylon	Exterior, Free-Standing, HSR-Enhanced Service, Medium, Internally Illuminated
	A6 Site Pylon	Exterior, Free-Standing, HSR-Enhanced Service, Large, Internally Illuminated
B Station Pylons	B1 Directional Pylon	Interior, Free-Standing, Base Service, Double Sided, Portable
	B2 Gate Pylon	Interior, Free-Standing, Base Service, Single Sided, LED Display
	B3 Gate Pylon	Interior, Free-Standing, Base Service, Double Sided, LED Display
	B4 Gate Pylon	Interior, Free-Standing, Base Service, Double Sided, LED Display, Poster Frame
	B5 Gate Pylon	Interior, Free-Standing, Base Service, Double Sided, LED Display, LCD Display
	B6 Directional Pylon	Interior, Free-Standing, HSR-Enhanced Service
	B7 Gate Pylon	Interior, Free-Standing, HSR-Enhanced Service, Single Sided, LED Display
	B8 Gate Pylon	Interior, Free-Standing, HSR-Enhanced Service, Double Sided, LED Display
	B9 Gate Pylon	Interior, Free-Standing, HSR-Enhanced Service, Double Sided, LED Display, Advertising
	B10 Gate Pylon	Interior, Free-Standing, HSR-Enhanced Service, Double Sided, LED Display, LCD Display
	B11 Information Pylon	Interior, Engaging Information Desk, Double Sided, Station Maps & Information
C Surface Mounted Signs	C1 Surface Mounted Sign	Overhead, Indicator Lamp, LED Display
	C2 Surface Mounted Sign	Overhead, Indicator Lamp
	C3 Surface Mounted Sign	Overhead, Indicator Lamp, LED Display, Static Text
	C4 Surface Mounted Sign	Overhead, Indicator Lamp, Static Text
	C5 Surface Mounted Sign	Wall-Mounted, Static Text
D Platform Signs	D1 Platform Sign	Overhead Hanging, Large, Double Sided, LED Display, Audio Speaker, Static Text
	D2 Platform Sign	Overhead Hanging, Medium, Double Sided, LED Display, Audio Speaker, Static Text
	D3 Platform Sign	Overhead, Free-Standing, Large, Double Sided, LED Display, Audio Speaker, Static Text
	D4 Station Identification	Overhead, Hanging, Double Sided, Static Text
	D5 Station Identification	Wall-Mounted, Single Sided, Static Text
	D6 Platform Sign	Wall-Mounted Projecting, Double Sided, LED Display, Audio Speaker, Static Text
	D7 Platform Sign	Overhead Hanging, Small, Double Sided, LED Display, Audio Speaker, Static Text
	D8 Platform Sign	Overhead Hanging, Small, Double Sided, Static Text

2.14

the DD phase progresses. For example, the need for new sign types may emerge, some sign types may be deleted, two sign types may merge into one, or the definition of a sign type may change.

Methods for defining sign types vary, but the two basic approaches are to type signs by:

- *Physical characteristics*, such as size, shape, material, mounting method, graphic application technique, and so on

- *Communication function*, such as whether the sign communicates identification, directional, or another kind of information, as described in more detail in Chapter 4.

At C&VE, we prefer to type signs by physical characteristics, as they most directly translate into drawings, schedules, and bid forms. Our thinking behind this is that the primary fabrication cost factor of a sign is its physical characteristics, not the kind of information it displays. For example, a 12″ square, wall-mounted aluminum plaque with silkscreened graphics costs the same to fabricate and install regardless of whether it

2.14 Preliminary sign type list for the Amtrak Acela Program.

displays identification or directional information. And a 12″ square, wall-mounted bronze plaque with silkscreened graphics costs more to fabricate than the aluminum plaque with all the same characteristics. In this example, the material—aluminum versus bronze—is the distinguishing factor between these two signs, so we define them as different sign types.

Other EGD practitioners type by communication function, rather than physical characteristics. And sometimes signs are typed using a combination of physical characteristics and communication function. There is no hard-and-fast rule for sign typing, but as recommended by EGD pioneers John Follis and Dave Hammer in their seminal book *Architectural Signing and Graphics* (Whitney Library of Design, 1979), "All signs in a given sign type should have the same size, shape, and method of attachment to the building." We agree with this recommendation.

Regardless of the sign-typing technique you choose, each sign type is assigned a code—typically alpha, numeric, or a combination of the two. This code is a shorthand way to refer to everything that comprises a given sign type. For example, the aforementioned Sign Type A is a code that succinctly refers to a large exterior internally illuminated ground-mounted pylon. As such, the sign type code is an essential element of the sign numbering system, which is used to track and inventory each and every sign in a program.

During phase 2, key signs may be numbered, but it is during phase 3 that the sign numbering system for tracking all the signs in the overall project is typically established, as that's when all the signs in a program need to be located on plans and entered into a message schedule. The sign

2.15 Design development phase: Full size in-house study model for assessment of sign graphic and hardware system sizes and forms.

2.15

numbering system identifies and distinguishes each sign unit on the location plans and the message schedule.

The sign numbering system is itself a coding system that conveys distinguishing information about each sign unit. To effectively track all the signs in a program, a sign number, at the very least, should be composed of a sign type and a unit number, and each sign should have a unique number—meaning it's not duplicated elsewhere in the program. Other information about the sign unit, such as which floor the sign is on or whether it's an interior or exterior sign, can also be coded into its sign number.

There are several approaches to sign numbering, some of which can be quite complex. A numbering system that's suitable for one project may not be for another, so it's wise to weigh various sign numbering approaches carefully before putting a given system to use, because it's tedious and time-consuming to completely revamp the sign numbering system once sign numbers have been entered on location plans and the message schedule.

The sign location plans indicate on plan drawings each sign in a program, along with its identifying sign number. This sign number is entered into the sign message schedule, which contains all the essential information about each sign unit, such as its:

- Message, including arrows and symbols
- Plan drawing number
- Construction drawing reference
- Mounting drawing reference
- Graphic layout reference, if applicable

2.16 Design development phase: Photomontage aids study of sign graphics and hardware in relation to viewing distances and angles on platforms at various stations.

2.16

Most message schedules also contain a Remarks column for tracking such items as changes, additions, deletions, signs for which client input is required, and so on.

Message schedules are formatted as tables, typically on $8^1/_2'' \times 11''$ landscape (horizontal) pages. Most EGD practitioners use a database or spreadsheet program for their message schedules because these programs provide more powerful, sophisticated tools for data entry, sorting, searching, and editing functions than a word processing program. And all of these functions are definitely required during the development of the message schedule.

A word about computer platforms: Most EG design offices operate on the Macintosh platform while most clients, including architects, are on the PC platform. This situation creates some file exchange issues, particularly with message schedule files and architectural CAD files.

2.17 Signage program message schedule. Sign numbers are keyed to sign numbers indicated on location plans.

In the case of message schedules, most clients don't have database programs in their desktop applications, but they do typically have

Sign No.	Plan	Mount	Const.	Layout	Message	Remarks
B2-05.07	SL.05	GL.15	1/GL.16A		MEETING SUITE 2	
B2-05.08	SL.05	GL.15	1/GL.16A		MEETING SUITE 2	
B2-05.09	SL.05	GL.15	1/GL.16A		MEETING SUITE 1	
B2-05.10	SL.05	GL.15	1/GL.16A		MEETING SUITE 1	
E-05.02	SL.05	GL.19	GL.19		(Side A & B) Directory (Updatable Map Directory)	Double-sided
E-05.03	SL.05	GL.19	GL.19		(Side A & B) Directory (Updatable Map Directory)	Double-sided
E-05.04	SL.06	GL.19	GL.19		(Side A & B) Directory (Updatable Map Directory)	Double-sided
E-05.06	SL.06	GL.19	GL.19		(Side A & B) Directory (Updatable Map Directory)	Double-sided
H1-05.01	SL.05	1/GL.12 4/GL.13	1/GL12A		Meeting Room 5D	
H1-05.02	SL.05	1/GL.12 4/GL.13	1/GL12A		Meeting Room 5C	
H1-05.03	SL.05	1/GL.12 4/GL.13	1/GL12A		Meeting Room 5C	
H1-05.04	SL.05	1/GL.12 4/GL.13	1/GL12A		Meeting Room 5B	
H1-05.05	SL.05	1/GL.12 4/GL.13	1/GL12A		Meeting Room 5A	

Project #0702 - Virginia Beach Convention Center
Sign Message Schedule

Calori & Vanden-Eynden/Design Consultants
130 West 25th Street, New York, NY 10001

Page 41 of 68
26 January 2004

spreadsheet applications, which is why many clients prefer message schedules in spreadsheet form. The PDF file format is becoming an essential tool in bridging this platform/application gap, by allowing EG designers to export database message schedules as PDF files that the clients' computers can read without the database application. Note that if the message schedule is exported as a PDF file, it will not be editable by the client. PDF format also facilitates the exchange of other kinds of files developed by the EG designer or the client for a project, particularly architectural CAD files.

Sign location plans are prepared by placing a marker indicating each sign's location, along with its identifying number, on base plan drawings of the project. Most clients possess or can provide architectural plan drawing files, so the designer should always request those files for use as the sign location base plans rather than going through the time-consuming effort of creating them anew.

The sign locations and numbers need to be clearly visible on the sign location plans, but this is easier said than done because plan drawings are typically cluttered with written information (such as notes, dimensions, symbols, etc.), which is necessary for construction of the project but tends to obscure sign locations. Nevertheless, there are several ways to increase the prominence of sign locations and numbers.

- Always request clean base plans with the written information removed, if possible. Note that cleaning up the plans can take some time, so this request may not always be granted.

- Whether the plans are clean or not, make sure they're "grayed back" so that they're still readily visible, but fade into the background relative to the sign locations and numbers, which are not grayed back.

- Enclose the sign numbers in a distinctive shape that stands out visually from the plan background and any architectural symbols or shapes on it.

Another important guideline is to avoid color coding on final plan drawings, as other parties using the signage drawings may not have color reproduction capabilities. Reserve color-coded sign locations for schematic studies. The techniques outlined here don't rely on color to distinguish sign locations and numbers, and therefore result in drawings that are readable when reproduced in either black and white or color.

When it comes to size, because plans are generated at small scales, the sign locations usually need to be indicated at a scale larger than that of the base plan in order to be visibly prominent. This alarms some clients, however, because they think the signs are going to be really large or that they're too close together, so some explanation of the scale discrepancy may be necessary. Another advance caveat: The sign locations and numbers can crowd each other on some plans, so give some thought to arranging them in an orderly fashion. Another recommendation is to pull

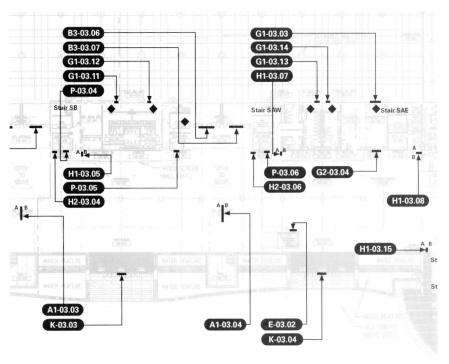

2.18 Detail of a sign location plan with
the base plan grayed back to make sign
locations and number more prominent.
Signs are typically indicated much larger
than actual size to be visible on location
plans.

2.18

the sign numbers out beyond the plan footprint, to help keep the plan itself
uncluttered and readable—but this, too, requires careful arrangement.

As the information content system is developed and tracked in the
DD phase, the design of the visual elements—the sign graphics and
hardware—also progresses, as shown in the figures related to the design
development phase. At this point, the EG designer begins to address the

2.19a, b Design development phase:
Preparation of full-size design prototypes
of two key Acela sign types in an outside
shop.

2.19a

2.19b

2.20a

2.20b

2.20c

2.20a, b, c Finished design prototypes assessed for size of graphics and hardware and for formal hardware details. These non-working prototypes are primarily for study and refinement of formal and color elements, so they are constructed of wood with simulated electronic displays.

details of the graphic system and the hardware system, to solve the subproblems that lie in those details. The EG designer can use scale and full-size models and mock-ups, drawings, and even design prototypes to study and refine those all-important details that contribute so much to the quality of the final sign objects. As the famed modernist architect Mies van der Rohe said, "God is in the details."

Phase 3 Goals and Results

The primary goal of the design development phase is to solidify and refine the conceptual direction selected at the end of phase 2, and to obtain client input and approval before proceeding into final documentation of the signage project.

Phase 3 results in several items that convey the evolution of the informational and visual aspects of the design concept to the client. At the very least, these items include:

- Sign location plans
- Message schedule
- Drawings showing development of sign graphics
- Drawings showing development of sign hardware

Other items that may or may not be reviewed with the client include:

- Study and/or presentation models
- Full-size mock-ups

Depending on the project's requirements, the EG designer may make a formal presentation during or at the end of phase 3, or may just submit a progress set of the location plans, message schedule, and design drawings for the client's review. In either case, client input on the development of the sign program's details is essential throughout the DD phase, and the EG designer should seek the client's review and approval of the sign program's development before proceeding into the documentation phase.

Phase 4: Documentation

The documentation phase, which is the final design-centered phase of the design process, begins upon the client's approval of the work accomplished in phase 3. Phase 4 continues the convergent activity of phase 3, honing in on detailed solutions and refinements to the subproblems of the sign program.

The goal of the documentation phase is to convey the design intent of the sign program to sign fabricators for pricing and production. In other words, the EG designer works out all the details and ties up all the loose ends of the sign program's design before it gets priced and built. The documents that work together to convey this design intent include:

- Sign location plans
- Message schedule
- Design drawings for the sign graphics and hardware
- Specifications

Note that work on most of these documents was started in the design development (DD) phase, and that the documentation phase is aimed at filling in and finalizing the information contained in these documents to provide fabricators with a complete picture of the sign program's design.

Before the documentation phase begins, the EG designer and client should agree on the format for the signage design documents, if that discussion has not already taken place. This includes the final sheet sizes of all documents in the package, whether the signage package is a stand-alone or part of the document package for an overall construction project—which often happens when signage is part of new construction. It also includes the titleblock, whether the EGD firm's own or that of another party, such as the project architect. Titleblocks appear on all drawings and contain general project and specific drawing information, such as drawing number, date, scale, and so on. (Remember: If the project is overseas, paper sizes and proportions will be different from those in the United States.)

As in phases 2 and 3, it's important to focus on the sign program's information content system in the early stages of the documentation phase. It's time to nail down every last sign location and message because, inevitably, a few will still be left open from the DD phase. Only when the sign locations and messages are finalized can the details of the sign graphics and hardware be finalized, as resolution of these visual aspects of the program is contingent on the quantity, kind, and viewing conditions of the information displayed on the signs.

Finalizing Sign Types

The documentation phase is also when sign types are finalized, to address the few that may have still been in a state of flux during phase 3. Keep in mind that the sign type is part of the sign number keyed on the sign location plans and the message schedule, making sign type revisions tedious, because they must be tracked and updated in the plans and schedule. That said, if sign typing was carefully considered during phase 3, the need to revise sign types during phase 4 should be minimal; but there's always the possibility that the definition of a given sign type needs to be changed or that a type needs to be added or deleted for the final project documents.

The sign message schedule is the master inventory list for the entire program, which is why it is updated and finalized during phase 4 with all changes, additions, and deletions to sign messages and sign types/numbers. Sign type/number changes must also be updated on the final sign location plans. Additionally, drawing reference numbers are entered into the message schedule as final drawings are generated for the sign graphics and hardware.

Just as the message schedule and location plans document the sign program's information content, the design drawings document the visual aspects of the sign program. Often called *working drawings* or *design intent drawings*, these drawings convey the details intrinsic to the design of the sign graphics and hardware.

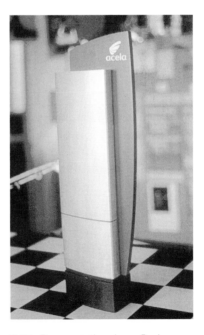

2.21 Documentation phase: Design refinements often continue into the documentation phase, as shown in this professionally made scale model with interchangeable vertical fins, to study and determine the final fin shape. Note that the top of the fin now features a subtle curve.

Deciding on Level of Detail in Drawings

The eternal question on design drawings is how much detail needs to be conveyed in order to obtain clear apples-to-apples pricing from fabricators; thus, this is where the distinction between design intent and working drawings comes into play. It's generally understood among EGD practitioners that design intent drawings contain just the amount of detail that's required to convey the intent or outward appearance of the sign program's design; in contrast, working drawings contain a higher level of detail, typically regarding how the signs could be built.

Along the continuum of design intent to working drawings detail, it's impossible to decree the appropriate amount of detail for any given project, design firm, or client. Accordingly, this section focuses on the core or essential information that needs to be conveyed in the drawings for a sign program.

As noted earlier about sign location plans, the design drawings should be prepared with black-and-white reproduction in mind. In other words, don't rely on the use of color to communicate important information. For example, if a sign background color is blue, it must be noted as such in writing on the drawing; if this is not so noted and the drawing is reproduced in black-and-white, there is no way to know that the sign background is blue. These annotations, which indicate colors, materials, finishes, and so on are referred to as *callouts*.

Dimensioning and Scale

Size is another essential piece of information that needs to be conveyed about each unit in a sign program, so all design drawings must be dimensioned. The extent of dimensioning depends on the complexity of a given sign type, but at the very least overall dimensions (height, width, and depth) should be indicated, as well as the dimensions of any components of the sign type. For example, the overall dimensions of a post-and-panel sign unit are indicated, along with dimensions for the post component and for the panel component. Dimensions indicating where signs are positioned relative to their surroundings are also important. For example, a typical wall plaque mounting elevation indicates dimensions for the plaque's mounting height and distance from door frames.

In addition to being dimensioned, all design drawings must be prepared at scales that can be measured with a scale ruler, typically an architectural scale ruler. The smaller signs in a program can be drawn at full or half size, but larger signs have to be drawn at a smaller scale to fit on the drawing sheet. Again, all drawings must be at a *measurable* scale—that is, not reduced an arbitrary percentage to fit on the sheet. The scale of each drawing should be indicated in writing, and anything that not drawn to a measurable scale should be clearly indicated as N.T.S., for "not to scale."

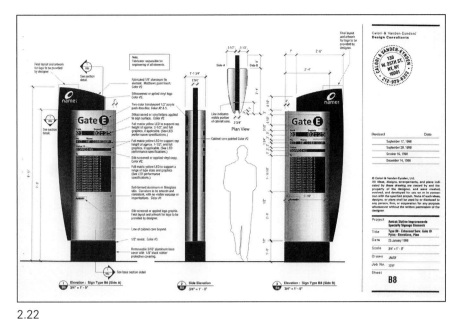

2.22

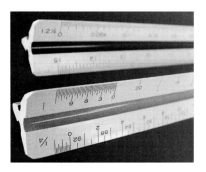

2.22 Documentation phase: The working drawings for the Acela sign program were highly detailed due to the complexity of the signs. On this sheet, front and side elevations have extensive dimensions and callouts.

The importance of measurably scaled, dimensioned design drawings cannot be overstated, particularly to graphic designers, who are not typically trained to work at scales less than actual size. Use of dimensions and measurable scales is the only clear, accurate way to convey the sizes of the various sign units within a program. And it's important to point out that the metric system *must* be used for dimensioning and scaling on any project outside the United States. You'll find the metric system, once mastered, to be much easier to use than the U.S. system.

Conveying Design Information

In addition to providing dimensional information, the design drawings contain a package of information about the sign program's visual aspects. A checklist guide for the drawings package content includes:

- Listing of the graphics vocabulary, including the full fonts of all typefaces, along with all symbols and arrows used

- Summary of all colors, materials, and finishes used in the program

- Front, side, and top views of each sign type, with callouts

- Representations of the different graphic layouts for each sign type, with callouts

- Mounting elevations, fixing signs in relation to architectural or site features

- Sign location plans, typically bound in with the design drawings package

Depending on the sign program's design, more or less detailed information may be required than indicated on this checklist. For example, if a sign is a simple, flat, square wall plaque, top and side views may not be required, since the thickness of the plaque can be conveyed by a callout rather than

2.23 Scale rulers: An architectural scale is shown in the foreground, a metric scale in the background.

be dimensioned on a side or top view. Similarly, if that plaque is simply glued to the wall, that can be called out as a note rather than shown in a side or top view. However, in the case of a sign that's more complex in form, say, with tapering or multileveled planes, all sides may need to be shown—front, back, top, right side, and left side, possibly even along with some sections through it. The drawing number of a sign type's primary elevation—typically the front elevation, since it's usually the most distinctive—is entered into the message schedule for each sign number. (See Chapter 6 for an explanation of these drawing views.)

The key to the drawings package is to include all the design information about the signs that will affect how they're priced, how they're built, and how they're installed. The goal is to cover all the bases for all the unique conditions in the program; the trick is to do this without being unduly repetitive. For example, several elevations may be required to show the different mounting conditions for a given sign type at different locations, but a typical mounting elevation can be used for a condition that's the same at many locations, such as wall plaques mounted next to doors. At this point, the drawing number for the mounting elevation corresponding to each sign number is entered into the message schedule.

In the graphics drawings, the EG designer controls the appearance of the sign graphics for a wide range of message content. The graphics drawings should show each unique layout configuration for each sign type, since a given sign type may display several different kinds of informational content, with each requiring a different layout. Keep in mind that a given layout configuration can be utilized for any number of similar messages, so it's inefficient to provide a layout for each and every sign message in a

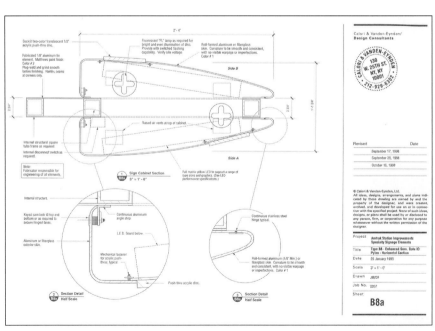

2.24 Documentation phase: Working drawing sheet with cross sections and even larger detail sections address fit of internal components such as LED displays, lighting, and fastening.

2.24

program, unless the sign program is very small. At this point, the drawing number for the graphic layout that corresponds to a given sign number's message content is entered into the message schedule.

Distinguishing between Drawings and Artwork

It's important to make the distinction here between drawings and artwork for sign graphics. The graphic layout drawings visually depict the graphic arrangement of various kinds of messages, but they are not the actual artwork for the final sign graphics. It's more efficient for the sign fabricator, rather than the designer, to produce the final digital artwork for each individual sign unit in a program, so digital art production is typically the fabricator's responsibility; but it's the EG designer who controls the visual appearance of the artwork by providing graphic layout drawings.

As design firms have adopted computers to produce their design documents, the content and nature of documents for the sign graphics have changed. In the precomputer era, it was typical to highly dimension the graphics drawings, because they served as layout grids that the sign fabricator used to produce and assemble the final artwork for each sign's graphics. But now that design firms produce their layout drawings as computer files, it's now fairly common for the designer to provide those files as templates for the fabricator to use in producing the final art.

And that brings up another important distinction: between template files and artwork files. Think of a template as a digital grid, which has typical graphic elements in their specified size(s) and arrangement, into which new messages are input to create individual artwork files for each unique sign message. Template files have active, editable fonts so the fabricator can input the various messages specified for a given layout template to create the final digital artwork file for each sign. Again, sometimes the EG designer will produce individual artwork files for a very small sign program or for a relatively small collection of signs within a larger program.

Once the messages have been input into the artwork files, the fonts are typically converted to paths or outlines, which renders the fonts uneditable (i.e., deactivated) in the final artwork files, to avoid font conflicts with computerized cutting equipment in the fabricator's shop. At this point, the fonts become mere geometric objects in the shapes of letterforms. But messages can't be edited in files with deactivated fonts, so it's important for the EG designer to maintain the source files with editable, active fonts in case artwork for additional or revised messages needs to be produced. (Chapter 5 has more on graphic layouts.)

Compiling Technical Specifications

Specifications serve as an adjunct to the design drawings, communicating verbally what the drawings can't communicate visually. As such, the specifications, or specs, can be thought of as the instructions to the sign fabricator. As with the design drawings, the appropriate level of detail and formality of the specifications varies with each project.

An entire book could be written about specifications—indeed, there are professional spec writers, who occasionally become involved with signage projects—so the purpose of this section is to provide only a general overview of specifications relating to signage.

As mentioned, signage fabrication is part of the construction industry, and the signage specs become part of the fabrication contract, which is let by construction industry professionals such as general contractors (GCs) or construction managers (CMs). The actual fabrication contract is a legal document that consists of many more general contractual items than the signage specs, including terms and conditions (often referred to as *boilerplate* or *up-front conditions*), bonding requirements, and others; thus, the specs that are concerned solely with the product to be constructed— that is, signage—are termed the *technical portion* of the specs.

The extent and formality of signage technical specs is dependent on the size and circumstances of each project. On small projects, the specs can effectively be incorporated into the design drawings. On larger projects, particularly those for large governmental or institutional clients, the EG designer may be required to provide highly detailed, formalized specs conforming to the MasterFormat established by the Construction Specifications Institute (CSI). CSI format specs are in the form of a letter-sized document independent from the drawings. (More information about CSI format can be found at www.csinet.org.)

Most signage specifications fall somewhere between drawing notes and CSI's MasterFormat in detail and formality. Usually the signage specs are wordy enough that they're easier to produce as a letter-sized word processing document than put on the drawings. And even if the client doesn't demand strict CSI language, the EG designers should not be surprised if they are told to label the signage technical specs as "Section 10 14 00," which is the section of the CSI MasterFormat devoted to "Signage". Note that the 2004 MasterFormat has further subcategories, such as "10 14 16, Plaques" under the Signage section. Nor should the EG designer be surprised to see the signage specs bound into a huge, comprehensive specification document for an overall construction project.

Two other important tips about the detail and formality of the technical specs:

- Unless all the specs are treated as drawing notes, there should be as little redundancy as possible between any drawing notes and the letter-sized spec document. There will always be some redundancy between the two, but it's time-consuming to indicate a spec twice, or to need to change a spec in two places rather than one.

- In the interest of clarity and brevity, spec language should be as definitive and concise as possible. Specs are definitely not a creative

Section 10400 – Project Name and Description

2.8 ILLUMINATION

A. It is the responsibility of the Sign Fabricator to provide bright and even illumination appropriate for the condition.

B. Code: Conform to State Electrical Code, National Electrical Code, and U.L. listings for all materials. All electrical components and wiring methods for internally illuminated sign units (by others) shall be properly insulated and UL Approved. Coordinate with architecture.

C. All internally illuminated sign units shall be adequately vented to dissipate heat generated by electrical components.

2.9 FABRICATION / GENERAL SIGN CONSTRUCTION

A. Fabricator shall fabricate signs and graphics following dimensions and details shown in the Contract Documents, accepted Shop Drawings, Graphic Layouts, and other Submittals, and as otherwise approved or specified.

B. Intent of Specifications: It is intended that all finished work be of the highest quality to pass eye-level examination and scrutiny by the Architect.

1. Construct all work to eliminate burrs, dents, cutting edges, and sharp corners.

2. Finish welds on exposed surfaces shall be of the correct type to eliminate distortions of flat surfaces, and to be imperceptible in the finished work. At exposed connections, all flux, oxides, slag, and discoloration shall be removed so that these areas match the finish of adjacent areas. Any damage by welding shall be repaired by grinding, polishing or buffing.

3. Except as indicated or directed otherwise, finish all surfaces smooth.

4. Surfaces that are intended to be flat shall be without dents, bulges, oil canning, gaps, or other physical deformities.

5. Surfaces that are intended to be curved shall be smoothly free flowing to required shapes and shall be without dents, bulges, oil canning, gaps, or other physical deformities.

6. Except where approved otherwise by Architect, conceal all fasteners.

7. Make polycarbonate LED access lenses tight-fitting, curved and flush with adjacent surfaces with no exposed fasteners or hinges.

8. Exercise care to assure that polished, plated, or finished surfaces are unblemished in the finished work.

Project Name   10400 - Page 11   Date

2.25

2.25 Technical specifications for a typical signage project.

writing exercise! Typically, sentences are formulated in a somewhat brusque, instructional, form, such as, "Use stainless steel fasteners for all sign attachments," and use the biblical-sounding verb *shall*, as in "All signs shall be attached with stainless steel fasteners." Words such as *must*, *should*, and even *will* are considered too indeterminate in intent for spec language.

Regardless of the level of detail or formality required, on one level or another, the technical specs for signage should cover at least the following:

- Quality assurance
- Required submittals
- Quality/workmanship standards
- Materials and products
- Fabrication and graphic application techniques
- Installation and cleanup

Quality assurance specifies the qualifications fabricators must provide to assure they're capable of performing the work required by the design. This is very important on projects that go out to publicly advertised bidding, as such projects often draw bids from unqualified fabricators. Qualifications requested may include length of time in business, list of similar projects in scope and cost, list of designer references, square footage of fabrication shop, list of shop equipment and personnel, percentage of work to be subcontracted, and the like.

Required submittals indicate which drawings, samples, and other items fabricators are to submit for design review as they produce the project. Submittals required for signage typically include shop drawings, artwork for all sign graphics, material/color/finish samples, product literature, and production prototypes.

Quality/workmanship standards describe general standards for the quality of work to be performed by the fabricator, such as tolerances, accurate fitting of parts, use of nondefective materials and components, production and finish standards, and more.

Materials and products specs indicate specific materials and products the fabricator is to use to produce the project, such as metals (e.g., stainless steel, aluminum, etc., plus specific alloy if necessary for the appearance or integrity of the design), plastics, paints, stock sign components, electronic displays, and so on. If a specific material or product essential to the design of the project is only available from one manufacturer, the material/product name should be specified, along with the manufacturer's name and contact information. Such *proprietary specs* are sometimes frowned upon by clients, necessitating addition of the term "or approved equal" in the proprietary spec.

Fabrication and graphic application techniques specify the techniques the fabricator is to use in producing the sign hardware and graphics, such as how parts are to be attached to each other, seamless or seamed assemblies, types of finishes and coatings, how graphics are applied, and others.

Installation and cleanup indicates how the fabricator is to install the signs and clean up after installation, such as coordinating sign installation locations with other trades or parties, installing signs level and plumb, restoring any adjacent areas damaged by sign installation, removal of fingerprints and dirt from installed signs, and the like.

Phase 4 Goals and Results

The primary goal of the documentation phase is to tie up all the loose ends of the sign program's design, and clearly communicate the program's design intent to sign fabricators, who will be bidding on and then producing the sign program. It's the last design-intensive phase of the design process before the design is handed off to the producer. As such, it's the last chance to finalize all outstanding detail, approval, and coordination issues, to avoid unpleasant—and, often, costly—surprises during the postdesign bidding and fabrication phases.

Phase 4 results in several documents that convey the final design intent to the client and other parties involved in procuring fabrication of the program:

- Final sign location plans
- Final message schedule
- Final sign graphics drawings
- Final sign hardware drawings
- Technical specifications

The EG designer wouldn't have progressed to phase 4 without client approval of big-picture presentations of the program's design in phases 2 and 3, therefore formal design presentations are rare during the documentation phase. Designer-client interaction during phase 4 is usually more in the form of coordination meetings and document review to resolve all the details of the program, culminating in the client's approval to release the design documents for the bidding phase. Coordination between the designer and the client's contracting representative should also occur during phase 4 to prepare for the bidding phase.

Phase 5: Bidding (Postdesign)

Finally, the project has been completely documented and the design work is done, for all intents and purposes. Bidding is the first of three postdesign phases in the overall design process, and it's the phase in which official, binding prices are competitively obtained for the sign fabrication contract, and a bidder is selected for the contract. As with previous phases, the formality of the bidding phase depends on the project at hand.

Remember, EG designers very rarely procure sign fabrication services because they don't have the hefty financial or legal resources needed to enter into a construction industry contract. Rather, the sign fabrication contract is let by an outside entity who represents the client, such as a GC, CM, or a government or corporate purchasing department; therefore, the EG designer's role during the bidding phase can be described as advisory.

After the designer releases the document package to the client's contract representative, it's that representative's responsibility to compile and assemble the overall bid document package, issue the documents for bidding, administer the bid process, evaluate the bids, and award the fabrication contract. Unfortunately, contract reps sometimes leave the EG designer out of the bidding loop. This is a mistake for two reasons. First, the project design firm can provide valuable technical assistance on signage issues during the bidding phase; second, many contract reps don't have experience with signage packages.

Bid phase items on which the design firm can advise the contract rep include:

- Bidder qualification
- Bid form development
- Invitation to bid
- Responses to information requests
- Bid review
- Contract award recommendation

Bidder Qualification

Signs are some of the most highly scrutinized objects in the built environment, making bidder qualification a very important step in the design process. Simply put, an inexperienced or poorly equipped fabricator can destroy a sign program's design value and create enormous headaches for the entire project team. Also, many owner reps, while experienced in heavy construction trades, lack the means to assess the capabilities of sign fabricators to successfully execute the type of signage project at hand. In fact, the owner's rep has the experience to assess the financial condition of potential signage bidders but it is the EG designer who has the experience to assess their technical production capabilities.

When possible, to achieve a high level of quality control, it's best to have bidders' qualifications reviewed *before* bids are solicited; the project then goes out for bids from a preselected group of quality-screened bidders. Many publicly funded projects, however, require open bidding without regard to prequalification. In such public-funding scenarios, the qualification requirements of the technical signage specs become essential for eliminating unqualified fabricators that have submitted bids.

Developing Better Bid Documents
Mark Andreasson

The quality and pertinence of the information that you include in your bid documents is the key to a good and fair result. From the fabricators' perspective, there is some essential information that will help them to determine whether they should pursue the project in the first place.

The Basics

Basic questions you should be asking as you begin to formulate your bid documents include the following:

- What date is the bid due?
- Is a prebid meeting required? If so, has it been scheduled?
- What is the anticipated project schedule? When would work be awarded and what is the project completion date?
- Is it a public or private bid?
- Are there any special contract requirements such as tax exemption, bonding requirements, union labor, off-hours work, Minority and Women's Business Enterprise (MBE/WBE) requirements or owner-controlled insurance programs (OCIP)?

The Bid Form

By providing a standardized bid form you will be better able to control the pricing information that you get back and allow you to more easily set up a more precise comparative analysis among bidders. At a minimum, the form should include these items:

- A list of the quantities, by sign type.
- Space for itemized sign type cost and installation cost, on a unit-times-quantity basis.
- Individual line items for taxes, bonds, and permits, or any other special considerations, including alternates.
- Space to list any general expenses that would be part of the project costs, regardless of how

the quantities may fluctuate—for example: management costs, shop drawings, shipping, travel expenses, equipment, and so on.

The Documents

Specifications

The written specifications should include a clear description of the scope of work. This may include identifying the party responsible for excavation and foundation work; bringing electrical service to the site; electrical tie-in; removal of existing signs; layout of artwork or maps; permit procurement; and others. Specifications will also encompass vendors and material and process information pertaining to metal alloys, coatings, surface finishes, light fixtures, adhesives, and the like. Bear in mind that the less control you, as a designer, will have over the final decision about which fabricator will be awarded the work, the more thorough you should be while writing specifications and preparing drawings.

Sign Location Plan

The sign location plan may not be an essential element at the time of bid; nevertheless, it will help the fabricator understand the site, and thus should be included—if it is accurate. In combination with the message schedule and the bid form, this gives the fabricator the opportunity to cross-check quantities between the three documents.

Message Schedule

The message schedule is an essential tool for the fabricator to reference while preparing pricing. Some of the information contained will tell the fabricator whether a sign has one or more sides with graphics, or how many lines of text there will be. Signs that contain individual dimensional letters are usually priced by the letter, so an estimator will need to count each letter in the various messages. The message schedule should also contain a location number that will, in turn, reference the location plan.

The Drawings

The drawings comprise the primary tool used to communicate the form and spatial relationships among the elements. Therefore, the more information that can be conveyed through the drawings, the better. The fabricator will be examining the drawings primarily to identify information that has a cost impact—such as color breaks, material thicknesses, relationships between parts, dimensions, face and edge finishes, fasteners, graphic applications (e.g., silk-screen versus vinyl versus digital print)—so every effort should be made to include this type of detail.

Another helpful piece of information communicated through the drawings is how each element is intended to interface with the architecture or landscape. Both exploded views and thumbnail perspectives are incredibly helpful to an estimator, making it possible to quickly understand a design. Moreover, often, they will help you, as a designer, to identify spatial or dimensional problems that may not be obvious in a typical front/top/side view. Color layouts, particularly when portraying elements with intricate color patterns, are always helpful, as well. And don't forget to check your scale. The most common errors found in design drawings usually involve incorrect dimensions or incorrect scale.

As a designer, the most valuable skill you can develop is a thorough understanding of the materials, technologies, and processes involved with the fabrication arts. This is the medium in which you work, and the better you understand the materials and the way things go together, the more options you will have at your disposal. In this way, you become more valuable to both your employer and to your clients.

Mark Andreasson is president of Design Communications Ltd., Boston, Massachusetts.

The designer's role in the qualification process may be as simple as providing a list of sign fabricators with whom the designer has previously worked as potential bidders for the project, usually a minimum of three. Or bidder qualification may entail much more work on the designer's part, such as reviewing qualification literature and information provided by potential bidders, visiting their shop facilities, conducting interviews with them, and contacting their references to assess past performance on similar projects. In either case, the designer should have no affiliations with, nor imply performance guarantees for, any recommended or reviewed fabricator.

Bid Form Development

Bid forms provide a standardized means for all bidders to submit their bids, easing the task of bid comparison and analysis. The EG designer can advise the contract rep on how to devise the bid form for the project, or can provide the bid form to the contract rep. At C&VE, we favor unit pricing for bid forms, since unit prices provide much more information for bid comparison than a single lump sum for the entire fabrication contract.

At their most basic, unit price bid forms are itemized by the unit price for each sign type times the quantity of each sign type, yielding a total price for each sign type and a grand-total, bottom-line price. Of course, there are many variations. Client reps may want any of the following:

- The fabrication and installation costs quoted together on a unit basis for each sign type

- Fabrication and installation costs quoted separately on a unit basis

- Fabrication quoted only on a unit basis, with installation quoted as a lump sum

- Costs quoted with sales tax included in unit prices

- Costs quoted with sales tax as a lump sum

The designer may want to include on the bid form quantities for each sign type, but with the caveat that each bidder is responsible for verifying all quantities.

Invitation to Bid

The invitation to bid provides specific information to bidders on preparing and submitting their bids. This information can include when and where to submit bids, contact information for the contract representative, brief scope of work, bid guarantee period, work completion dates, and any other information that may be pertinent to bidding the project.

Responses to Information Requests

Responses to information requests are just that. Bidders sometimes have questions or need clarifications about the design documents—although generally not too many if the EG designer produced a thorough document package. These questions can come up in a prebid conference, where the EG designer is present to respond, or in the form of official requests for information (RFIs). Bidders are typically required to send an RFI to the owner's representative, who in turn routes the RFI to the EG designer, often via the project architect, if one is involved. The designer then responds via the same channels, usually within a requested time period.

A word about protocol during the bidding phase: To ensure a fair bidding process, all bidders should have access to the same information. Accordingly, unless otherwise arranged, the designer should avoid responding directly to any given bidder's questions and route all communication with bidders through the contract rep.

Bid Review

Bid review involves the analysis of the bids submitted by fabricators. The client's rep will usually organize the numerical bid results in some form, such as a table, and the designer should review this information for discrepancies or red flags among the field of bids, such as an unusually high or low unit price for a given sign type, or a wide spread between the lowest and highest bids. The designer should advise the contract rep of such anomalies and have the rep request clarification.

Contract Award Recommendation

The contract award recommendation is typically a joint decision involving the contract rep, the client, and the designer. Depending on the project, factors other than price may play a role in the contract award decision. These factors can include the bidders' conformance with the formal contractual requirements, qualifications, understanding and responsiveness to the project at hand, financial status, and others.

Phase 5 Goals and Results

The main goal of the bidding phase is for the client's contract rep to award a contract to a fabricator qualified to produce the sign program at a competitive price. This process involves the contract rep's solicitation, administration, and review of bids, with the EG designer performing an advisory role to the rep and client.

Depending on the project, phase 5 can result in the designer providing or advising on certain documents for the bidding process, such as:

- Bid form
- Invitation to bid
- Responses to information requests, including prebid meeting

During phase 5, the designer should also be involved in reviewing the bids received by the contract rep and in contract award decision making. Additionally, the designer should attend the prebid conference and be involved in reviewing the qualifications and capabilities of the bidders.

Even though the designer's role is advisory during phase 5, all parties— including the designer—should feel confident that the selected bidder is capable of fabricating the sign program to the highest-quality standards at the lowest possible price. This sense of confidence is the most important result of phase 5.

Phase 6: Fabrication/Installation Observation

In this second postdesign phase of the design process, the client's contract rep has contracted with a qualified sign fabricator to produce the sign program, and the EG designer's creative solution to the signage problem is physically embodied. This is the exciting moment of truth for the designer, when all the planning, vision, and hard work literally take form.

In the fabrication/installation observation phase (subsequently referred to here as "observation"), the designer reviews the fabricator's work and progress for technical conformance with the design intent, while the contract rep administers the overall mechanics of the contract, such as payment schedules, time schedules, coordination of signage with other trades, routing of project communications, and so forth.

In the architectural profession, this phase of the design process is often termed *construction administration* (CA) or, simply, *construction phase services*. Note that the use of the word *administration* is somewhat misleading, because the overall administration of the contract, including payment of subcontractors such as sign fabricators, is primarily the responsibility of the client's contract rep, not the architect. The EG designer's role during this phase is similar to the architect's during the construction phase: observing and reviewing the fabricator's work, and advising the contract rep on its quality and progress in relation to the design intent. Thus, the designer's role is of an advisory rather than an administrative nature (which is why this book uses the term *observation* rather than *construction administration*). That said, the EG designer's role during this phase should, however, be much more active than that of a passive, disinterested observer.

Activities in which the EG designer should be involved during the observation phase include:

- Coordination meetings
- Submittal review
- Shop visits
- Site visits
- Postinstallation punch list inspection

Although some clients, in an attempt to reduce design fees, request little or no designer involvement during the observation phase, it's important to note that the designer's involvement is a key quality control measure during sign fabrication. EG designers are far more experienced with the details that comprise a signage program, and they have the greatest expertise of anyone on the project team to review and assess the fabricator's fidelity in executing the design intent. Certainly, the designer's involvement may be limited in some of the activities listed, to reduce design fees, but at the very least the EG designer should review all of the fabricator's submittals, which include shop drawings and samples, during phase 6.

Coordination Meetings

Coordination meetings are important tools during the observation phase, starting with a fabrication kickoff meeting at the beginning of the phase, which the client's contract rep, the fabricator, and the designer attend, along with any other interested project team members, such as the client or project architect. The kickoff meeting helps set the stage for an efficient observation phase, covering such items as the expectations and responsibilities of all parties, identification of any potential problem areas, identification of coordination points and processes, definition of project communications protocol, and so on.

After the kickoff meeting, periodic coordination meetings are necessary as sign fabrication progresses, and the designer's involvement with them can vary with the project at hand. In addition to face-to-face meetings, other tools can be utilized for project coordination, such as teleconferencing, e-mail, an FTP site, or dedicated project collaboration Web sites.

Submittal Review

Submittal review is the key role for the EG designer during phase 6. As noted in the discussion of phase 4, submittals are items the fabricator prepares to indicate how the sign program will be fabricated, and these items are submitted for the designer's review and approval. Submittals required for signage typically include shop drawings, artwork for all sign graphics, material/color/finish samples, product literature, and production prototypes.

Each kind of submittal provides a different piece of information about the sign program's fabrication.

- *Shop drawings* indicate how the fabricator will construct and install the signs.
- *Artwork* shows the size and layout of graphics for each unique message/sign type combination within the sign program.
- *Material/color/finish samples* show the actual materials, colors, and finishes the fabricator will be using on the signs.
- *Product literature* provides information and specifications on signage components, such as lighting fixtures or electronic display devices, which the fabricator purchases from outside manufacturers.
- *Production prototypes* are, effectively, samples of the actual, completely fabricated and assembled signs, with one prototype typically provided for each sign type. Obviously, production prototypes are usually submitted after all the other submittals have been approved, giving the fabricator the green light for actually producing the signs on a trial basis. Approved production prototypes then become the quality standard for the remaining production run, and may also be part of the total sign product the fabricator delivers and installs.

2.26a, b Observation phase: Shop drawings indicate how the sign fabricator intends to build the signs. These final revision shop drawings have been reviewed and approved.

Submittal review is a checkpoint process that facilitates coordination and helps catch mistakes, inaccuracies, and defects, and resolves misunderstandings before the sign program is built. It's in the best interest of every fabricator to provide meaningful, complete submittals for design approval, because approved submittals indicate that the fabricator is on the right track in interpreting the design intent of the sign program, thereby

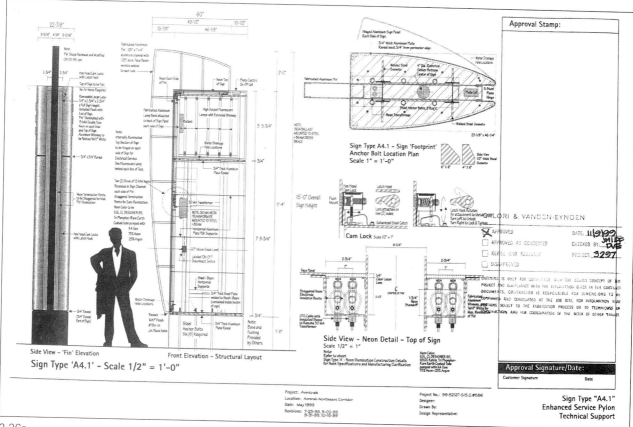

2.26a

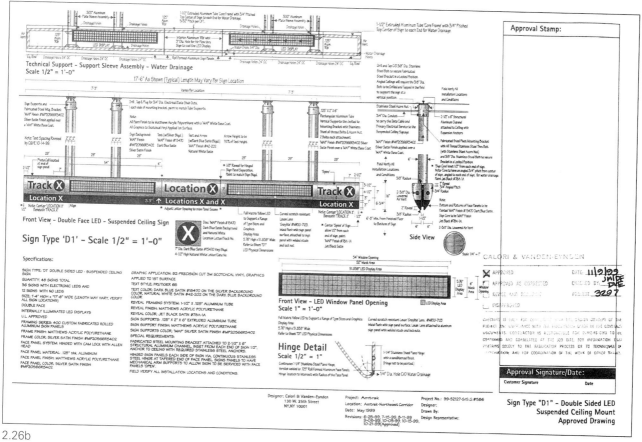

2.26b

2.27a, b Observation phase: Production prototype of gate pylon with LED displays in test mode. Sign cabinets were designed to provide service access to LED and lighting components while also protecting them against the elements and providing convection ventilation.

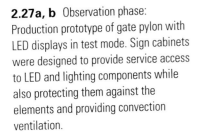

2.27a

2.27b

minimizing the chances of design rejection after the entire program is fabricated.

Most kinds of submittals are sent to the EG designer's office for review via a routing protocol set up for the project. The one exception may be production prototypes, as the prototypes for some sign types may be far too large to transport to the designer's office. Prototypes for smaller-sized sign types, however, can be reviewed in the designer's office.

The formality of the submittal review process varies from project to project, as does the protocol for routing the submittals. The key is to keep all interested parties in the loop so they're aware of all comments and approvals on all submittals. For this reason, it's best for the fabricator to issue all submittals to the contract rep, who in turn routes them to the proper parties for review. The routing order is reversed after the submittals are reviewed. Although such protocols can be cumbersome, they are vital, as they help prevent mistakes and misunderstandings by ensuring that all project communication is transparent and that all key players are aware of the status of the submittals. It is definitely bad form for the designer to discuss submittals directly with the fabricator without inclusion of the client's contract rep and/or architect—although in certain cases the contract rep and/or architect will authorize such direct contact.

Even when the design document package for a program is very thorough, many of the infinite details of the sign program are worked out during the observation phase. As such, sign fabrication is a give-and-take process that requires mutual respect between the designer and fabricator, assuming the fabricator is properly qualified. The two must work together to ensure that the design intent is executed as faithfully as possible, and that requires reasonableness—and, sometimes, compromise—on both sides regarding submittals.

The fabricator shouldn't try to "pull any fast ones"—for example, trying to convince the designer that substandard workmanship is within acceptable industry standards. The fabricator should also prepare meaningful shop drawings, which provide an accurate picture as to how the signs will actually be produced with that fabricator's equipment, shop practices, and personnel, rather than an unconsidered rehash of the design drawings. This is now more important than ever, since it has become more common for some fabricators to try to pass off design drawing rehashes as shop drawings. Conversely, the designer shouldn't be unreasonably fussy—for example, objecting to fabrication details that don't compromise the appearance or functionality of the design intent.

That said, the designer should review submittals very carefully, for once a submittal is approved it is considered an acceptable standard for fulfillment of the fabrication contract. In most cases, submittals are stamped or tagged with a review stamp that has check boxes for indicating the submittal's approval status. Typically, these boxes are labeled in a range from Approved (outright approval) to Approved as Noted (conditional approval) to Revise and Resubmit to Rejected. Note that some EGD and architectural offices avoid the use of the word Approved on their stamps because it may imply the designer's guarantee of the fabricator's performance; in such cases, a less definitive word, such as Reviewed, may be used. Depending on project protocol, the review stamp may belong to the EGD office or to another firm on the project team, such as the architect, or the review stamps of both may be used. In addition to the

2.28a

2.28b

2.28a, b Observation phase: Production prototype of station/site identification pylon showing hinged sign cabinet for lighting component access. Internally illuminated acrylic letters are flush with the face of the vertical fin and pushed through beyond the face of the curved airfoil sign body. Note the horizontal reveal, which points out, rather than conceals, joints between the sign panels.

status check boxes, the review stamp typically contains a disclaimer of the reviewer's responsibility, along with spaces for the reviewer's signature and review date.

The review stamp status is accompanied by any applicable review comments written on the submittal. On paper submittals, such as shop drawings and graphics artwork, the drawings are marked up with review comments in red pencil—hence the terms *markups* and *red lines* for reviewed drawings. On some projects, other project team members, such as the architect, will mark up the drawings with comments additional to those of the EG designer.

It's rare for all the various submittals on a signage program, particularly shop drawings and graphics artwork, to be approved, outright or conditionally, on the first round. It's often a process of revise and resubmit based on the design review comments, or, less commonly, outright rejection, when a submittal is so off base that it doesn't even warrant the EG designer's time and consideration. The key is that the fabricator is required to resubmit, in a timely manner, each submittal item until it is approved. As such, the resubmittal process can become a war of the wills, which requires judiciousness—and, sometimes, compromise—on behalf of both designer and fabricator.

Shop Visits

Shop visits are performed during the course of fabrication to observe the quality and progress of sign production in the fabricator's shop. The need for, and number of, shop visits varies with each sign program. Smaller, relatively simple programs, with just a few sign types that are physically

2.29a, b Observation phase: Production prototypes of gate pylon and platform canopy signs. Internal illumination of push-through gate identifier flashes to indicate boarding trains. Platform canopy signs were designed in modules that were configured to fit canopies of varying width from station to station.

2.29a

2.29b

small in size, may require no shop visits since production prototypes can be sent to the designer for review. Larger, more complex programs, with many sign types that are too large in size to transport to the designer, may require several shop visits.

When shop visits are warranted, they are conducted by the EG designer, often accompanied by the contract rep and/or the client. The purpose of the first shop visit is typically to review production prototypes, although on some larger projects the first shop visit may be devoted to project coordination and review of other kinds of submittals. The need for additional shop visits varies with each project, but if only one shop visit is covered in the design budget, it's most effectively allocated to production prototype review, during which the designer can discuss any design or fabrication issues directly with the shop-floor personnel involved in building the prototypes.

The observations and conclusions of shop visits are documented in a memo or the meeting minutes, which can be recorded by the EG designer, the contract rep, or the fabricator. In projects where the shop visit records are produced by others, the designer should review them for accuracy and completeness before they are distributed to the project team.

Site Visits

Site visits are typically concerned with coordinating sign installation, such as verifying sign locations and mounting heights, and coordination of sign installation details with the adjacent site conditions. As with shop visits, the need for and number of site visits varies with the sign program's size and complexity. Site visit participants can include the EG designer, contract rep, client, and other members of the project team, such as the

2.30 Observation phase: After the production prototypes are approved, the full fabrication run commences. Here, aluminum sheet for side and top panels is cut on a computer-controlled routing table.

2.30

2.31 Observation phase: Aluminum panels rolled into the airfoil shape await assembly.

2.31

architect. The observations and conclusions of site visits are documented similarly to shop visits.

Postinstallation Punch List Inspections

Postinstallation punch list inspections are also site visits, but now the EG designer and/or contract rep walks the project site to inspect the signs after they've been installed, and enters any defects onto what is termed a *punch list*—which is why this inspection process is also called *punching out.* On some projects, the fabricator may accompany the punch lister(s) for at least part of the inspection. (Note that the term *defects*, as used here, includes not only fabrication defects but a whole host of other problems such as missing signs, signs damaged in shipping, signs mounted crooked or in wrong locations, sign installation damage to adjacent construction, and others.)

The message schedule, which already exists as a complete itemized inventory of every sign in the program, can be readily adapted for punch list comments. The contract rep forwards the completed punch list, often accompanied by a memo summarizing general comments, to the fabricator to make any necessary corrections to the defective signs.

Obviously, on a large signage program, the punch list inspection can be very time-consuming—and exhausting—so it's important to point out that the design budget may not accommodate the EG designer performing an exhaustive inspection of each and every sign. There are, fortunately, a couple of ways to adhere to the design budget in such instances. For one, the designer could inspect all of the signs that receive the most public scrutiny and just spot-check the less noticeable signs. Or the designer and the contract rep or client can spend a day together spot-checking each sign type, with the designer pointing out what to look for and then handing off the inspection of all the remaining signs to the contract rep or client.

2.32

2.32 Observation phase: Assembly of a platform canopy sign.

As with submittal review, the punch list inspection requires reasonableness and, sometimes, compromise. The punch lister needs to know where to draw the line between acceptable and unacceptable products, hence the punch list can become an instrument of negotiation. There's also the thorny issue of signs that have been damaged by other trades after the signs were installed but before they were punched out. For this reason, the sign program should be punched out as soon as possible after installation.

After the fabricator has taken action to remedy any defects, the corrected signs should be punched out in a follow-up inspection. This inspection is best performed by the designer, but can also be handled by the contract rep, if necessary. After all the work is completed to everyone's satisfaction, the contract rep arranges the final payment to the fabricator, and the new sign program is up and running! It's time for congratulations, handshakes, and photography to document the final product of the signage design process.

Phase 6 Goals and Results

The main goal of the observation phase is to observe and review the fabrication and installation of the sign program. It is the contract rep who handles the general administration of the fabrication contract, with the EG designer taking on the dual roles of advisor and facilitator on the technical issues relating to the fabricator's fulfillment of the design intent.

Phase 6 should result in the EG designer participating in the following activities that provide review checkpoints for the sign fabricator's quality, progress, and compliance with the design intent:

- Coordination meetings
- Submittal review

2.33a

2.33b

2.33c

2.33a, b, c Observation phase: Uncrating, lowering, and attaching the primary exterior identification sign at Philadelphia's 30th Street Station.

- Shop visits
- Site visits
- Postinstallation punch list inspection

At the very least, the designer should be thoroughly engaged in submittal review and approval, providing review comments and approval status marked up on the submittals. The designer's involvement is also key to more effective coordination meetings, shop and site visits, and punch list inspections. Depending on the project, the designer may also be involved in providing coordination memos and meeting notes.

Phase 7: Postinstallation Evaluation

The signage program solution that took so long to evolve, to become reality, has been built and installed and is, everyone hopes, a huge success. It might seem, then, that the design process has been concluded in the observation phase and that it's time to move on to another project. Not so fast. Whether formally or informally, paid for by the client or not, every design solution should be evaluated.

In phase 7, the EG designer evaluates the effectiveness and functionality of the operational signage program. The major goal of evaluation is to learn which aspects of the signage program are successful and which aspects, if any, could use improvement. The results of the evaluation phase of a given sign program can be applied to both the program at hand and to other programs the EG designer develops in the future.

It should go without saying that, in fact, evaluation takes place throughout the design process, as various solutions and processes are explored, considered, presented, and either selected or rejected. But only after installation can the sign program as a whole be evaluated in its real-world environment.

Most often, evaluation takes place informally and without the direct involvement of, or compensation to, the designer. So how can the designer obtain evaluation input? The two most basic ways are through client feedback and direct observation. After living with the operational sign program—and people's responses to it—for a while, the client gains insights into the program's strengths and (ideally, few) weaknesses. Accordingly, it's useful to contact the client a few months after the sign program is installed to request the client's assessment of the program's effectiveness. At this point, the client may commission the designer to develop any additional signage or make any modifications to the in-place signage that may be needed to fine-tune the program.

The designer can also visit the project site and directly observe how people interact with the sign program and how the program fits with its environment. This approach may also include interviews with site staffers who interact with the site's users. The depth and formality of the direct observation approach tend to depend on whether or not the designer is being compensated by the client for assessing the project.

Phase 7 Goals and Results

The primary goal of the evaluation phase is for the EG designer to learn how effectively the sign program solution functions in its operational environment. Phase 7 results in insights and findings that can be applied to the sign program being evaluated, as well as to other sign programs developed by the designer.

As noted, the designer may or may not be compensated for performing an evaluation of the sign program, and this tends to determine the depth and formality of the assessment. In either case, client feedback and direct observation are helpful evaluation tools. If the designer is being compensated for phase 7, a report may be produced that summarizes the conclusions and recommendations of the evaluation process. In any event, after the sign program has been operational for a period, the client may engage the designer to fine-tune the program with additional and modified signs.

Chapter Wrap-Up

That's it for the design process. It's quite a journey, even when delineated in somewhat simplified form, as in this chapter. And no two projects are ever quite the same, so it has myriad variations and nuances.

Design is an evolutionary, creative, problem-solving process, so plan thoroughly, don't jump the gun, keep the ideas flowing, and follow through on everything. From the initial project research to conceptualization to development and documentation of the design to advising on bidding and fabrication to evaluating the final sign program, the design process involves a lot of work. It makes concepts become reality and, ideally, results in a successful sign program—and, perhaps, lasting friendships with other members of the project team.

Overview of the Signage Pyramid Model

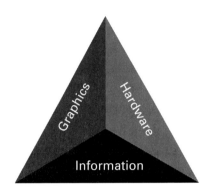

3.1 The three components of the Signage Pyramid model.

As explained in Chapter 2, "The Design Process," the design of a comprehensive signage and wayfinding program is a very complex undertaking, more complex than most people—including those in the broad-spectrum design community—might imagine. So how can EG designers approach a signage problem and begin to chase down a successful solution? By using the Signage Pyramid, a methodology I outline in this chapter and delineate further in the next three chapters. It is an effective, systematic, proven approach to mediating the problems and subproblems associated with the design of a comprehensive signage program.

I initially developed the Signage Pyramid approach in my graduate school studies and thesis, and have since noodled with and fine-tuned it through years of practice at my design office. Although many people think I'm crazy to share this proprietary tool with my fellow designers (and competitors!), I think the time has come to contribute it to the growing body of knowledge about EG design.

As pointed out in Chapter 1, when I developed this approach, the terms *signage* and *environmental graphic design* were just coming into use, and the field was just progressing from its infancy to toddlerhood. The Society of Environmental Graphic Designers, now the Society for Environmental Graphic Design (SEGD), had been formed a few years prior to my graduate studies, and very little information was available on how to approach EGD problems. The notable exception to this knowledge gap was the seminal book, *Architectural Signing and Graphics*, written by esteemed pioneers of the field, John Follis and Dave Hammer, in 1979.

Genesis of a Design Approach

In my professional career, after receiving my undergraduate degree, I gravitated from two-dimensional print to three-dimensional signage design because I found the 3D aspect of signage to pose more interesting design challenges than print work. My first foray into the signage world was as a member of a design team that was developing the signage for a large, new international airport being built overseas. The team consisted of graphic designers and architects working within the corporation that was designing and building the airport.

In the early project phases, we focused primarily on the design of the sign graphics, based on a rudimentary list of messages, and the sign objects that would display those graphics. During the design development phase, we began to develop the actual sign messages and locations that would be needed for people to find their way through this very complex airport environment. In the process, the number of messages that had to be displayed on the signs grew from one to many, and this required a fundamental alteration in the design of the signs from the one conceived during the schematic design phase. I somehow believed that this amount of backtracking shouldn't be necessary, and so decided to take my budding professional EG design experience to graduate school to analyze what's involved in EG design and to figure out a way to approach it more seamlessly. Thus, the Signage Pyramid approach was born.

The Signage Pyramid's Component Systems

During my graduate ruminations, I deduced that the primary purpose of a sign program is to communicate information about a given environment to users of that environment, and that that information is conveyed via graphics displayed on physical sign objects or hardware. From that, I came to realize that the design of a signage program is composed of the design of three constituent yet interrelated systems:

- Information content system
- Graphic system
- Hardware system

Comprehensive sign programs consist of many types of signs, from large exterior freestanding pylons to small interior wall-mounted plaques. A key design problem is how to create a unified family resemblance, both informationally and visually, among all the various types of signs in a comprehensive program. The Signage Pyramid does just that: It provides a balanced, three-prong solution to this problem.

Basically, the Signage Pyramid approach is a classic divide-and-conquer strategy for solving a complex problem. By breaking down a complicated, nebulous, seemingly insurmountable signage problem into its component parts, each of those parts can be more readily solved. The Signage Pyramid method views all signage programs as composed of the three distinct but interactive systems, just itemized, that must be balanced in the design process. Each of these systems is outlined briefly here.

The Information Content System

The communication of information is the functional essence of any signage program; therefore, the information content system consists of:

- The information displayed on the signs
- How the sign messages are worded

3.2

- Where the sign information is located
- How the messages and locations of the various signs in the program relate to each other in a consistent, cohesive network of information

The Graphic System

The graphic system is the two-dimensional vehicle that visually encodes and displays the information content system. The graphic system consists of:

- What two-dimensional graphic elements—typography, symbols, arrows, and color—are used to encode the sign information
- How the graphic elements are arranged into layouts, to organize the information content, emphasize messages, and create a visual identity
- How the graphics are applied to signs

The Hardware System

The hardware system is the collection of three-dimensional, physical sign objects that display the sign information as encoded by the sign graphics. The hardware system consists of:

- The three-dimensional shapes of the signs
- What sizes the signs are
- How the signs are mounted or connected to other environmental objects
- The materials, coatings, finishes, and lighting techniques used
- The stylistic relationship of the sign objects to one another and their surroundings

System Roles

Each of these systems plays a distinctive role in the development of a sign program, yet they all interact with each other. The information content

3.2 The Information Content System consists of sign locations and the messages they contain.

3.3 The Graphic System communicates the information content of a signage program with two-dimensional graphic elements and their arrangement.

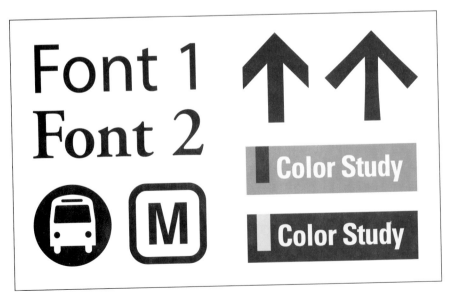

3.3

system is the underlying reason for a sign program to exist. Sign information is not tangible, per se; it's the raw communication material that makes a sign program work. In this respect, the information content system can be thought of as the software of a sign program—you can't see it or touch it but the sign program wouldn't be functional without it. In contrast, the graphic and hardware systems exist to make the program's information content visible and concrete in the built environment.

Given that the information content system is the bedrock of a sign program, the development of this system—often called *programming*—is a more planning-oriented than design-oriented activity. As such, the information content system should be mapped out and planned before design of the graphic and hardware systems begins in earnest. Why? Because any design activity will be somewhat meaningless and, therefore, wasted if the extent of the information content system, for which the graphic and hardware systems are being designed, is unknown.

Take, for example, the design of a drinking vessel as a very simple analogy: The type of liquid content—whether water, coffee, beer, wine, or a cocktail—and the quantity of liquid it can contain will, obviously, have a profound influence on the design of the vessel. Should it be thick- or thin-walled, stemmed or not, large or small, glass or ceramic or plastic, equipped with a handle, and so on? Without knowing the intended contents, the designer would very likely spend a lot of time designing a vessel that's completely inappropriate to its required function. The same applies to designing a sign program's graphic and hardware systems before the EG designer has developed the information content system.

Accordingly, the information content system is the foundation, the planning that takes place before design of the graphic and hardware systems commences. Thereafter, design of the graphic and hardware systems takes place concurrently, in a back-and-forth manner. Additionally, the information content system may be further refined or tweaked as design of the graphic and hardware systems progresses.

System Interactivity

So much for the differences between the three systems of the Signage Pyramid. Now, how do they interact? The information content system is

3.4 The Hardware System consists of the three-dimensional physical objects—their shape, structure, arrangement, and materials—that display the sign graphics.

3.5 Just as the kind and quantity of liquid content affects the design of a drinking vessel, the kind and quantity of information content affects the design of a signage program.

3.5

the bedrock, the raw informational material that is communicated by the graphic system, which in turn is displayed on the hardware system. Let's examine a few examples of this interaction. For starters, sign locations and messages, part of the information content system, have a profound effect on the size of the graphics for a given sign, as determined by the reading distance for the graphics and the length and quantity of messages. The size of the sign graphics, in turn, affects the size of the sign hardware that displays the graphics.

The sign location aspect of the information content system can also directly affect the hardware system, in that the location of a given sign can determine how the sign is mounted, and sign mounting is a primary formal factor in the hardware system. The graphic and hardware systems interact in terms of visual appearance factors, such as style and color.

There are many other ways in which the three systems of the Signage Pyramid interact with each other, as will be seen in Chapters 4 through 6.

The Signage Pyramid and Resource Allocation

There's no doubt that all design activity, including EG design, involves a certain amount of backtracking—one step backward for each two or three steps forward—as the designer progresses from initial concept to final product. But the Signage Pyramid approach can help reduce the amount of backtracking encountered when solving complex signage problems, and this translates into more efficient use of the EG design team's time and, therefore, design budget.

At the outset of any EG design project, there's a big temptation, on behalf of both the designer and the client, to rush into creating design concepts— that is, the pretty pictures for sign graphics and hardware. But too often this just results in finding out later that the concepts won't work at various sign locations or for the quantity and nature of information various signs need to contain. Don't fall prey to this temptation! Keep in mind, the sign information content system is intangible, meaning it doesn't lend itself to sexy visualizations; nor is the planning of this system as creative as design of the graphic and hardware systems. But, by gritting your teeth and tackling the information content system first, you'll find the subsequent design of the graphic and hardware systems to be far more focused, hence effective.

Think of trying to design a book or a Web site without having the information—or at least a good idea of the information—these items are to contain. Without the content, designing that book or Web site would be a waste of time, because the design of these items is so intrinsically linked to the quantity and nature of the information they contain. The same holds true for designing a signage program: It's a waste of both time and money

3.6a

3.6b

3.6a, b Examples of graphics-driven signs, in which richly detailed graphic treatments enliven flat, rectilinear sign hardware panels.

to design the program's graphic and hardware systems without the informational content.

Not only can the Signage Pyramid approach help allocate design resources and budgets, it can also help in the allocation of fabrication budgets. The way the information content system affects fabrication budgets is essentially a numbers game: the more sign units required to communicate the sign information, and the bigger the signs must be to hold all the required information, the more expensive the job will be to fabricate. The point? Take care not to oversign an environment.

The graphic and hardware systems affect fabrication budgets differently. Generally speaking, sign quantities and sizes aside, more of the cost of fabricating a sign is tied up in the three-dimensional hardware system than the two-dimensional graphic system. This is due to the cost of the hardware system's raw materials, such as aluminum and steel, the cost of working those materials into the final sign objects, and the cost of installing the sign objects at the project site. In a freestanding overhead freeway sign, for example, most of the cost goes into building and installing the three-dimensional hardware structure that supports the sign panel that displays the message graphics—even though, often, these sign panels contain only a few words! In general, the simpler the detailing of the hardware system forms, the less expensive the sign objects are to fabricate. For example, a flat sign panel is cheaper to produce than a curved one. Rich detailing of the graphic system, however, has less impact on fabrication costs.

These facts can help the EG designer allocate fabrication budget resources. If the fabrication budget for a given project is limited, the EG designer may consider designing the sign program to be driven by the

3.7 Flat graphics directly applied to columns create visual impact at less expense than three-dimensional graphics or highly detailed sign hardware.

3.8a, b This program features a single showcase or centerpiece sign, whereas other, more commonplace signs have related but simpler materials and details.

3.9a, b Limited fabrication budgets can be stretched by concentrating high-end materials and details into a showcase or centerpiece sign that becomes the focal point for all the other signs in a program.

3.8a

3.8b

3.9a

3.9b

graphic rather than the hardware system. In such a case, the sign graphics are the primary design feature, as applied to simple, flat sign panels.

Another strategy for allocating limited fabrication budgets is to concentrate the more expensive hardware system details on a few, highly visible showcase or centerpiece signs, and design the rest of the signs in the program with simpler hardware system details. The key in such cases is to maintain a formal resemblance among all the sign objects in the program's hardware system—from the splashy showcase signs to the less obvious room number plaques, for example.

Chapter Wrap-Up

This chapter has provided an overview of the Signage Pyramid model for approaching the design of a signage program. This model divides and conquers the complexities of a signage problem by splitting it into three different yet integrated systems that are more readily managed and solved. These three component systems are the information content, graphic, and hardware systems.

This chapter has also stressed the importance of *planning* a sign program's information content system before *designing* its graphic and hardware systems, and has explained some of the ways in which these systems interact.

Finally, this chapter has described how the Signage Pyramid model can aid in the allocation of both design and fabrication budget resources. The next three chapters are devoted to a detailed explanation of each of the component systems of this model, with the aim of providing the EG designer with the tools to effectively solve even the most complex signage problems.

The Information Content System

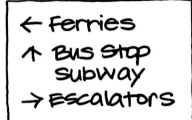

4.1 The information content system.

Signs are meaningless without information. What good is a blank sign?

Signs exist for one purpose and one purpose only: to communicate information to people about their environment. Unlike other objects intentionally placed in the built environment such as light fixtures, walls, flooring, landscaping, and so on, signs literally speak to viewers, in that they convey meaningful information that people, in turn, act upon. In this respect, a sign is one of the few truly interactive elements of the built environment. And because people have to engage in the act of reading the information on signs, signs also are among the most scrutinized objects in the built environment. Other environmental objects, by their very form and existence, may connote an inherent message (e.g., a fence or high wall connotes "stay out"), but they do not do so in a literal, denotative manner as do signs.

Put simply, a sign program's information content system consists of what the signs say—the information they communicate—and where that information is located in the environment. The information content system of a signage program can be compared to the operating system of a computer. Like all those unseen 0s and 1s in a computer program, the information content system makes the sign program function; indeed, it is the essence of signage, but it's intangible, in that it doesn't take physical form. Put another way, a sign program's information content system is the program's communication infrastructure, the network of content that links all the signs in a program together informationally.

As explained in Chapters 2 and 3, it's essential to plan and develop the information content system—an activity often called *programming*—early on in a project. Programming is critical because before meaningful design activity for the graphic and hardware systems can take place, the EG designer has to have a good idea of the amount of information each sign will display, the physical conditions of each sign's location, and the viewing conditions for each sign.

Unlike other graphic design projects, it's typically the responsibility of the EG designer to take the lead in formulating the informational content of a signage program, with the input and approval of the client. In contrast, in collateral, Web, advertising, and other graphic design projects, the informational content is typically provided by others, such as professional copywriters.

Why do EG designers generate the informational content for sign programs? Because they possess the skills to analyze a site's plan, its circulation paths, and the informational needs of its users, all necessary to map out where signs are needed and the kinds of information content the signs should convey. More traditional content providers, such as copywriters, do not possess these skills.

It's important to reiterate that information content system development consists primarily of locating signs and generating their messages. Typically, the EG designer plays a lead role in locating signs, with the EG designer and the client playing a mutual role in the formulation of the sign messages. In some projects, the sign message content may be almost entirely developed by the client, with the guidance of the EG designer; in other projects, the sign message content may be almost entirely developed by the EG designer, with the client's advice and approval.

Kinds of Sign Information Content

The information content system serves many functions in a signage program and provides many kinds of informational content. For example, in wayfinding signage, the information content system is the "bread-crumb trail" that helps people find their way through an environment. The various types of informational content communicated by signage are categorized in this section, along with an indication of who may generate the message content and locations for each type of information. In a comprehensive signage program, all or many of these kinds of information will be displayed on the program's various sign types. But before we delve into these categories, keep in mind that every signage program and every EG designer is different, so some EG designers may use different terms than the ones used here to refer to the various kinds of sign information content. Additionally, some of these informational content categories may overlap.

- *Identification signs* are located at a destination to identify that destination or place in an environment. Identification signs confirm that "you have arrived" at a destination; and they may or may not have directional signs leading to them. Identification sign message content— that is, destination names—may be generated by the EG designer and/or the client. But identification sign locations are typically mapped out by the EG designer; and message content and locations for identification signs related to life safety, such as stair identification signs in high-rise buildings, may be mandated by code authorities.

- *Directional signs* are located remotely from destinations to direct people to the various destinations within a given environment. Directional signs are also often referred to as *wayfinding signs* because they help people

4.2 A "bread-crumb trail" made permanent in the red brick paving of Boston's Freedom Trail.

4.3 Identification signs confirm that "you have arrived" at a destination, such as this building address at Royal Executive Park in Rye, New York, one of New York City's northern suburbs.

4.4 Identification and directional signage combined on one sign unit at McCarran International Airport in Las Vegas, Nevada.

4.3

4.4

find their way to destinations. Directional signs almost always display arrows to point out specific paths—such as, left, right, straight ahead— to destinations. Directional sign message content—that is, destination names—may be generated by the EG designer and/or the client. Directional sign locations are typically mapped out by the EG designer.

• *Warning signs* alert people of hazards or safety procedures within an environment. Two common examples are Danger: High Voltage; and In Case of Fire, Use Stairs Unless Otherwise Instructed. Warning sign message content and locations may be developed by the EG designer and/or the client, and often are mandated by code authorities.

4.5 Directional signage guides drivers to civic facilities and major highways in the city of Summit, New Jersey.

4.6 Primary and secondary directional signs at Lambert-St. Louis International Airport's long-term parking facility.

4.5

4.6

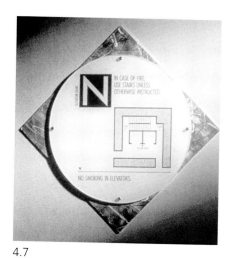

4.7

4.8

4.7 Warning sign at a New York University dormitory conveys building evacuation procedure at elevator lobbies, along with elevator bank identification, smoking prohibition, and map showing stair locations, all per New York City code.

4.8 Warning sign for the One Raffles Quay office tower complex in Singapore.

- *Regulatory and prohibitory* signs are intended to regulate people's behavior or prohibit certain activities within an environment. Two common examples in this category are Authorized Personnel Only and No Smoking. Regulatory and prohibitory sign message content and locations may be developed by the EG designer and/or the client, as well as be mandated by code authorities.

- *Operational* signs inform people about an environment's use and operations, thus may often be quite detailed, requiring some time to study and absorb. One example is directory signs, also called directories, which list the location of tenants within an environment, often accompanied by a locator map. Other examples include signs listing days and hours of operation, such as for a retail store; and the All Visitors Must Be Announced signs, which are ubiquitous in Manhattan apartment buildings. Message content and locations for operational signs may be generated by the EG designer and/or the client.

- *Honorific* signs confer honor on people associated with an environment. A prime example is donor signage, which displays the names of financial benefactors of a site or facility. Another example is a building

4.9 Regulatory/prohibitory sign at the FDR Memorial in Washington, DC.

4.10 Regulatory/prohibitory sign at Lema Ranch in Redding, California.

4.9

4.10

4.11

4.12

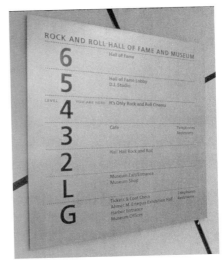

4.13

4.11 Operational signage explains use of municipal parking lots in Summit, New Jersey.

4.12 Operational sign announces security procedures at Philadelphia's Cira Centre office tower.

4.13 Operational signs, such as this building directory at Cleveland's Rock and Roll Hall of Fame and Museum, often convey detailed information that requires close study.

cornerstone, which typically displays the date of erection, along with the names of the building's developers, architects, and other notables. Honorific signage is most common at institutional and civic sites and facilities. The message content for honorific signage is typically provided by the client, but sign locations may be mapped out by the EG designer or the client.

- *Interpretive* signage helps people interpret the meaning of an environment, or places within it, by providing information on its history, geography, inhabitants, artifacts, and more. Examples include plaques that commemorate the event(s) that took place at a historical site, such as a battlefield, and signs that provide information about the animals at

4.14 Honorific signage includes donor recognition signage such as this Donor's Circle of granite columns at MidState Medical Center in Meriden, Connecticut.

4.14

4.15

4.16

a zoo or aquarium. Research—often quite scholarly and detailed—is usually required to develop the information content for interpretive signage, and the research, content development, and locations of interpretive signs may be undertaken by the EG designer, the client, and/or experts in the subject matter of the interpretive program.

Hierarchy of Content

Not all informational content is equal in a signage program. Some sign messages and locations are more important than others, therefore, the designer must impose a hierarchical ranking on an environment's sign messages and locations, based on relative importance. In this process, signs are ranked in regard to whether the information they display is primary, secondary, tertiary, or even less important. The general principle is that the more important the information, the higher the rank. This, in turn, translates into the size of the graphics conveying the information and, correspondingly, the size of the sign itself. Logically then, signs communicating primary information are larger than those communicating secondary information, and so on. Additionally, the ranking of the information determines how visually prominent the sign that displays it should be. Generally speaking, the higher up a sign is displayed, within limits, the more visually prominent it is. (Chapter 6, "The Hardware System," has more on sign mounting heights.)

There are two basic, related reasons why a sign information hierarchy is necessary:

- To enhance communication effectiveness.

- To conserve space on sign faces.

Regarding the first, communication effectiveness, consider an airport terminal, which has many destinations, some of which are more important

4.17

4.15 This donor recognition wall, which honors financial benefactors to Philadelphia's Wharton School of Business, features glass panels to which the names of additional donors can be added.

4.16 Interpretive signage provides information on aquatic wildfowl at the Port of Los Angeles.

4.17 Interpretive panels on the back sides of map signs in Washington, DC's citywide signage program inform citizens and visitors about neighborhood points of interest.

to a greater number of people than others. For example, more people will be seeking out check-in, gate, and baggage claim areas (primary destinations) than the nursery (secondary or tertiary destination). To give all of these destinations equal importance on a primary directional sign— or, indeed, even to include all of them on such a sign—leads to information overload and communication breakdown. Particularly with directional signs, which often list multiple destinations, there is a limit to how much information people can absorb while moving through an environment, especially if they are in vehicles.

A similar circumstance occurs with signs displaying content other than directional information. Continuing with the airport example, it would be confusing if the airport's hours of operation were signed with the same prominence as the ticketing area or other major destinations. Similar confusion and overload would arise if the nursery and janitor's closet were identified as prominently as the gate numbers.

Related to communication effectiveness, sign information hierarchies help conserve sign space. As the old saying goes, "You can't pour 10 pounds of flour into a 5-pound sack." The amount of space a sign has for the display of information is often constrained by various physical site factors, such as low ceiling heights, which limit the height of overhead signs to allow adequate vertical clearance for people or vehicles to pass underneath. A sign that's limited in size is also limited in informational capacity; therefore, it should not contain messages other than those that are the most important. Even where there are fewer physical site constraints on sign face size, loading too much information on a sign is dysfunctional.

Developing the Sign Information Content System

As noted at the beginning of this chapter, developing a sign information content system is often called *programming* and this process is best introduced with a question: What information do sign users need and where do they need it? Essentially, this process entails mapping out sign locations and establishing the message nomenclature that will be displayed on the signs at each location.

Sign Locations

Sign locations are determined by analyzing circulation routes and decision points within the project environment. This process, too, can be addressed by posing a question: "Where are the pathways that people move along, and where along those pathways must people decide whether to make a turn or proceed straight ahead?" The EG designer answers this question by reviewing the project's plan drawings, which depict a site or building from above, and marking out where the circulation routes and decisions points are. If the project at hand is new and not yet built, plan drawings will be the only tools for analyzing circulation and decision points. If, on the other hand, the project site exists, the EG designer has an additional tool: He or she can visit the site to survey circulation and decision points in situ. Obviously, it takes more skill to envision circulation and decision points for a site that doesn't yet exist and is defined solely by drawings than for a site that can be directly experienced. Whether or not the project site exists, however, plan drawings are the medium for sign location analysis.

Although plan review focuses on lateral circulation, it's necessary to keep in mind that for many project environments vertical circulation routes are just as important as the lateral ones. A great many sites, such as rail stations, airports, hospitals, retail malls, and parking garages have multiple floor levels and the vertical circulation pathways between these levels present key decision points for navigating the site. Section drawings, which are vertical slices through a building that reveal the stacking of its levels, can aid vertical circulation analysis.

After studying decision points and user circulation, the EG designer begins to map out the signs on plan drawings, making a mark to indicate each sign on the plan. This initial go-round of the sign location plans may include just primary signs, for simplicity and clarity, and they may be color-coded

4.18 Circulation analysis of primary and secondary pedestrian pathways, as well as vehicular pathways, in Washington, DC.

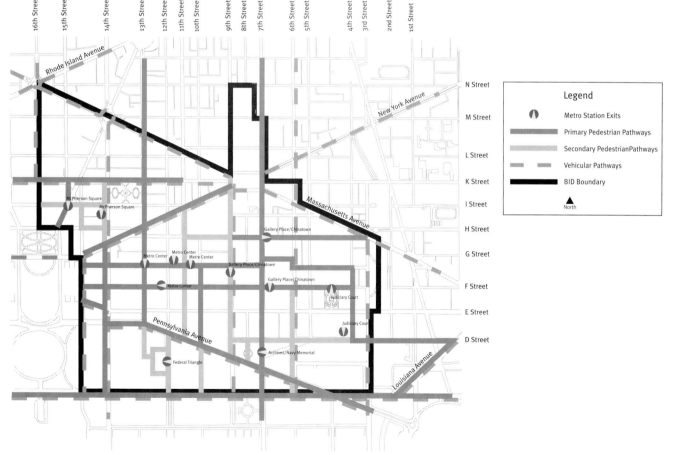

4.18

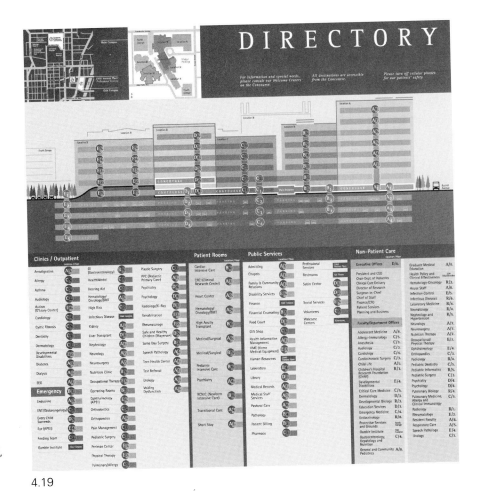

4.19 The directory for the Cincinnati Children's Hospital indicates vertical circulation routes in the interconnected, multibuilding complex.

4.19

4.20 A unique three-dimensional directory for the cruise ship Radiance of the Seas provides orientation to lateral and vertical circulation, as well as to the ship's fore and aft.

by communication function—for example, red for directional signs, blue for identification signs, and so on. Remember, though, as pointed out in Chapter 2, color coding can be useful for the initial sign location plans, but the final sign location plans should not rely on color coding to communicate important information about each sign, as the final location plans may be reproduced in black-and-white only.

Keep in mind that like the design process itself, developing sign location plans is also an evolutionary process, so expect to go through several iterations of the sign location plans and corresponding messages before they are finalized.

Tips for Determining Sign Locations

- Always locate signs perpendicular to the viewer's line of movement and sight, as people can't see signs located parallel to their line of movement/sight without turning their heads. This can be dangerous, particularly in driving situations, when drivers need to keep their gaze focused on the road ahead.

- Always locate directional signs at decision points; and on long paths, reinforce the information on additional signs to assure people they're heading in the correct direction to their destination, as shown in Figure 4.22.

- In certain situations, particularly those involving vehicular signage where reaction time is a factor, use advance directional signs (e.g., Departing Flights Next Left) to give people enough time to maneuver to the decision point. Use these in tandem with confirmatory directional signs (e.g., Departing Flights with a left directional arrow) at the actual decision points, as shown in Figure 4.23.

- Place identification signs at the destinations to which people have been directed, to confirm their arrival at the destination they've been seeking, as shown in Figure 4.23.

Thus the wayfinding bread-crumb trail has been laid: Directional signs point to the various destinations at each decision point along a circulation route, and each destination is identified to confirm that it has been reached.

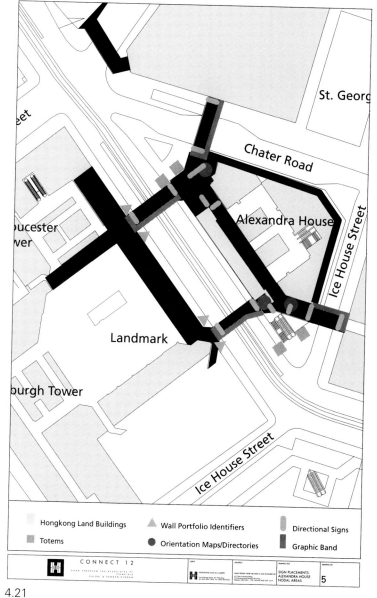

4.21

4.21 Initial sign location plan maps out primary sign elements, defined by communication function.

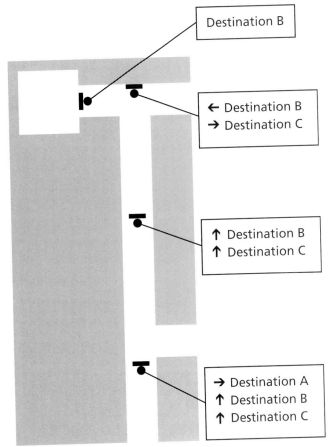

4.22

4.22 Directional signs should be located at decision points, and directional information should be reinforced with additional signs on long paths.

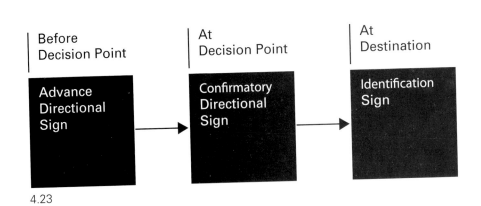

4.23

4.23 Advance directional signs give people time to maneuver for turns at decision points, which are signed with confirmatory directional signs. Identification signs verify arrival at the destination.

After the initial sign location plans have been developed, the EG designer should examine the site conditions at each location. These site condition factors include:

- Viewing distances

- Viewing angles

- Physical limitations on sign sizes and/or mounting heights, such as low ceiling clearances or narrow corridor widths

- Physical sight-line obstructions, which can be fixed, such as columns or trees, or movable, such as people or vehicles

- Lighting conditions
- Sign mounting opportunities
- Adjacent surfaces, finishes, and functions

As with circulation analysis, it's easier to determine conditions at each sign location when the project environment actually exists and can be surveyed in person, rather than having to rely solely on drawings. But on projects whose sites are not yet built, again, drawings will provide the only reference for site conditions, so all available architectural and/or engineering drawings need to be studied carefully. In addition to plan drawings, these architectural drawings will include elevations and sections, with elevations showing vertical surfaces such as walls and doors, and sections showing vertical slices through the site. On projects that require ceiling-mounted signs, those drawings will include reflected ceiling plans (RCPs), which should be consulted to ascertain ceiling conditions at each sign location. Renderings, models, photos, and other visualizations of the site can also be helpful in assessing sign location conditions.

Another important design guideline has to do with scale. That is, even if the final sign location plan documents aren't prepared at a measurable scale, early sign location studies should take place on plans of a measurable scale so that viewing distances can be accurately measured with a scale ruler. Why is viewing distance so important? Because the farther the distance from which a sign must be viewed, the larger the sign typography must be; and the larger the typography, the larger the sign size must be to accommodate it. (Chapters 5 and 6 go into greater detail about sizing sign typography for viewing distances.)

By identifying site parameters and constraints, the information gathered in studying sign locations begins to set the stage for designing the sign program's graphic and hardware systems, as well as for defining the program's sign types. It also aids in identifying and coordinating sign locations that require additional support systems to be brought in, such as electrical or structural.

As the EG designer learns more about the conditions at each sign location, the sign location plans will be refined and filled in with all the signs necessary for the program. Concurrently with mapping out sign locations, the EG designer is also mapping out messages to be communicated at each location, which leads to a discussion of message nomenclature development.

Sign Messages

Each project site requires a message nomenclature vocabulary. This should be a consistent and concise collection of messages to be displayed on the site's signage. The operative words here are *consistent* and

Wayfinding: Passive and Active
Wayne Hunt

In an act of wayfinding, we respond to two kinds of environmental design. The first is the environment itself—sight lines to destinations, objects that help us maintain orientation, intuitive location of entrances, even lighting and sounds. These built-in features in the natural and man-made environment are the passive tools of wayfinding. The best places and spaces are rich with these integrated attributes that foster orientation, understanding, and self-guiding.

The second category of wayfinding design is the group of added active elements: signs, directories, color-coding, and other more literal tools that help guide us. These proactive elements are needed to supplement and clarify the as-is, or passive, environment. It is in this second category of design, active wayfinding design, that most environmental graphic designers operate. We plan, design, and implement systems of physical tools that are added to or overlaid onto and into existing or planned places and spaces.

This combination of passive and active information allows us to navigate freeways, find our way in museums, stay oriented in malls, and even find the party in an apartment building—"After you get to our building, just follow the noise to our place." However, the best environments have a higher percentage of passive wayfinding qualities. These are the intuitive, self-guiding places that need relatively few directional signs: the museum with a formal heroic entrance; the European town with a large clock tower in the center; the theme park with restrooms right where we expect them (and when we need them); hotel corridors with distinctive art, and so on.

Lost in the Woods

If you have ever become lost while hiking, you suddenly became dependent on the passive native things in the natural world—the position of the sun, a distinctive rock formation you passed that morning, a distant mountain range, and the like. Regaining orientation is critical, often a matter of life or death. You are without active wayfinding elements until you stumble upon a trail sign.

Note that a trail map is an active tool, but its utility depends on users matching the features shown on the map with their real-life counterparts in the environment, a melding of passive and active wayfinding processes. But even with a good flashlight, a trail map is of little use after dark.

Where Is the Cave?

Ancient humans were wholly dependent on reading the natural environment for wayfinding information. Heading out for a day of hunting, ancient man intuitively recorded his route and could quickly retrace the path back to safety in an emergency. Survival depended on this innate ability to wayfind by means of a wide variety of passive elements. Some wayfinding experts contend that even things as subtle as regionally unique, tiny wind-shaped patterns in desert sand could signal nearness to an important destination or the location of water.

Ever More Active Elements

Modern urban development has covered over many of the natural wayfinding cues, so much so that our daily world is largely a human-constructed place, but we still have a built-in, innate need to be oriented—to know where the cave is. To meet this powerful need, we are more and more dependent on the hard and literal tools of active wayfinding. To interpret and navigate through today's complex built spaces and places we need organized systems of signs: signs to direct, signs to identify, signs to inform and signs to regulate.

While this proliferation of signs solves immediate problems, often the real problem is the place itself, if it has been designed without important passive wayfinding qualities. A parking garage has been set back from the street with no view to the entrance; the second floor in a hospital aligns with the third floor in the connected garage; the four corridors leading from an elevator in an office building look identical; the sections in a stadium have a counterintuitive numbering system. Unfortunately, the familiar remedy for all of these all-too-common situations is signs and more signs—that is, active elements added to make up for the missed opportunities of passive wayfinding.

Improving the Active; Influencing the Passive

As wayfinding designers, we continually try to improve the design of signage, but we also look for opportunities to participate in the early stages of projects and help design in passive wayfinding

elements. Such integrated elements and strategies include:

- Building entrances that look like entrances.
- Providing clear sight lines to decision points wherever possible.
- Incorporating the fewest turns in routes between destinations.
- Centrally locating elevators.
- Making elevator doors visible from a distance.
- Differentiating paint and artwork schemes in similar corridors.
- Adding views to exterior features.
- Heightening lighting near entrances, both exterior and interior.
- Using intuitive numbering systems for rooms, gates, and buildings.
- Using descriptive building and department names.
- Designing understandable paths through landscaped areas.

The active wayfinding design skills and strategies developed over the years by graphic designers can and should be applied earlier, during the planning and preconstruction stages of the passive environment. This up-front approach can enable user understanding and self-guiding, hence necessitate fewer active wayfinding elements—signs.

Wayne Hunt is the principal of Hunt Design Associates in Pasadena, California.

concise, for a nomenclature vocabulary that is both consistent and concise is essential for clear communication of the sign information system.

A consistent sign message vocabulary is key to maintaining the bread-crumb trail of information. Once a destination name has been determined, it should be used on *every* sign relating to it. As the saying goes, "Don't change horses in midstream"—developing the sign message nomenclature system is not an exercise in creative writing. Also, never use synonyms! Imagine the confusion of users if some signs in a program display the message Downtown and others display the message Center City. Both have the same basic meaning, but using the terms interchangeably within a sign program causes confusion. Hence, rigid adherence to consistency of message nomenclature is essential for clearly communicating the sign information system.

The sign message vocabulary must also be concise, for two previously stated reasons: to conserve sign space and to prevent information overload. Accordingly, a message should communicate the essential information needed by the sign user in as concise a manner as possible. For example, often, the official names of destinations are quite lengthy, such as Ford's Theater National Historical Site, and such messages take up a lot of real estate on a sign face. The more concise message Ford's Theater communicates the core information necessary for sign users far more clearly and effectively than the lengthy, official message. Accordingly, destination names must be reviewed and edited for conciseness and clarity, and consistently used once edited. Note, however, that it may be difficult to build consensus with clients on the use of the edited versions of destination names.

Related to the conciseness of the message nomenclature vocabulary is the use of abbreviations, which is sometimes necessary to conserve sign space. The rule of thumb is that abbreviations should only be used in sign nomenclature when they are highly recognized by the general public. Examples of highly recognized abbreviations include:

- St., for street
- Hwy., for highway
- Fl., for floor
- Int'l., for international
- Dept., for department

Stay away from less recognized abbreviations, such as:

- Arpt., for airport
- Term., for terminal
- Stn., for station
- Dntn., for downtown

Again, once the decision has been made to use a given abbreviation, use it consistently throughout the sign program. One more point: Don't hyphenate sign messages; while hyphenating words may be acceptable in large blocks of newspaper or book text, it is unacceptable in signage.

Another critical element in achieving consistency of message vocabulary is message syntax, which refers to how the sign messages are structured. For example, there are two common ways to indicate a numerical series, such as levels of a building:

Levels 1 to 5

Levels 1–5

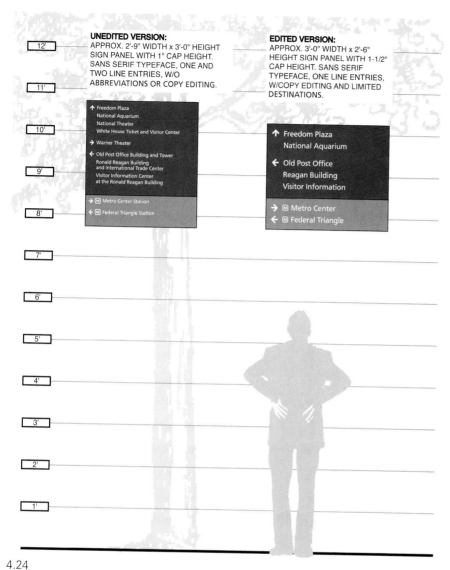

UNEDITED VERSION:
APPROX. 2'-9" WIDTH x 3'-0" HEIGHT
SIGN PANEL WITH 1" CAP HEIGHT.
SANS SERIF TYPEFACE, ONE AND
TWO LINE ENTRIES, W/O
ABBREVIATIONS OR COPY EDITING.

EDITED VERSION:
APPROX. 3'-0" WIDTH x 2'-6"
HEIGHT SIGN PANEL WITH 1-1/2"
CAP HEIGHT. SANS SERIF
TYPEFACE, ONE LINE ENTRIES,
W/COPY EDITING AND LIMITED
DESTINATIONS.

↑ Freedom Plaza
   National Aquarium
   National Theater
   White House Ticket and Visitor Center
→ Warner Theater
← Old Post Office Building and Tower
   Ronald Reagan Building
   and International Trade Center
   Visitor Information Center
   at the Ronald Reagan Building

→ Ⓜ Metro Center Station
← Ⓜ Federal Triangle Station

↑ Freedom Plaza
   National Aquarium
← Old Post Office
   Reagan Building
   Visitor Information

→ Ⓜ Metro Center
← Ⓜ Federal Triangle

4.24

4.24 Lengthy, official destination names are typically edited to more clearly and concisely communicate the essential information. The number of destinations must also be limited.

Both the word *to* and the dash are widely recognized, hence acceptable to use, but one method or the other must be chosen and employed consistently throughout a sign program, to prevent confusion.

As stated previously, the EG designer is the lead orchestrator of the information content system for a sign program. In some cases, this entails structuring and editing message content such as destination names provided by the client. In other cases, the EG designer generates an entirely new message nomenclature vocabulary to impose on the project site; that is, he or she develops a new destination naming system that relates directly to the informational needs of the project's sign users. The most straightforward example of this is the development of a signage room numbering system for a building in which the room numbers on the architectural plans must be superceded by a different numbering system for signage purposes. The need for this arises when the room numbers assigned during the architectural design process (which properly fulfilled

4.25 The major interior circulation spine of Boston's Brigham & Women's Hospital complex was named the "Pike," after the Massachusetts Turnpike, with people directed to various buildings and facilities at numbered "exits."

4.25

their architectural function) do not make sense from a communication standpoint to a person navigating the building. For example, rooms are commonly added or deleted during the architectural design process, resulting in room numbers on the plans that aren't in any logical sequence for a sign user; thus, the EG designer is called upon to develop a new, more logical room numbering system for sign program use.

The EG designer may also generate and impose even more comprehensive new signage nomenclature vocabularies for complex, multibuilding sites, with the goal of organizing the site's nomenclature to simplify and clarify user orientation and navigation. These vocabularies are almost always hierarchical and are developed for unbuilt as well as existing sites. A classic example is a new signage nomenclature vocabulary for a hospital complex that has grown from its original building to several buildings, often with complex, interconnected lateral and vertical circulation routes.

Navigation: Message Hierarchy and Proximity

People navigate from general to specific destinations, and the sign information system needs to be organized accordingly. Navigation is a process of zeroing in on a specific target destination in ever more discrete, nesting steps. In a simple example, consider the steps involved for a woman who lives outside of a city's downtown district who is visiting a friend in a downtown hospital complex. She must:

1. Find her way to the downtown district within the city.
2. Find the hospital within the downtown district.
3. Find the proper wing within the hospital complex.

4. Find the proper floor within the wing.

5. Find the proper room on the floor.

Obviously, when this woman first enters the freeway to head downtown, she isn't going to see her friend's hospital room number on the freeway directional signs. She is likely to see the word "Downtown," which is the first, most general, layer of the informational hierarchy leading to her friend's hospital room sign. The point here is that it's completely inappropriate, let alone impossible, to display every single, specific destination within an environment on all directional signs within the environment. Therefore, sign information must be organized so that it builds from less detailed to more detailed the closer the sign user gets to his or her target destination.

In another example, consider a traveler entering a city environment. Hundreds or thousands of destinations, ranging from major to insignificant, lie within the city, but they couldn't—and shouldn't—all be listed on directional signage. For a cohesive, comprehensible sign information system, the destinations need to be organized on two bases: *hierarchy* and *proximity*.

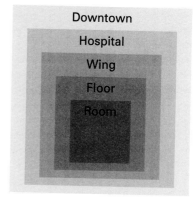

4.26 People navigate from general to specific destinations.

Hierarchy

Developing a sign information hierarchy starts with reviewing and analyzing all the various destinations within the project environment. The first step is to make a list of these destinations and then begin to rank them in order of importance for the sign user. Some rankings will be obvious, such as in an airport, where a janitor's closet would be a less important destination than the security checkpoint. In a city wayfinding example, the municipal sewage plant would be a less important destination than the city government offices or the train station.

In determining the ranking of destinations, the client's input is extremely valuable, and often essential, particularly for projects such as urban or campus signage programs. In these cases, the client often has hard and/or anecdotal data regarding which destinations are most sought out or visited by the most people, and this data can be used to determine which destinations appear on which signs. This data is often referred to as *trip generation* data.

Keep in mind that some destinations are just not important enough to be displayed on directional signs. Nevertheless, people will seek out these less important destinations, so they can be included on map signs or paper map handouts, space permitting. A good example of this sort of sign information hierarchy is found at large regional shopping malls. The primary directional signs typically display only the major anchor store destinations, because listing all the smaller specialty shops would overload the signs with information too detailed to be absorbed effectively. Instead, the specialty store names are displayed on the mall directory maps, which contain detailed information that requires more time to study and absorb.

Proximity

Along with hierarchy, sign information can be organized and displayed according to its proximity to the destination. Again, signs have limited message capacity, so not all destinations can be displayed on all signs within an environment. However, destination names are dropped from signs once they have been reached, freeing up capacity for new destinations, so that as the information system courses through a site, messages are added and deleted from signs.

The general objective of proximity-based messaging is to add a destination to a sign when the sign's location is near to the destination. Just how near to the destination is a judgment call that varies with each project, and depends on the hierarchical ranking of a given destination. A very high-ranking destination such as Downtown may be displayed on a sign quite far away from the destination, along with less highly ranked destinations in closer proximity to the sign location. For all but the most highly ranked destinations, however, a standard should be established stating at what point a destination will be added to a sign. That standard may be different for each project. It might, for example, state that the destination name will be added to all signs located within a 500-foot radius of the destination, or within a .5-mile radius, depending on the size of the sign program's environment and the density of destinations within it.

4.27 Destinations located within a fixed radius from sign location number 42. Different destinations will be located within the same radius from other sign locations.

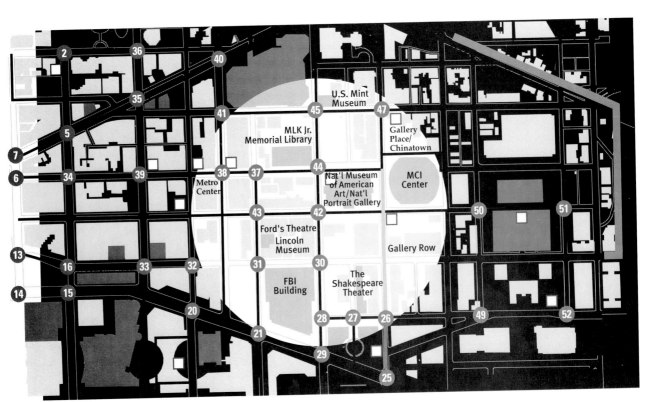

Other Factors Affecting the Sign Information Content System

By now it should be obvious that developing the sign information content system is not a simple process, so it shouldn't be surprising to learn that there are still other factors that make it even more complex. These factors are primarily related to various government regulations and guidelines, as well as multiple language considerations.

Unlike most graphic design projects, the information, graphics, and hardware systems of a signage program are affected by federal, state, and municipal codes and regulations of various forms. It is beyond the scope of this book to delve into the details of these regulations, which are numerous and constantly being revised; rather, the objective here is to raise awareness of the fact that signage must be designed with government regulations in mind, in order to help both the EG designer and the client to avoid pitfalls.

To begin, it is important to note that regulations and guidelines, including those affecting signage, are typically written in cumbersome legal language that can be interpreted in several ways. It is therefore advisable for the EG designer and the client to thoroughly research and review the applicable sign regulations and then develop viable compliance strategies, with the input of legal counsel, code consultants, regulatory officials, and professional organizations, as deemed necessary.

Signage and the Americans with Disabilities Act

The Americans with Disabilities Act (ADA) is a federal regulation enacted by Congress to secure the civil rights for disabled Americans, and these rights include physical access to the built environment. To that end, the ADA includes numerous provisions that affect signage at buildings and transportation facilities. These provisions are contained within the Americans with Disabilities Act Accessibility Guidelines (ADAAG), which are available from the U.S. Department of Justice Web site, www.access-board.gov/adaag/about/index.htm. (Note: The ADAAG was updated in July 2004 but, as of this writing, the updated guidelines have not yet been completely adopted. Check the Access Board Web site periodically to check on the status of their adoption.) In addition to the federal regulations, it's important to be aware that a number of states also have accessibility regulations and guidelines that affect signage, sometimes more stringently than the federal regulations.

The intent of the ADA signage provisions is to promote equal access to the built environment for visually impaired persons, as well as to point out accessible routes for those with mobility impairment. For the visually impaired, the signage provisions stipulate standards that must be complied with in the display of sign information; they do not, however, mandate specific messages that must be displayed on signs. For example,

Regulations and Architectural Signage
Ken Ethridge

I'll bet that no matter where you studied design the subject of regulation was never brought up. You're not alone. When I studied architecture it was hardly ever discussed either. There was, though, a tacit understanding that we'd have to "learn all that stuff later—in practice."

It's all very well to say, "I'll just design and let the drones make it compliant." The problem is that your client actually thinks you know this stuff, and is betting good money on that risky supposition. So here's a very abbreviated version of what I wish someone had taught me in school.

Architecture, and its handmaiden architectural signage, is governed by four major groups of regulation:

1. *Land use (i.e., zoning regulations and ordinances)*: This addresses the questions what can be built and how big it can be, depending on where it is. It is enforced, for example, by a municipal planning and zoning department, with reference to a local zoning code.
2. *Structural (i.e., Building Code)*: This addresses the question how strong it has to be to resist likely forces, including wind and gravity. It is enforced, for example, by a municipal building code department, with reference to both state and local building code requirements.
3. *Escape and egress (i.e., fire and/or building code)*: This addresses the question how people normally exit a facility and during an emergency. It is enforced, for example, by a municipal fire marshal, with reference to a state and local fire or building code.
4. *Accessibility (e.g., Americans with Disabilities Act Accessibility Guidelines (ADAAG) and state and local accessibility codes)*: This addresses the question how should it be built

to make it available to the entire population, no matter what their physical condition. Enforcement for this group is more complicated than the previous ones. The federal government ultimately takes precedence, as the ADAAG supports a federal civil rights law and is enforced by the Department of Justice. The ADAAG, however, may have been formally adopted, in whole or in part, by a state building code. Additional, so-called higher standards may have also been adopted into that code. Local building officials, by logic, should enforce the federal ADAAG as the "law of the land." In practice, however, they will enforce the letter of state and local codes.

In the case of architectural signage, the first two groups, land use and structural, are most likely to affect exterior signs (because they're public and large), whereas the latter two groups, escape and egress and accessibility, will almost always affect interior signage.

Escape and egress signage is, by definition, interior. As is the case for accessibility, local and state fire codes are based on so-called model codes, developed by independent bodies whose members are drawn not only from public agencies but also from the ranks of experts and other interested parties. Enforcement is most often concentrated in the hands of local fire marshals, who function as the inspection division of the local fire department. Such enforcement agents have a great deal of leeway in their interpretations. For example, although fire codes are often very clear about the requirements for signage both inside and outside stairwells, the necessity and location of fire egress maps are often at the discretion of the individual inspector.

Accessibility is also an interior game, simply because although the guidelines define what's permitted under the federal law, the Americans with Disabilities Act (ADA, 1991) refers only to interior signs. As a practical matter, it's easier to assure that disabled persons (mainly the blind or severely visually impaired) have a better chance of finding an interior sign in the first place, much less be able to read what it says.

Notice that I wrote *guidelines*, not *regulations*. They can't be fixed regulations because of the nature of civil rights law. At base is the idea that an individual can bring civil suit against an alleged violator, saying, "The guideline was not enough for my case. The guideline should be changed to include me (and people like me)." Therefore, unlike a regulation, such a guideline can be a moving target, more dependent on the spirit rather than the letter of the law behind it. This

may seem a fine point, especially since *meeting* the *guidelines* and *complying* with the state building code's accessibility *regulations* is usually enough for mere mortals. However, this fundamental difference accounts for most of the confusion in an environment where we expect hard-and-fast rules but are faced, in the case of accessibility, with an array of gray areas. If that weren't enough, both guidelines and regulations change over time, arguably representing the best of current knowledge.

An overall, if not detailed, knowledge of accessibility regulations is now assumed to be part of a design professional's toolkit. Welcome to the adult world.

Ken Ethridge, AIA, RIBA, is vice president, Marketing, for iZone, a manufacturer of digital high-pressure laminate signs and graphics, located in Temple, Texas.

identification signs for all permanent rooms and spaces must display the room or space identifier in raised tactile lettering, accompanied by Grade 2 Braille, which is a shorthand form of Braille. The typographic styles for the tactile lettering are limited: lettering must be in all capitals, and the size of both the tactile and Braille lettering must meet those specified in the provisions. The ADA also mandates the mounting heights and locations of permanent room identification signs.

Signs that contain nonidentification information content, such as directional signs, are subject to compliance with only some of the ADA requirements for identification signs. For example, directional signs are not required to display messages in all-caps tactile lettering or Braille, but typographic style and size requirements must be met.

Similarly, sign information of a changeable nature, such as directory listings and employee names, is not required to comply with the ADA signage provisions. Room functions may also be considered changeable information in certain environments, such as office or academic buildings, where a conference room or classroom may become an office, or vice versa. In such situations, EG designers often employ a two-pronged compliance strategy, in which the room number is the permanent identifier, meeting the ADA's tactile/Braille provisions, and the room function message (e.g., Conference Room or Departmental Office) is the

4.28 Room names on permanent room identification signs must comply with the ADA's tactile/Braille provisions, one of which stipulates lettering in all capitals.

4.29

4.30

4.29 Bathroom signs should be identified by name, not room number. In such cases, the name must comply with the ADA's tactile/Braille provisions.

4.30 A room identification sign with tactile and Braille room number as the ADA-compliant permanent room identifier, plus changeable room information panel.

changeable information not subject to the ADA provisions. This strategy allows flexibility in both the design of the sign and the ability to easily change room functions. Bathrooms, however, are best identified by name, not room number, so in such cases, the room name must comply with the ADA's tactile/Braille provisions.

The ADA signage provisions also address aspects of a sign program's graphic and hardware system design, among them figure/ground contrast, symbol use, and material finishes. These are discussed further in Chapters 5 and 6.

When it comes to ADA signage compliance, an indispensable resource to guide EG designers and their clients is the SEGD's "ADA White Paper," which is discussed in greater detail in Chapter 5, "The Graphic System."

Local Codes and Interior Signage

Local codes, be they on the state or municipal level, contain regulations that affect the information content system of certain signs in a building environment, typically those relating to life safety. These codes can mandate both the locations and messages to be displayed on signage.

The local building code is the most obvious and common source of interior signage regulations, but these may also be buried in local administrative and health codes. Building codes are usually adopted on a statewide basis and they can vary from state to state—although building code standardization efforts among the states are underway. Certain large municipalities, such as New York City, have their own building codes that supercede the state building code.

It can be difficult to identify the local codes that apply to signage, and then to find the regulations on signage within the applicable codes. For example, even though some building codes have a section dedicated to signage, don't be fooled into thinking that all the code's signage regulations are neatly contained in that section, because there's a good chance that other signage regulations are scattered throughout other sections of the code. For example, a requirement for an elevator emergency evacuation sign may be buried in the elevators section of the code. And don't trust the code's index to capture all of the regulations pertaining to signs or signage, because they often don't. The only reliable solution is to visually scan the entire code for the words *sign* or *signage* if the code is in print form, or use the search function (if available) if the code is in electronic form.

Many states and cities adopt standard building codes formulated by independent code councils, such as the International Building Code (IBC) code developed by the International Code Council (ICC). Other localities adopt a standard building code, with amendments/addenda tailored to the locality. Still others have their own proprietary building codes. A word of warning: Building codes are updated on a regular or sporadic basis, so it's always necessary to ensure that you're consulting the edition of the code that affects your project. It's wise to verify the applicable code edition— which is not always the most current one—with the client or project architect.

Standard building codes, which are available in book and, increasingly, digital form, can be purchased from the independent councils that develop them. Some proprietary city building codes, such as the New York City code, are available for purchase through city government channels. Still other building codes are available without charge on the Internet.

As stated at the beginning of this section, local codes pertaining to interior signage typically mandate location and message content of life safety information for building emergencies. This includes information at elevator lobbies which directs people to use the fire stairs instead of elevators to exit the building during emergencies. The exact wording for this elevator safety message may be mandated by the code, as well as the size, color, and/or style of the typography used to display the message. Other content that may be required on an elevator safety sign can include:

- A symbol or pictograph that visually reinforces the typographic emergency stair usage message
- A map diagram showing the locations of the fire stairs relative to the elevator lobby, sometimes with route indicators
- An identifying letter or number for the elevator bank
- A no-smoking message or symbol

The location, mounting height, materials, and colors for the elevator safety sign may also be mandated by local code.

Local building codes also typically specify information that must be displayed on both the occupancy side and stair side of fire stairs, to orient both evacuees and emergency personnel to the stairwells. This may include the word EXIT, a stair identifier letter or number, the floor level number on each stair landing, the floor level on which to exit the building, whether the building can be reentered from the stair, whether the stair has roof access, which levels the stair serves, and other information. As with elevator safety signs, the building code may also mandate the location, mounting height, message wording, typographic style and size, and color and material of stair safety signs. Additionally, because these signs can identify permanent spaces, any identifying information must also meet ADA provisions.

Outside the scope of work of EG designers are standard illuminated building exit signs and illuminated signs identifying designated areas of refuge or areas of rescue assistance. The reason? These signs are usually required to be illuminated, often on dedicated circuits with backup power, so electrical engineering professionals are best equipped to handle them.

In addition to life safety signs typically mandated in the building code, other local codes may affect locations, message content, size, and so on, of other kinds of interior signs. Examples of such local code related signage abound, but two of the most common are no-smoking signs and maximum occupancy signs for public assembly spaces. The State of California, for example, mandates the message content, location, size, pictograms, and so on, of bathroom identification signs, making its bathroom signs the most distinctive in the nation.

With so many codes affecting interior signage, it's no wonder that code conflicts occasionally arise, typically between local and national requirements. In such circumstances, strategies must be developed to comply with both. For example, a local building code may require that a fire stair be identified by a sign mounted directly on the stair door, while the ADA requires that all identification signs be displayed on the wall next to the latch side of the door. The only solution in such cases is to "double sign," with one sign on the door to comply with the local requirements and the other sign on the wall next to the door to comply with the ADA requirements.

Local Codes and Exterior Signage

Exterior signs, too, come under the auspices of various local codes. Specifically, state and municipal building codes are typically concerned with the safety of exterior signs themselves, such as the structural integrity to withstand prescribed wind forces and the soundness of electrical systems and connections.

Other local codes, usually municipal sign or zoning ordinances, are concerned with aesthetics—that is, controlling the visual character of a community's signage. Such ordinances, which vary from locale to locale, have been enacted in response to the mostly unattractive hodgepodge of sign styles that have mushroomed along the commercial strips of so many American towns and cities.

These ordinances typically apply to commercial signs, but also sometimes to directional signs, and can range from highly to loosely restrictive, depending on the locale or zoning district within the locale. Sign ordinance restrictions can include square footage, height, location, quantity, form, materials, illumination, and other elements. An example is a community whose commercial signs are all small, low-lying, externally illuminated, carved-wood panels with painted and gilded graphics, sitting on twin carved-wood posts.

It is not the intent of this book to focus on commercial signage or on the ordinances that may control them within any given community, so suffice it to say that sign ordinances are definitely well intentioned; but they can also be open to interpretation, hence causing contention. More to the point of this book is that sign ordinances can pose problems for the EG designer, especially when an ordinance places restrictions on directional signs. For example, an ordinance that places unrealistic size restrictions on directional signs can limit either the amount of informational content that can be displayed on the sign, or the size of that information, to the point at which the sign fails to carry out its communication function.

Usually, before a sign can be erected, sign ordinances require filing a permit application at the local jurisdiction, accompanied by an illustration of the sign, to demonstrate that the sign will comply with the ordinance. Some communities may additionally require that any proposed exterior signage be presented to a local governing body for approval, particularly if a *variance* is being sought for the sign or signs. A variance is, basically, an official permission for the sign to vary from the ordinance, and they can be difficult to obtain. On certain projects, the EG designer may be involved in providing renderings or plan and elevation drawings of the exterior signs for local approval, as well as in making presentations to local authorities.

The square-footage aspect of sign ordinances, in particular, is open to interpretation, raising the question of what the square footage applies to: Is it just the message area or the overall sign face? Does it include exposed support structures, such as vertical posts, that are unsuitable for carrying message content? These are important questions because the message area footprint takes up far less than 100 percent of a sign's square footage, because it is almost always surrounded by *dead space*, or

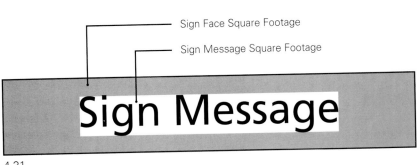

Sign Face Square Footage

Sign Message Square Footage

4.31 A sign message footprint, or *live space*, always comprises less square footage than the entire sign face, which consists of the live space plus dead space, such as margins.

4.31

white space, in the form of margins and any spaces between lines of typography, that contain no message content. The point is, one can make a valid argument that dead space—including exposed support structures—should not be included in the square-footage calculation.

There are various resources for additional information about exterior sign ordinances. These include the United States Sign Council (www.ussc.org), and the International Sign Association (www.signs.org).

Bilingual and Multilingual Sign Information

Undoubtedly all EG designers will become involved in signage projects that require bi- or multilingual sign information, whether those projects are in the United States or in other countries. English, of course, is the standard language used on signage in this country, but in certain regions, cities, and neighborhoods, additional languages may be required on signs due to large populations for whom English is not their first language. In the United States, Spanish is the most common second language that's displayed on signage; in many other countries, English is widely employed

4.32 Bilingual ceiling-hung directional signage at Brigham & Women's Hospital in Boston.

4.33 Bilingual directional signage at the Doctor's Hospital of Laredo, Texas, utilizes a stock hardware system in an innovative manner.

4.32

4.33

as a second language to the native language of the country, particularly on signage at international facilities, such as airports, train stations, exposition centers, and so on.

Designing sign programs to provide effective wayfinding and orientation in environments that serve speakers of multiple languages presents unique challenges to EGD professionals. Obviously, the more languages that need to be displayed on a sign the larger the sign must be, and this can lead to difficulties or trade-offs at sign locations that present physical constraints on sign sizes. Furthermore, in addition to requiring much larger sign faces, research has shown that signage displaying more than three languages is confusing and ineffective. Another issue is that sign messages in many other languages, such as Spanish, French, and German, are lengthier than those same messages in English, making it incumbent on the EG designer to obtain translations of the sign message content concurrent with the development of the English information content system.

To help address these language-related design issues, the Society for Environmental Graphic Design (SEGD) participated in the Hablamos Juntos initiative, which examines and presents strategies for effective orientation of multilingual users to U.S. health care environments. These strategies include use of symbols, maps, and human assistants to augment signage in a "total communication" package for speakers of languages other than English. Although the Hablamos Juntos initiative is geared toward health care environments, its findings and recommendations can be applied to other environments serving speakers of multiple languages. For more information, and to access documents from this initiative, go to www.segd.org.

For signage programs in the United States, messages in English are almost always displayed above or before their translations into other languages. For signage programs in other countries, the opposite is usually the case—messages in the country's native language take precedence over their English versions.

Another language-specific design issue that EG designers must account for is reading direction. Consider that while English and most other languages read from left to right, others, such as Arabic, read from right to left. And Chinese, which traditionally read vertically from top to bottom, is now also commonly read horizontally from left to right.

Even within the English language there are differences that can cause signage dilemmas—specifically, in spelling and nomenclature between American and British English. The British version is typically standard for signage in countries that historically were in the sphere of British influence, such as Singapore and India, as well as for some countries that were not, such as Mainland China. Common examples of these variations are listed here.

American Usage	British Usage
Exit	Way Out
Restroom	WC (for water closet or wash closet) or Toilet
Elevator	Lift
Garage	Car Park
Center	Centre
Theater	Theatre

Pictorial Information Content

Thus far, this chapter has focused on word-based information content, but some sign information can be communicated pictorially, without words. Pictorial content includes symbols, which are pictures that represent things or concepts, and diagrams, such as maps. Note that in this context the words *symbol, glyph, icon, and pictogram* are basically synonymous and used interchangeably, although this book primarily uses the term *symbol*.

The intention of this section is to give a general overview of pictorial information content for signage; it is not intended as a technical dissertation on semiotics.

Symbols

Symbols are used on signs as a shorthand substitute for words, but to be effective, they must be easy to understand. For example, the symbol of an airplane can substitute for the word Airport, and a symbol in the figure of a man can substitute for Men's Restroom. Directional arrows, too, can be considered symbols, in that they serve as a pictorial shorthand for directionals such as Straight Ahead, Turn Left, and the like.

Symbols are very useful in signage programs for three reasons:

- They conserve sign space.
- Their meaning can transcend language barriers, as the airplane symbol does.
- They can sometimes communicate more clearly than words, as arrows do.

The meaning of certain symbols is immediately obvious to most people on the planet, such as directional arrows and the airplane symbol. The meaning of other symbols has to be learned, and can vary by culture. For example, consider the symmetrical red cross symbol on signs, which connotes first aid in most Western cultures; yet, worldwide, its connection to first aid isn't as obvious as the airplane symbol is to airport. That is because the red cross derives its connection to first aid from its use by the

4.34

4.34 Options for communicating sign information include use of a symbol only, use of symbol paired with text, and use of text only.

International Federation of Red Cross and Red Crescent Societies, and this is a learned connection. In predominantly Muslim cultures, however, the International Federation of Red Cross and Red Crescent Societies uses a red crescent symbol on signs to connote first aid. (Note: To protect the trademark rights of the Red Cross relief organization, the red cross symbol used in signage has been replaced recently by a green cross symbol to indicate first aid.)

Even the seemingly universal symbols of male and female figures for men's and women's restrooms don't transcend all cultures. Typically, these symbols are based on Western dress, with the man in slacks and the woman in a skirt; but these depictions are less effective—and can even be offensive—in cultures where both men and women wear long robes, such as certain countries in the Middle East.

As useful as symbols are, many concepts are too complex to be readily communicated by them. For this reason, it's almost impossible to design a sign information content system that consists entirely of symbols. But judiciously used, symbols can streamline communication on signs. And because symbols can transcend language barriers, they can be very useful on signage at facilities where users of many languages and cultures gather, such as airports, medical facilities, and theme parks.

In some cases, symbols can be used alone, without words, to communicate the necessary information, but again, only if they are well-understood and culturally appropriate. In other cases, symbols can be used to reinforce the word messages, or to serve in a sense as a second language to help users not familiar with the written language displayed on the signs. In still other cases, symbols may not be used at all to communicate the sign information. And, finally, all three of these alternatives are possible within a given sign program.

There are several vocabularies of symbols, some of which have been adopted for official, standard usage by governing and regulatory bodies. A more in-depth discussion of symbols is contained in Chapter 5.

Diagrams

In addition to symbols, diagrams also convey sign information content in a pictorial manner. By far, the most common diagrams used in signage are maps. The fascinating and deep subject of maps in general, and in signage in particular, could comprise a book unto itself. The purpose here is to provide a brief overview of the information content role maps play in signage programs.

Maps are exceptionally useful in communicating the position of places and spaces—including transportation links such as train and bus routes—in relation to each other, and therefore as wayfinding and navigational aids. Maps can visually substitute for a complex series of directions in words, as they do on evacuation route map signs in hotel rooms. As stated earlier, however, many people do not understand maps; moreover, maps require detailed study because most people cannot interpret them quickly. Accordingly, from a design standpoint, maps should generally be considered as adjunct information content for a signage program.

Of course, maps also usually require legends in order to communicate effectively, and those legends are in the form of words and/or symbols. To prevent confusion, it's imperative that map legend nomenclature match the nomenclature used in the program's overall information content system. More on maps in the next chapter.

Another example of diagrammatic sign information is the interstate highway signs that depict the positions of the various traffic lanes and turnoffs at complex interchanges.

Signage Master Plans

A signage master plan, at least as defined in my office, is often the result of the information content development process. It is a document in which sign locations and messages are planned for the long term, a plan that is, in many cases, adopted in phases over time. The point is that it takes a long-term view, considering the informational needs of a site over time, minimizing informational or nomenclature changes as the site itself changes.

Signage master plans work best for planned environments that have predicted growth patterns. The EG designer develops an information content system for the planned environment, rather than taking a piecemeal, reactive approach as each site within it is built. Signage master plans take a holistic approach—the big-picture viewpoint regarding informational needs. In this way they are a proactive rather than reactive means to predict the informational needs of a site. Simply put, signage master plans provide for and predict the future informational needs of a site in an effort to minimize changes to the signage as the site changes.

Chapter Wrap-Up

The dedicated purpose of signage is to communicate information, therefore, the development of the information content system—what the signs say and where they say it—is the foundation of all sign programs. You can use the methods and advice in this chapter to plan any program's content infrastructure, after which you'll be well prepared to jump into actual design activity for the program's graphic and hardware systems, the subjects of the next two chapters, respectively.

The Graphic System

Graphics make sign information visible and give the information "voice."

The word "graphic" has ancient roots in the Greek word *graphikos*, which means "writing." The evolution of written and visual, or graphic, communication—as opposed to spoken communication—is one of humankind's greatest cultural achievements. No doubt humans communicated in spoken words before they invented ways to write those words, but the world's great civilizations didn't really begin to advance until humans developed writing systems to record, preserve, and accumulate knowledge.

The graphic system for a signage program is part of this great cultural legacy of visual communication. The sign graphic system makes the sign information content system tangible, in that it embodies and conveys the sign program's informational content. The graphic system gives structure, form, and style to the information being communicated on signs.

The EG designer utilizes and manipulates a vocabulary of visual communication devices in developing the graphic system for a sign program. These include typography, symbols, color, diagrams, and other graphic elements such as rules, bars, circles, squares, and other geometric and decorative elements. The EG designer then arranges these graphic devices into a unified system of layouts for the various sign types and messages in the signage program.

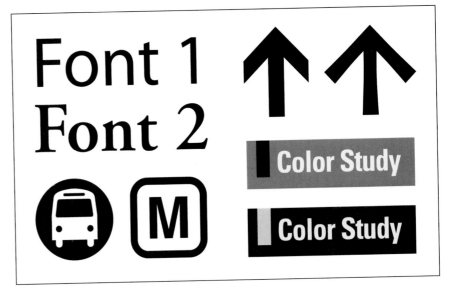

5.1 The graphic system.

5.1

This chapter discusses the vocabulary of graphic devices used for signage and how they are arranged into layouts; it also offers an overview of methods for applying graphics to signs. The intent here is to introduce the basics of graphics as they pertain to signage, not to serve as an exhaustive treatise on graphic design.

Typography Overview

Typography is the backbone of the sign graphic system because, as stated in Chapter 4, "The Information Content System," most of the informational content of a sign program is conveyed by words rather than pictorial elements. The word "typography" has its roots in a Medieval Latin word *typographia*, meaning "letterpress printing," but also referring to the style, arrangement, or appearance of typeset matter. The latter is the subject of this chapter, as it applies to signage.

The invention of printing from movable type is credited to Johannes Gutenberg (1390–1468) who implemented the idea of casting individual letters into metal type. Printers composed these individual metal letters into words, sentences, paragraphs, and pages, then locked the composed type into a printing press, inked the type, and pressed it into contact with paper to transfer the ink to the paper. Gutenberg is also credited with much of the typographic measurement and terminology still used today, which has its origins in the era of metal type, which spanned close to 600 years, until digital type supplanted it in the late twentieth century.

Every written language has a set of characters that comprise the language. In Western alphabetical languages, many of which are based on the ancient Roman alphabet, the character set is relatively small, consisting of upper- and lowercase letters, numerals, and punctuation marks. In American English, which has a Roman-based alphabet, the standard character set consists of about 225 characters, including punctuation and diacritical marks. In nonalphabetical Eastern languages, such as Chinese, Japanese, and Korean, the character sets can consist of upward of 20,000 characters.

Whatever the language, these character sets are expressed in *typefaces*, which vary in the way they depict the characters stylistically. Note that, today, the terms *type font*, or just *font,* are often used interchangeably with *typeface*, but this book uses the more correct term *typeface* when referring to the unique visual characteristics of any given set of typographic characters. Think of a typeface in the same way you do a human face: each has its own unique distinguishing stylistic features. In contrast, *font* simply refers to a complete assortment of type of a given size and face. Thus, correctly, *font* is closer in meaning to the term *character set* than it is to *typeface*.

5.2 A piece of metal type. Metal type, now obsolete after five centuries of use, formed the basis for the currently used typographic measurement system.

A plethora of typefaces exist for those languages that have Roman-based characters, including English, Spanish, French, Italian, and German. There are fewer typefaces for Western languages using non-Roman alphabets, such as Greek and Russian, or for Middle Eastern alphabetical languages such as Arabic. And when it comes to nonalphabetical Asian languages, such as Chinese, Japanese, and Korean, there are even fewer typefaces. This is understandable, given the difficulty of designing a unified yet distinctive typeface for the thousands of characters that comprise these languages. It is for this reason that typography for non-Western languages will only be touched upon in this section; the focus here is primarily on Roman-based typography, as that used in the United States. The anatomy of Roman type is depicted in Figure 5.3.

Keep in mind that with such a wide range of typefaces available, particularly for Roman-based character sets, typically, EG designers utilize existing typefaces for signage programs, rather than designing new ones. There are three very good reasons for this.

- Some signage projects, such as those that are part of a larger graphic standards program, actually *require* the use of a specific typeface(s), to create or maintain a consistent graphic or brand identity at the client's various facilities and sites.

- Use of existing typefaces is standard practice for signage programs because typeface design is a painstaking, time-consuming process, requiring specialized skills that are, in most cases, beyond the EG designer's range of expertise.

- Many existing faces are highly legible and well-proven in signage applications.

The creation of a new, customized typeface for a given signage program is exceptionally rare. Should the client wish to include custom typeface design for a signage project, the project design fees must take into account this additional, highly specialized service.

Choosing a Typeface

Typeface selection is key to the visual appearance of a sign program's graphic system, particularly as typography is the predominant graphic element for communication of sign information. Selecting a typeface can

5.3 Anatomy of type.

seem an overwhelming task, however, because as just noted, typefaces abound for Roman-based character sets. Generally, there are three factors that can aid in selecting typefaces for a signage program:

- Formal suitability
- Stylistic longevity
- Legibility

Formal Suitability

Formal suitability refers to how well a typeface suits a given project, both in terms of how visually compatible it is with the project environment and its stylistic longevity. Regarding visual compatibility, in broad terms, there are two basic typographic styles: *serif* and *sans serif*, each of which has broad stylistic connotations.

The primary distinguishing feature of serif letterforms is the presence of serifs, or "feet," the short horizontal strokes at the upper and lower ends of the main letterform strokes. Serif letterforms were invented by the ancient Romans, and elegant, beautifully carved serif letters still can be seen gracing the archaeological sites of the Roman Empire. Most serif letters also exhibit varying, thick-thin stroke widths within each letterform. It is thought that both serifs and thick-thin strokes were the result of the acts of carving letters into stone with flat-nosed chisels, and of calligraphic writing on paper or skins using flat-nosed reeds as pens. Some of the earliest serif typefaces, whose design is rooted in ancient Roman carved letterforms, date back to the 1570s.

5.4 Serif letterforms carved into the entablature of ancient Rome's Pantheon.

5.4

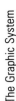

Serif Faces	Sans Serif Faces
Typography	Typography
Bodoni Roman	Avenir Roman
Typography	Typography
Caslon 540 Roman	Futura Book
Typography	**Typography**
Adobe Garamond Regular	Gill Sans Regular
Typography	**Typography**
Goudy Oldstyle	Gotham Medium
Typography	Typography
ITC New Baskerville Roman	MetaPlusLF Normal Roman
Typography	**Typography**
Times Roman	Myriad Roman
5.5	

5.5 Examples of serif and sans serif typefaces.

Sans serif means without serifs, so it should not be surprising that the primary distinguishing feature of these typefaces is the lack of serifs, or "feet." Most san serif letters also have relatively uniform stroke widths within each letterform, so uniform or near-uniform strokes are another distinguishing feature of sans serif letters. Although sans serif letterforms are visually simpler than serif letterforms, sans serif typefaces are relative newcomers to the typographic scene, with origins in the early 1800s.

Given the ancient origins and visual complexity of serif letterforms, contrasted with the relative newness and visual simplicity of sans serif letterforms, it's no surprise that serif typefaces have traditional connotations and sans serif typefaces have contemporary connotations. Therefore, serif typefaces are generally better suited for use on signage projects where a traditional look is desired, whereas sans serif faces are better suited for projects where a contemporary look is desired. Sometimes, of course, visual contrast or juxtaposition is desired, which can be created by using a sans serif typeface in a project with a traditional context, by using a serif typeface in a project with a contemporary context, or by combining serif and sans serif typefaces in the same program. One of the first questions we ask at my office when we start designing the graphic system for a signage project is: "Is this a serif or sans serif project?"

Typefaces for languages with non-Roman character sets also fall into serif or sans serif styles to a greater or lesser extent, depending on the language. Those for the more Western Cyrillic (Russian) and Greek languages are available in styles that can be clearly identified as serif or sans serif; those for languages such as Arabic, Chinese, and Korean are available in calligraphically derived thick-thin styles. In the latter case, though these typefaces do not feature serifs per se, they have the more traditional connotations of Western serif type styles, as well as typefaces with more uniform stroke widths, which have the more contemporary connotations of Western sans serif type styles.

Though there are endless stylistic variations and subcategories of Roman letterforms and typefaces, most can be broadly classified as either serif or sans serif. This does not, however, include the large number of typefaces that are categorized as novelty faces, those that are so distinctive and quirky that they can usually be ruled out for use in a signage program. And this brings us to the matter of stylistic longevity.

Stylistic Longevity

While trendy, novelty typefaces may be desirable for advertising and other relatively ephemeral, short-lived graphic campaigns, signage programs tend to have comparatively long life spans. In fact, it's not at all uncommon for sign programs to endure for years, if not decades. For this reason, stylistic longevity of typefaces is an important selection factor for signage programs. Trendy typefaces often become quickly dated, thereby prematurely dating a sign program. This is not to say that novelty typefaces should never be used in a signage project, for every project is different; nor is it to say that the EG designer has no creative freedom in typeface selection. There are several timeless typefaces, serif and sans serif—some designed centuries ago, others only a few years ago—that have the stylistic longevity suitable for signage programs.

Legibility

Legibility is the third crucial factor in typeface selection for sign program graphics, and it's linked to both formal suitability and longevity. Simply put, a legible typeface is easy to read, and since the objective of the graphic system of a sign program is to communicate information, it must be easy to read and understand so that viewers can act upon the information easily and seamlessly. Legible typography is essential for clear communication, and many novelty typefaces are so stylistically errant that they fail to meet the primary purpose of a typeface: to be legible.

Scientific studies have been conducted on typeface legibility, but it's not the purpose of this book to go into such technical detail. However, there are some basic parameters that help to determine the legibility of a typeface. Legible typefaces tend to exhibit the following characteristics:

- They have clearly defined, easily recognizable letterforms.
- They have a large x-height.

Typography
Typography
Typography
Typography
Typography

5.6 Examples of novelty typefaces.

- They are of medium weight, with stroke widths that are neither too thick nor too thin.
- They are of medium or normal character width, with letterforms that are neither too condensed nor too expanded.

There are also considerations regarding the legibility of serif versus sans serif type in signage. The horizontal strokes of serif letterforms are generally regarded as an aid to reading large blocks of small text, such as in a book or a newspaper, whereas serif faces are often considered to be too delicate in form for signage graphics in critical communication applications such as highway signs. Think about it: You rarely see book or magazine text set in sans serif type and, conversely, you rarely see vehicular-related sign graphics in serif type. This is not to say that serif typefaces can't be used for signage, but that their legibility should be carefully studied for vehicular signage applications.

Typographic Treatment

In addition to the inherent legibility, or lack thereof, intrinsic to the design of any given typeface, typographic treatment can also affect legibility. Typographic treatment refers to variables that can be manipulated to affect how a typeface looks when it is set, such as *case* and *letterspacing*.

Most Roman-based typefaces are composed of two versions of the same characters: an uppercase ("capital" or "cap") version and a lowercase version. *Case* refers to which version or combination of versions is used, and this significantly affects both the legibility and appearance of typography. Case treatments include:

- ALL UPPERCASE (CAPITALS or CAPS)
- Title Case (Initial Caps)
- Sentence case
- all lowercase

Good Legibility	Poor Legibility	
Hoplitux Clearly defined, easily recognizable letterforms	 Letterforms not clearly defined	
Hoplitux Large x-height	Hoplitux Small x-height	
Hoplitux Medium weight or normal stroke width	**Hoplitux** Stroke width too thick	 Stroke width too thin
Hoplitux Medium or normal character width	**Hoplitux** Character width too condensed	**Hoplitux** Character width too expanded

5.7 Characteristics of good and poor legibility in typefaces.

5.7

Legibility and the Aging Driver: Development of the Clearview Type System Improves the Visual Landscape for All

Don Meeker

The ubiquitous highway sign system in the United States looks dreadful, but it is one of those things that seems beyond the control of anyone. That was my assumption in 1989 when I was commissioned to design a guide sign program to advance tourism in the state of Oregon. My field review, taking over 1,000 photographs of highway sign installations, only confirmed that there was little consistency among similar sign types, as well as a clutter of many disparate sign types at decision points. I concluded that it was not possible to add another layer to the cluttered roadscape unless the existing road signing could be organized in a more systematic way.

After the Oregon project my questions remained, particularly about typography. I wanted to know why most messages on conventional road signs—from street name signs to motorist service signs—were displayed in all capital letters when in other parts of the world these are often in mixed case. And why the mixed case lettering used on U.S. freeway signs is so crude, that is, not based on any established typographic design conventions. I found that the all-capital-letter alphabets originated when highway signs were hand-lettered, with no change in letterforms as technology advanced from the hand to the computer generation. The mixed case freeway lettering evolved from Leroy lettering, which was used by engineers for labeling drawings.

These questions led to my partnering with researcher Martin Pietrucha and Phil Garvey at the Pennsylvania Transportation Institute (PTI). After 18 months of work we received a research grant from 3M Corporation. We came to realize that with a system that had not been upgraded

since 1961 and still incorporated many items from the 1940s, the research problem was more complex than originally envisioned. Factors included a ballooning population of older drivers, who have reduced visual acuity and contrast sensitivity, combined with a longer reaction time than younger drivers. Another factor: the new high brightness retroreflective materials that create greater halation, making the signs more difficult to read. Yet another factor: the recently published federal older driver study which recommended that all signs be made 20 percent larger to aid older drivers—an impossibility due to physical constraints of lane and shoulder widths, plus prohibitive implementation expenses.

Our original study compared existing FHWA highway typeface standards to commonly used san

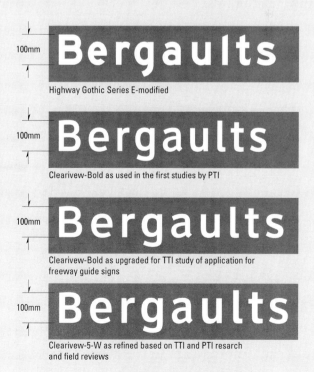

100mm **Bergaults**
Highway Gothic Series E-modified

100mm **Bergaults**
Clearivew-Bold as used in the first studies by PTI

100mm **Bergaults**
Clearivew-Bold as upgraded for TTI study of application for freeway guide signs

100mm **Bergaults**
Clearivew-5-W as refined based on TTI and PTI resarch and field reviews

serif typefaces. After careful analysis we found that no existing font families—most of which had text based origins—were suitable to roadway signage applications. This included the few typefaces designed for signage such as Jock Kinneir's "Transport," and Adrain Frutiger's "Frutiger."

Based on that review, we elected to design new fonts from scratch. We originally designed two versions for comparison: bold regular to replace the freeway font FHWA E-modified and a condensed weight to replace FHWA Series D. Both were designed for mixed case display and were named Clearview.

The initial outdoor, day and night older driver study of Clearview was conducted on a controlled test track. The results were very positive with 16 percent improvement in legibility and recognition ease for the bolder weight, and a 14 percent improvement in the condensed version using same size mixed case in lieu of all capital letters.

TexasDOT and the Texas Transportation Institute (TTI) learned about this research, which had been done primarily for conventional road (nonfreeway) applications, and decided to conduct their own comparative study of Clearview for freeway applications. This pilot study indicated that more letterform and spacing refinements were required. In three separate studies over six years, and two new versions refined by type designer James Montalbano, who had joined the project team, Clearview's performance significantly improved against current FHWA type standards.

Based on this work, PennDOT and TexDOT began implementing Clearview for freeway guide signs. However, we still needed to reach our 20 percent legibility improvement goal for same size signs, and while we knew it could be reached we did not know how, and we were unable to acquire the research funds to make this refinement.

In an unrelated effort to design a road sign typeface for the National Park Service, we reduced the proportional relationship of the lower case to the initial capital letter by 4 percent that resulted in a 12 percent improvement in readability and legibility. This paralleled the earlier Clearview study described above. Based on this finding, Montalbano made a similar change to the heavy weight Clearview. This allowed the stroke width to be increased while not compromising halation control in use of high brightness retroreflective materials.

We unveiled the new Clearview designs at a workshop with state and federal highway engineers at PTI in April 2002, and the observers recognized very significant improvements. We also introduced two versions of each weight, a positive contrast version (light on dark), and a negative contrast version (dark on light). Based on that review, we developed the ClearviewHwy Type System, which includes six weights of each version. In September 2004 the FHWA granted "approved alternative" status, allowing highway departments to use the typeface nationwide in positive contrast applications.

Based on this work, Meeker & Associates, in conjunction with PTI, have developed proportionally based systems for freeway and conventional road guide signs that will create a more uniform and much easier-to-read system of signs on the roadscape. The FHWA has now requested that these designs be considered for FHWA adoption, which with the use of Clearview will make the first significant improvement in road sign design in over 45 years and the first typeface change in 55 years.

This has been a 16-year process—involving no federal funds—with five peer review studies published by the National Research Council. The results of this effort will make signs 20 percent more legible and add one to two seconds to drivers' reaction times, with the greatest benefit to older drivers at night—all with no additional cost for larger signs. This has been an interdisciplinary team effort that fostered fresh thinking, teamwork, and perseverance.

Don Meeker is principal of Meeker & Associates, Inc. in Larchmont, New York.

The most common, and most legible, case treatment for sign typography is title case, in which all words, with the exception of so-called "helper" words such as conjunctions and prepositions, have their initial letters set in uppercase with all subsequent letters of the word set in lowercase. Much like book titles, most sign messages are single words or a short series of words—for example, Restrooms and Food Court—therefore, title case is the most appropriate treatment.

Title case treatment may seem counterintuitive to nonpractitioners of graphic design, who often have the mistaken notion that all capitals are somehow more legible because they're bolder or simpler. In fact, for people without vision impairments, the reality is that because lowercase letters have more distinctive shapes and greater variation among those shapes than capital letters, lowercase letters form a more distinctive word footprint that is easier to read than an all-caps footprint. As confirmation of this fact, consider the difficulty of reading a book or newspaper with text set in all caps. Such text is set in sentence case, with an initial cap on the first word of each sentence, because it's more legible than all caps.

Sentence case treatment of signage typography is usually reserved for detailed information that is in whole sentences, such as operational or interpretive text. And all lowercase treatment of sign typography, while occasionally seen on sign programs in Europe, is rare in the United States.

Although sign messages in all caps are less legible than messages in title case, particularly for the nonvisually impaired, all-capital messages can have a commanding, magisterial, even elegant appearance, à la the ancient Roman letterforms—which were all capitals—that were carved into the edifices built by that civilization. Indeed, certain sign messages, such as STOP and EXIT

Typography
TYPOGRAPHY

5.8 The title case treatment of the word "typography" aids legibility because it has a more distinct "footprint" than the all-capitals treatment.

5.9a, b, and c Signs with different case treatments

5.9a

5.9b

5.9c

are mandated by various codes to be displayed in all caps. Additionally, the ADA requires identification sign messages to be in all capitals. So, there's no doubt that all-caps case treatments can be appropriate for all typography in some sign programs, or for some of the typography within a program. Keep in mind, however, that since the capital letters are larger than the lowercase letters of any typeface, messages set in all caps take up more of the sign face than messages set in title case at the same type size.

Letterspacing is another typographic treatment variable that affects the legibility and visual appearance of typefaces. Letterspacing, also known as *tracking*, is the spacing among all the letters in a word. Letterspacing and tracking, which affect spacing throughout a word, should not be confused with the term *kerning*, which refers to spacing between individual character pairs within a word.

Most type fonts are engineered to set, by default, with so-called "normal" letterspacing, typically indicated as zero (0), which is the "not too much, not too little" spacing people need to comfortably read text. Normal letterspacing can be varied by increments on the plus, or positive (+), side of zero, to increase the space between letters, or on the minus or negative (−) side, to decrease the space to the point of making the letters touch, or even overlap.

To aid legibility, signage typography should be set at normal or slightly open, positive letterspacing. Negative or tight letterspacing treatments, while they can add drama and immediacy to the appearance of typography, impair legibility and so are best employed in other graphic design applications than signage. Two specific instances in which more open typographic letterspacing treatments should be studied are for vehicular-related signage and for internally illuminated signage. Both situations can pose viewing condition and human factor issues that can be mediated by increased letterspacing.

The openness or tightness of normal, default letterspacing varies from typeface to typeface. Some faces are engineered to "set tight" at normal letterspacing, while others "set loose." Therefore, it's important to study letterspacing variables for each typeface being considered for a signage program to be able to select the appropriate letterspacing treatment for optimum legibility. And, generally, once a letterspacing standard is determined for the chosen typeface, the spacing standard should be utilized consistently for all typography throughout the program to foster visual unity.

It's important to note that letterspacing increments vary with different computer programs. For example, +10 spacing for a given typeface in Adobe Illustrator is not as open as +10 letterspacing for the same face in QuarkXPress. Even the increments for normal or zero letterspacing can vary among computer programs. It's also important to remember that regardless of computer program increments, the more open the letterspacing, the more space it will take up on the sign face.

Hoplitux

Tracking at -100

Hoplitux

Tracking at -10

Hoplitux

Tracking at 0

Hoplitux

Tracking at 10

Hoplitux

Tracking at 100

5.10 Typographic letterspacing can be made tighter or looser than normal by adjusting tracking.

201	202	2 0 3
Student Affairs	Admissions Office	B u r s a r ' s W i n d o w

5.11

5.11 Sign layouts with inconsistent letterspacing impair visual unity.

Typography

Helvetica Regular Set at Track 0

Typography

Univers 55 Roman Set at Track 0
5.12

5.12 Helvetica is a typeface that sets tight, whereas Univers is a typeface that sets loose.

One typographic treatment will be mentioned only in passing here because it is considered by graphic design professionals to be amateurish and, therefore, should be strictly forbidden in any sign program's typography: horizontal or vertical scaling. Most computer graphics programs allow typefaces to be scaled more or less than 100 percent in the horizontal or vertical axis; but this grossly distorts typeface proportions, and is usually done in an effort to cram a too-long message onto a sign face of limited size, by reducing the typeface's standard character width. Some graphic designers consider horizontal or vertical scaling of type to be

Typography

Helvetica Bold Set Normal

Typography

Helvetica Bold Set at 70% Horizontal Scaling
5.13

5.13 Typeface proportions distort badly if character widths are manipulated to fit long messages onto signs of limited width.

so heinous as to dub it a "type crime." As we say in our office, just like Mr. Whipple, "Don't squeeze the Charmin, and don't squeeze the type."

Typographic Considerations in Signage for Nonsighted and Low-Sighted People

Thus far, we've covered typographic treatments for sighted sign users, but as discussed in Chapter 4, the ADA specifies provisions to improve signage accessibility for visually impaired people. Again, it's not the intent of this book to exhaustively delineate the ADA's signage provisions, but to provide highlights of its impact on signage design, including sign typography.

ADA guidelines require that identification signs for all permanent rooms and spaces display the room or space name in raised tactile typography, accompanied by Grade 2 Braille. The tactile typography and Braille are required for people with no or very limited vision who read the identification sign messages by touch rather than sight, and for this reason the ADA places other limitations on the tactile typography for permanent identification signs. Currently, these limitations include the following aspects of typography:

- *Character width*, which must not be too condensed (narrow) or too extended (wide), and must fit within the specified character-width-to-height ratio range of 3:5 and 1:1.

- *Stroke width*, which must not be too light (thin) or too bold (thick), and must fit within the specified stroke-width-to-height ratio range of 1:5 and 1:10.

- *Typographic style*, which is limited to sans serif or *simple serif* typefaces. Note that the term *simple serif* has no technical meaning in the lexicon of typography, but has been interpreted to mean straightforward, unembellished serif typefaces, such as Garamond, Times Roman, Bodoni, and other similar faces.

- *Case*, which is limited to all capitals.

As explained earlier in this chapter, title case is more legible for sighted people than all capitals. So why does the ADA require all capitals, as well as the other limitations, for tactile typography? Simply, because tactile typography is read by touch rather than sight. The variety of form that makes lowercase letters easier for nonvision-impaired people to read by sight makes lowercase letters harder to read by touch than all caps. Similarly, straightforward, nonornamented letters are easier to read by touch, as are letters that don't deviate much from "normal," in character width or stroke width.

Typography for signs that aren't permanent room identification signs, such as directional signs, does not have to comply with all of the aforementioned ADA limitations on identification sign typography. The ADA does not require nonidentification sign typography to be read by touch, so type for such signs isn't required to be tactile or displayed in all capitals. The ADA limitations on character width, stroke width, and typographic style do apply to nonidentification sign typography, however. The ADA also specifies sizes for sign typography and symbols, and these provisions are discussed further in the "Layout" section of this chapter.

As noted in Chapter 4, the SEGD's "Americans With Disabilities Act (ADA) White Paper," which defines the SEGD's official interpretation of the ADA as it relates to signage, provides highly useful guidance on sign typography and ADA compliance. The 1993 edition of this document can be obtained through the SEGD. (Note: Although the federal government published updated ADA Accessibility Guidelines in 2004, as of this writing the new guidelines have been adopted only by selected agencies. The signage provisions of the new ADAAG differ considerably from the original version, and both can be viewed at the Guidelines and Standards section at www.access-board.gov. Until the new guidelines are adopted by a given agency, the original ones remain in effect, so it's advisable to periodically check the new ADAAG status at the Access Board Web site. Presumably, the SEGD will issue an updated White Paper on the new signage provisions when appropriate.)

Symbols and Arrows

Recall from Chapter 4 that symbols and arrows are graphic devices that communicate information pictorially—that is, without words. Also recall that the words *symbol, glyph, icon,* and *pictogram* are all basically synonymous and are used interchangeably to refer to a picture that represents a word or concept—for example, how a picture of a taxi represents the word *taxi,* or a picture of an airplane represents the concept of *airport.* As a reminder, this book primarily uses the term *symbol* to refer to these pictorial devices, and considers directional arrows as kinds of symbols, in that they are pictorial representations for directional indicators such as Straight Ahead, Turn Left, and the like.

Humankind's use of simple pictures to communicate visually predates the development of written languages. Some of the earliest examples of pictorial communication are the Lascaux cave paintings, circa 15,000–10,000 B.C., in southern France. It is thought that these paintings tell hunting stories. As cultures advanced, many early written languages were based on the use of pictures in an organized fashion, such as the hieroglyphic language of ancient Egypt. The Chinese language was, and still is, pictorially based, with each character representing a complete word or concept, as opposed to English, an alphabetical language in which words are assembled from alphabetical characters. And even the Roman alphabet, as used in most Western European languages, including English, evolved from a series of pictorially based characters.

| Left | Diagonal/ Upper Left | Up/Straight Ahead | Diagonal/ Upper Right | Right | Diagonal/ Lower Right | Down/ Straight Ahead | Diagonal/ Lower Left |

5.14

5.14 Arrow directions.

In signage, symbols can replace typography to communicate certain messages, or augment typographic messages. For example, an airplane symbol can replace the word *airport* on a sign, or a wheelchair symbol next to a destination name can indicate the wheelchair-accessible route to that destination. Symbols can also be paired with typographic messages on signage to reinforce the typographic message, such as when the airplane symbol is paired with the word *airport*. This typographic/symbol pairing can be useful in multilingual signage environments such as airports, hospitals, exposition centers, and theme parks, to reduce the need for multiple languages on the signs.

Some symbols, such as the airplane or wheelchair symbols, are almost universally understood, because they directly depict relatively simple concepts, as explained in Chapter 4. Other words or concepts, such as *outpatient clinic* or *passenger drop-off* are not as easily depicted in a symbol, so the meaning of symbols developed for such concepts often needs to be learned for the symbols to be understood. And, remember, cultural differences can affect symbol recognition and understanding.

Arrows are symbols that are well understood worldwide as directional devices, replacing lengthy verbal indications of direction. For example, an arrow pointing left is clearly understood to mean "turn left"; therefore, the words *turn left* are typically replaced by a left arrow in sign graphics. The same is the case for other arrow directions, as depicted in Figure 5.14.

Symbol Vocabularies

Just as a given typeface can be considered a vocabulary of characters of a given, unified style, EG designers should consider the symbols they use for sign graphics as a vocabulary. In order to communicate clearly, the vocabulary of a sign program's symbols and arrows require visual unity, clarity, and simplicity in their graphic design. And keep in mind that even if other symbols are not used for the graphic system of a given sign program, at the very least that program will require a vocabulary of arrows.

The EG designer has two basic sources for symbol vocabularies:

• A completely new symbol vocabulary created for a specific project

• An existing symbol vocabulary or vocabularies adopted for the project

The first source is far less common than the second. As pointed out earlier in this chapter, there are three reasons for this, primarily because developing a new symbol vocabulary is a labor-intensive process, requiring much testing and revision. Second, a new symbol vocabulary may not be as readily understood as an existing one. Third, use of an existing symbol vocabulary may be required for a given signage project. For these reasons, just as it's not common for EG designers to include the design of a new, custom typeface in the design services for a signage program, design of a custom symbol vocabulary is typically not part of signage design services. And, remember, should the client request the design of a custom symbol vocabulary, the design fee must cover the research and development time involved with this task.

Given that design of a new symbol vocabulary is the exception rather than the rule, we'll turn the focus here to use of existing symbol vocabularies. By far the most commonly utilized symbol vocabulary in the United States is the AIGA/DOT symbol system, which was developed by the American Institute of Graphic Arts, in conjunction with the U.S. Department of Transportation for U.S. transportation facilities. Development of this symbol vocabulary, which took place in the 1970s, was a major undertaking, involving considerable research and development on behalf of several parties, including various teams of distinguished graphic designers. Examples of the 50 symbols in AIGA/DOT vocabulary are shown in Figure 5.15; the various display formats are shown in Figure 5.16.

5.15

5.15 Selected symbols from the AIGA/DOT symbol vocabulary, which is composed of 50 symbols.

5.16

5.16 The five different display formats for the AIGA/DOT symbol vocabulary.

5.17 SEGD symbols for accessibility.

5.17

5.18 The meaning of the word *access* is the same regardless of its typographic treatment, just as the meaning of the wheelchair access symbol is the same regardless of its stylistic treatment.

5.19 A more active accessibility symbol is gaining usage.

5.18

5.19

The AIGA/DOT symbols, which have been adopted for signage use by various transportation authorities and facilities, are now in such widespread use they're generally well recognized by travelers throughout the United States. This symbol vocabulary is available as digital artwork from the AIGA and SEGD.

In addition to the original AIGA/DOT symbol set, the SEGD developed a set of ADA Symbols for Accessibility, which includes the four symbols specifically developed for signage and graphics associated with the ADA. These SEGD accessibility symbols, shown in Figure 5.17, which have been designed to be stylistically compatible with the AIGA/DOT symbols, are available from the SEGD.

The most recognized of the SEGD accessibility symbols is the wheelchair accessibility symbol, which varies stylistically from the less visually sophisticated version depicted in the ADAAG guidelines, both of which are shown in Figure 5.18. I point out this distinction because some clients have been known to object to the use of the SEGD symbol because they feel that it isn't the "official" version. An effective rebuttal is that the informational and visual content of both the SEGD and ADAAG symbols is the same—a wheelchair—and that they differ only in the graphic style in which they're treated, just as the word *access* has the same informational content whether it's treated in a serif or sans serif type style, also shown in Figure 5.18. In other words, regardless of the graphic treatment of the wheelchair accessibility symbol, the meaning is the same—and is clear. Another fact supporting the use of the SEGD version of the accessibility symbol is that it has been adopted into the symbol vocabularies of various official entities. Also note that a more active accessibility symbol is beginning to gain usage, and that version is shown in Figure 5.19.

The AIGA/DOT symbol vocabulary is particularly appropriate if you're designing a sign program for a transportation facility. Many of these symbols, such as those for restrooms, escalators, and stairs, are not specific to transportation and are used on signage for a wide range of facilities. But what about symbol vocabularies that venture beyond the transportation focus of the AIGA/DOT symbols? The SEGD has developed a vocabulary of 108 symbols for recreation-related facilities, which were designed to be stylistically compatible with the AIGA/DOT symbols and are available from the SEGD. Additionally, as noted previously, the SEGD has participated in the Hablamos Juntos Universal Symbols in Healthcare initiative, sponsored by the Robert Wood Johnson Foundation, and headed

5.20

5.20 Selected symbols from the SEGD recreation symbols vocabulary.

5.21

5.21 Selected symbols from the Hablamos Juntos healthcare symbols vocabulary.

by Hablamos Juntos with JRC Design. The 28 symbols in the Hablamos Juntos Healthcare vocabulary also are available from the SEGD.

There are also commercial sources for symbol vocabularies beyond the AIGA/DOT and SEGD transportation, ADA, recreation, and healthcare vocabularies just discussed. A major source is *Official Signs & Icons 2* by Ultimate Symbol/Mies Hora, which is a compilation of more than 4,800 EPS vector files on CD-ROM, accompanied by a 240-page, four-color hardcover reference book. This definitive resource is the most comprehensive compendium of current standard signs, symbols, icons, and labels ever assembled, and it includes most of the aforementioned symbol vocabularies.

Other symbol and arrow sources include type foundries, many of which have fonts that are symbol vocabularies, and clip art libraries. Note, however, that symbol vocabularies from type foundries and clip art libraries are typically not stylistically compatible with the AIGA/DOT and SEGD vocabularies.

Arrows

Arrows are specialized, yet quite simple symbols, typically comprised of a pointed head and a shaft, that are graphic representations of physical arrows, such as those used for sport or hunting. The AIGA/DOT symbol vocabulary also contains a vocabulary of arrows, as shown in Figure 5.22, which is one of myriad stylistic treatments for arrows. Several arrow treatments are shown in the illustration accompanying the sidebar "Human Factors Researchers Can Improve Environmental Graphic Design Products" by Phil Garvey.

EG designers tend to favor arrows with open heads and clear, orderly geometrical styles such as the Helvetica parallel, Helvetica perpendicular, and Optima perpendicular styles shown in Figure 5.23, or some variation thereof. The Helvetica arrows feature uniform stroke widths for the head and shaft, which refer to the basically uniform stroke widths of the Helvetica typeface. The Optima arrow features slightly curved, thick/thin strokes similar to those of the Optima typeface. The Helvetica-style arrows

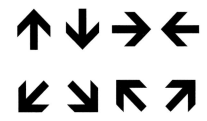

5.22 The AIGA/DOT arrow vocabulary.

5.23 Helvetica parallel, Helvetica perpendicular, and Optima-style arrows.

5.24 Arrows without shafts can be confusing.

← Classrooms	◀ Classrooms
↑ Financial Aid	▲ Financial Aid
→ Computer Lab	▶ Computer Lab

5.24

are compatible with sans serif typography, whereas the Optima-style arrow is compatible with serif typography.

Of course, EG designers don't limit themselves to using only Helvetica- and Optima-style arrows, not when such a wide range of stylistic treatments is possible. One word of caution in arrow usage is in order, however: Arrows without shafts communicate less clearly than those with shafts, for the shafts reinforce the directionality of the arrows. Also, some people may interpret a triangular, shaftless arrowhead as a geometric sign layout element rather than as a directional device. Every project is different, of course, so this is not to say that shaftless arrows should never be used; it simply points out the shortcomings of shaftless arrows.

As with other kinds of symbols, the two primary sources for arrows are the creation of a new vocabulary of arrows for a given project and the adoption of an existing arrow vocabulary. Unlike an entire typeface, an arrow is a relatively simple geometric shape, and it can be easily constructed in any kind of vector drawing program and rotated in 45-degree steps for the various directions in the arrow vocabulary. Arrows can also be adopted from several existing sources, including:

- Arrows in the AIGA/DOT symbol vocabulary
- Various typefaces that include arrows, such as Zapf Dingbats
- Symbol and clip art libraries, including the aforementioned *Official Signs & Icons 2*

Diagrams

Diagrams, particularly maps, often comprise another element of a sign program's graphic system. As stated in Chapter 4, the subject of maps and diagrams is a deep one, so this section will only touch on map and diagram design as they relate to a sign program's graphic system.

Maps used in signage are site-specific; therefore, they are best custom-designed for the project at hand, either by the EG designer or a commissioned specialist such as a cartographer. It's important to point out, however, that maps and diagrams can be difficult and time-consuming to prepare; furthermore, the need for, or extent of, these elements is often unknown when a fee proposal is prepared for a signage project. That is why EG designers often treat map and diagram design as an additional service to the signage program design.

Stylistic Treatment of Maps

Why should maps be custom-designed for a signage program when there are often many kinds of existing maps for a given environment, including architectural floor plans? The simple answer is that most existing maps were developed for purposes other than signage and are, therefore, unsuitable for the communication purposes of a signage program. Sometimes, however, a suitable existing base map can be adapted and customized to a sign program's purposes. At the very least, existing maps and floor plans can often be used as a starting point for development of signage-purposed maps.

Whether designed by the EG designer or an outside specialist, the communicative and stylistic treatment of maps and diagrams is as unlimited as the communicative and stylistic spectrum of the graphic design field. Map design, in particular, can vary from highly realistic and geographically accurate to highly diagrammatic and abstract. Several examples of different styles of map design are shown in Figures 5.25 to 5.29. The key to map design is for

5.25 Route map at Zion National Park in southwestern Utah.

5.26 Street map of the Portland, Oregon, downtown district.

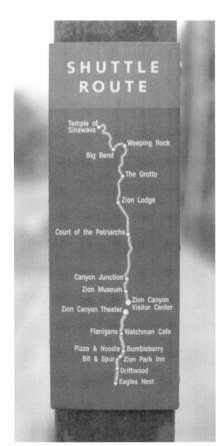

5.25

5.26

5.27

5.28

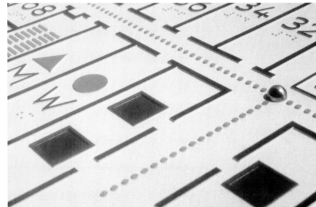

5.29

5.27 Park map with symbol legends at the Coney Island Boardwalk in Brooklyn, New York.

5.28 Campus map with symbol and typographic legends at Crotched Mountain Hospital in Greenfield, New Hampshire.

5.29 Detail of a tactile interior map for the vision-impaired at the Lighthouse in New York City.

the map and other diagrammatic elements of a sign program to be as stylistically unified with the program's overall graphic system as possible.

Ways to promote visual unity among a sign program's diagrams and other graphic system elements include using typeface(s), symbols, and colors that are the same as, or at least compatible with, those elements in the program's overall graphic system. For example, if the Times Roman typeface is used for the sign program's typography, it should also be used for map legend typography. Obviously, stylistic unity is easier to control when the EG designer is preparing the maps or diagrams. If, on the other hand, the maps are being prepared by an outside specialist, the EG designer should thoroughly brief that person on the graphic system's stylistic elements, as well as review his or her work in progress.

Map Orientation

Map orientation is a major issue in any signage program. When the top of the map is oriented in the direction the viewer is facing, it's termed as a *heads-up orientation*. The heads-up orientation aids map comprehension because viewers are facing what's directly ahead of them on the map. Everything else is also logically oriented to the viewer, too: What's on the right side of the map is on the viewer's right, what's on the map's left is on the viewer's left, and what's toward the bottom of the map is behind the viewer. Paper maps, which are printed with North at the top, are flexible—viewers can easily rotate them into a heads-up orientation. Not so with signage maps. They're fixed to sign hardware structures and can't be rotated in the hands of the viewer like paper maps.

Although the heads-up map orientation on signs is best for viewer comprehension of a map, it does pose two logistical problems from a design standpoint. First, multiple rotations—typically four, with North, South, East, and West at the top of the map—are required to orient a map heads-up with the viewer. These multiple rotations of the underlying map also require rotation of any legend typography and symbols, so they don't have to be read sideways or upside down, and rotating the legend graphics is a time-consuming task. The second logistical problem has to do with the proportions of a map's footprint. If the footprint is anything other than a 1:1 height-to-width proportion, the map will take up either more vertical or more horizontal space on the sign panel, depending on which way the map is rotated to be in the heads-up orientation. This, in turn, can affect sign panel proportions, as well as the layout of other graphic elements on the sign.

Due to these logistical problems, which definitely make heads-up map orientation more costly, many sign programs must make do with all maps oriented with North at the top, regardless of which direction the viewer is facing. This is less than optimum, as the viewer has to go through mental gymnastics to interpret the map's orientation relative to which way he or she is facing.

Regardless of whether maps on signs have a heads-up or North orientation, it's essential to have a prominent graphic indicating where the viewer's location is on the map. This is typically a triangular shape pointing in the direction the viewer is facing, with the legend "You Are Here."

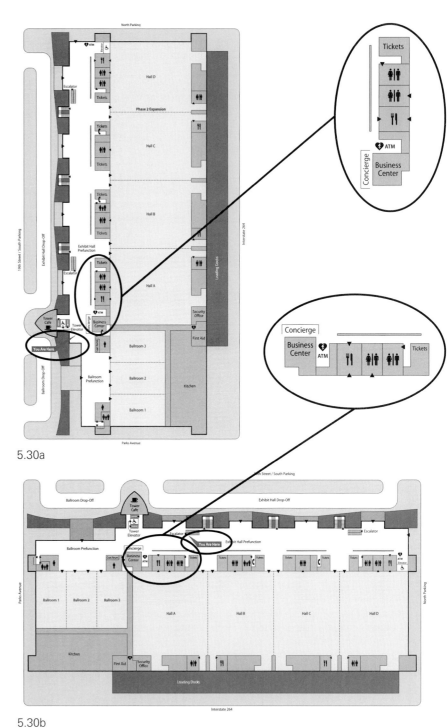

5.30a

5.30a, b Two different heads-up orientations of the same map, with details of legend rotation. In a heads-up orientation, the top of the map is positioned in the direction the viewer is facing. Note changes in the map footprint proportion depending on orientation.

5.30b

Other Graphic Elements

In addition to the communicative graphic elements of typography, symbols, and arrows, all of which purposefully communicate information, there are other noncommunicative graphic helpers that organize and distinguish the graphic presentation of information on signs. These include rules, bars, boxes, circles, and other simple or

5.31a

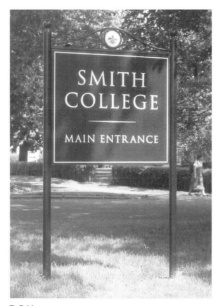

5.31b

5.31c

ornate shapes and patterns. These various shapes can also be used as decorative features.

5.31a, b, c Uses of rules, shapes, and patterns as organizing and decorative graphic elements.

Color

We do not live in a black-and-white world, so color is as much an element of a sign program's graphic system as it is of the hardware system. There are many ways in which color can be used in signage programs, as illustrated in the completed projects shown in the color insert of this book.

As with all the other graphic system elements discussed thus far, the intent of this section is to give an overview of color selection as it relates to a sign program's graphic system, rather than to provide an extensive discussion of the complex and multihued subject of color.

The Roles of Color in Signage

Color plays several roles in a sign program's graphic system, and it can play these roles individually or severally:

- To contrast or harmonize with the sign environment.
- To augment the meaning of sign messages.
- To distinguish messages from one another.
- To be decorative.

Before looking at each of these roles of color in sign graphics, it's important to know that the EG designer doesn't always have free rein when it comes to selecting a color vocabulary for a sign program. For certain signage programs, use of specific colors may be mandated by official bodies,

Navigating State Departments of Transportation*
Craig Berger and Bob Trescott

What can happen when everyone in the process feels involved, respected, and appreciated?

Almost every city and county in the United States has state roads cutting through them. U.S. Route 1, for example, slices through nearly every major city on the east coast from Maine to Florida. That means that state Departments of Transportation (DOTs) have purview over major roads in cities with urban systems. Every state Department of Transportation is different, but they all have two things in common. They take almost all their cues from the Manual for Uniform Traffic Control Devices. This continuously updated document has room for states to make their own decisions on urban signs. Some states (like New Jersey) are adventurous enough to do that; some are not. Secondly, most state DOTs do not like to be surprised, especially by a sign system they have not seen before.

Working with a DOT can be difficult, but working from a base of prior knowledge will definitely give you and your client an advantage in achieving success.

Design Issues to Consider
Color Contrast

Until a few years ago, most DOTs accepted any color provided it was green, blue, or brown. Now at least fifteen states, including New York, New Jersey, Texas, Florida, California, Pennsylvania, and Arizona, have allowed sign systems with a wider palette of colors. Always keep in mind that all state DOTs want a color contrast between foreground letters and background sign of at least 50% and preferably 70%. This is similar to the recommendations of the Americans with Disabilities Act.

Letter Height

Many DOTs require a minimum 4" letter height on state roads. While a good idea, it is often impossible on tight city signs. Fight for 3" or $3^1/_2$" (the smallest heights advisable), but if that isn't feasible, specify 4" heights as a requirement on state roads and 3" or $3^1/_2$" on nonstate roads.

Letter Type

Most DOTs have no clear rules on the selection of type fonts for urban signs. The requirements vary considerably from state to state. So check if there is a specific DOT type requirement. If there is some leeway, select type from the narrow band of fonts that are well known for vehicular legibility and have precedence in other cities. These fonts include Clearview, Futura, Franklin Gothic, and British Transport.

Message Schedules

Most states follow the "three destination maximum" rule, with four used in some extreme cases.

Height of a Sign

The Americans with Disabilities Act requires a 7' minimum height for a blade sign in the public right of way, except if clearance below is not blocked.

Arrows

Many DOTs do not focus on using specific arrows, but like to see arrows with a wide head and long tail. Arrowheads and other narrow head arrows are strongly discouraged.

Position of Arrows

Testing in this area is still inconclusive, but some states require the left arrow to be on the left side of the sign and the right arrow on the right side. Most DOTs have allowed arrows below the destination.

Planning Issues to Consider

The most important thing DOTs would like to see has nothing to do with the design of the individual sign, but the hierarchy of the entire system. When submitting work to a DOT, remember that the most important thing for them to see is a clear and efficient system. The system must have a destination hierarchy that can prevent future disputes and a management plan that allows for accountability.

Precedence Matters

States like Florida, Pennsylvania, and New Jersey have already passed rules for implementing urban signs, but most states have not. When implementing a system in a state that has few written rules, be sure to study successful efforts in other cities in that state and other states. Engineers like to base future results on past successes.

Start Early and Communicate

Cities and design firms have a bad reputation with many DOTs because they often submit their plans at the last minute and plead ignorance on many issues. Conversely, most DOTs have a bad reputation among designers as a result of a general lack of responsiveness until a project is forced on them. In this situation, it always pays to be the bigger person, invite the local district officials to your meetings, and submit the needed paperwork early.

Respect and Cooperation

You will be surprised to see what can happen when everyone in the process feels involved, respected, and appreciated.

Craig Berger is Director of Education and Professional Development for the Society for Environmental Graphic Design (SEGD).

Bob Trescott is an urban planner in Tallahassee, Florida, with extensive experience in the layout, content, and function of community wayfinding systems.

Reprinted from SEGD Design number 09 (2005), with permission.

or dictated by corporate or institutional color identity standards. And the EG designer should always investigate cultural connotations of color when designing a sign program for overseas projects.

An example of a situation where colors may be mandated by official bodies include cases where local codes require the use of red for typographic or pictorial sign messages of a warning or emergency nature. Another case in which official bodies may be involved in color selection is in city signage programs that interface with public roadways. Such programs almost invariably involve the participation of local Department of Transportation (DOT) officials, who may or may not insist that the city sign program colors conform to the color standards indicated for various categories of roadway signs in the Federal *Manual of Uniform Traffic Control Devices* (MUTCD). The MUTCD is the bible of official U.S. traffic and roadway signage, and should be on the reference list of any EG designer involved with city or urban signage programs. The MUTCD, which is an unwieldy document, can be accessed at www:mutcd.fhwa.dot.gov.

Even when a given sign program isn't affected by official bodies, the EG designer still isn't necessarily free to explore a rainbow of colors. If the client is a large corporation or an institution, such as a university or a transportation authority, it may have instituted graphic standards programs to promote a consistent graphic or brand identity. And these standards programs typically dictate specific colors that can be used for sign graphics, as they often do with typefaces and symbol vocabularies.

One last word about official restrictions on color usage: The current ADA recommends a minimum of 70 percent contrast between the figure and the ground of sign graphics. Here, the word *figure* refers to the typographic and pictorial graphic elements, and *ground* refers to the background on which they appear. Note that this is a recommendation, not a requirement, but good contrast between figure and ground is essential for good legibility of sign graphics.

Theoretically, white figures on a black ground, or vice versa, have a 100 percent contrast ratio, even though white never reflects 100 percent of the light that hits it and black never reflects 0 percent. Nevertheless, how does one determine the contrast of black or white graphics on a color background, or one color of graphics on a different-color background? Light reflectance values (LRVs) are helpful in this determination, and are available for most paint color systems by manufacturers such as Benjamin Moore and Sherwin Williams—which don't, by the way, actually manufacture paints for the sign industry. LRVs aren't available for other color systems that many EG designers use, such as the Pantone system. So, to determine an approximate LRV for a color swatch from a non-LRV color system, one must find the closest visual match for the non-LRV color from an LRV color system. There are other, more scientific methods for determining the LRVs of non-LRV rated colors, and such methods may be warranted for certain signage programs.

Color Selection Considerations

Now that I've discussed a number of the constraints on color selection for sign graphics, it's time to move on to the color considerations on projects for which the EG designer does have some freedom to select colors for the sign graphic system.

Color can play a role in whether signs contrast or harmonize with the sign environment. For those projects where navigation decisions must be quickly and easily made, such as transportation facilities, a goal may be to make the signs stand out from their surrounding environment so that they can be easily distinguished, read, and acted upon. In such cases, color can be one of the most obvious factors to set the sign program apart from its surrounding environment. For other projects, a goal may be to make the sign program blend in more closely with its setting, which can be achieved through the use of sign colors that harmonize with the environmental setting. In general, depending on the overall color palette of a given sign environment, bright, saturated colors can enliven and stand out from the environment, and neutral, more subtle colors can blend with or recede from the environment.

Color can also play roles in augmenting the meaning of sign messages and in distinguishing sign messages from one another. Obvious ways color can augment the meaning of a message is when the color red is used for warning or emergency messages, and yellow is used for attention-getting messages. When color is used to augment or distinguish sign messages, the color can be used for either the message graphics themselves (the figure) or the message background (the ground). Sometimes color is used in other graphic elements such as squares, bars, or circles to augment or distinguish sign messages.

Color-Coding

The use of color to communicate meaning in sign graphics leads to the topic of *color-coding*, which will be discussed briefly here. Color-coding links a given message with a given color to reinforce the message and to distinguish it from other messages. For color-coding to be effective in signage, a message and color must be linked, because color by itself is too ambiguous to communicate a specific message clearly.

One of the few instances where color alone communicates a clear message is with traffic signals, but that's because the driving population worldwide has been trained over time to stop on red and go on green. Yet even this clear-cut response doesn't translate to uses of red and green in signage. For example, in many countries, green is used for exit sign graphics because of its association with the concept of *go*, as in "Go out through this exit." In other countries, however, exit sign graphics are red because of its association with danger, warning, and emergency, regardless of the seeming illogic that red is also associated with the concept of *stop*, as in "Do not proceed through this exit." There are two points here: first, the meanings associated with colors are learned and, second, that those meanings vary with geographical location and culture.

Most transit systems worldwide use some form of color-coding—in association with numbers, letters, or names—on maps and signage to help users distinguish one route from another. The New York City subway signage program also color-codes its exit signage with a red background to command attention and to reinforce the meaning of the word *exit* with the red warning/emergency color. Color-coding can also be useful for signage programs for large, complex, nontransit-related sites, such as in cities, airports, hospital complexes, and arenas and stadiums.

Coming back to the MUTCD and DOTs, color-coding is also used officially for the backgrounds of traffic and roadway signage throughout the United States, even though many drivers in this country don't really realize the significance of the background colors. These official road sign background colors are:

- Green, for guide and orientation messages
- Blue, for motorist services messages

- Brown, for recreational and cultural interest messages
- Yellow, for warning messages
- Red, for prohibitory messages, such as Stop, Yield, Wrong Way, and Do Not Enter
- White, for regulatory messages
- Bright orange, for construction messages

Clearly, color-coded sign graphics can be useful for both transit-related and large nontransit sign programs, but they should be used thoughtfully and judiciously, for excessive or inappropriate use of color-coding can actually impair rather than enhance the communication effectiveness of a sign program. Color-coding is not a panacea for unclear message nomenclature and should never be relied on to substitute for a poorly formulated sign information content system. Keep in mind, too, that many people have color perception problems and cannot distinguish between certain colors. And, of course, the more colors that are used in a color-coding vocabulary, the more visually complex the vocabulary becomes, making it difficult for even normally sighted people to distinguish among the various colors and to learn the meaning associated with each color.

In addition to aiding communication and helping sign programs contrast or blend with their environments, color in sign graphics can also play a decorative role. Sign graphic color schemes can range from bold and playful to subtle and sophisticated. As always, every project is different so the key is to select a color palette that meshes with the goals of the project at hand.

Color Palette Sources

There are several sources for the selection and specification of the color palette for a sign program's graphic system. One source commonly used by EG designers is the Pantone Matching System (PMS), which offers a large range of color swatches, each coded by a number for specification use.

The Pantone system was developed as a color standardization and mixing guide for inks used on presses in the commercial printing industry, and is therefore perhaps not the best source for color palettes used in the sign industry. However, most EG designers with a graphic design background are familiar with the PMS system and it resides in the color swatch libraries of the vector drawing programs typically used by EG designers. Most manufacturers of sign coating materials such as paint and vinyl can analyze a Pantone color swatch and create a dead-on or acceptably accurate match for it in paint and other coating media. Additionally, some standard vinyl colors are cross-matched to commonly specified Pantone colors.

Although the Pantone system does contain a seemingly mind-boggling range of color swatches, it sometimes just doesn't offer the exact color

Amtrak Acela Specialty Station Signage

Northeast Rail Corridor, Boston to Washington, DC

Calori & Vanden-Eynden / Design Consultants

The Comprehensive Breast Center at Bryn Mawr Hospital

Bryn Mawr, Pennsylvania

AGS

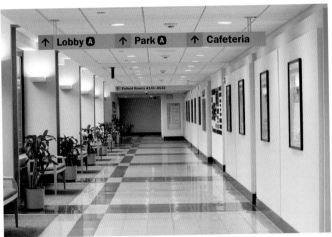

For information in Hospital, look for this symbol.

PARK A
LEVEL G

Remember where you are parked.

For access to Lobby A take elevator or stairs up to Level 1.

Please take a parking card to remember where you are parked.

ZONE A FLOOR 2

Rosengarten Elevators access the following destinations:

NO ACCESS to Emergency from these elevators. ← Use Pew Elevators

NO ACCESS to Radiation Oncology from these elevators. ← Use Service Elevators

Floor G		Floor 1	
A7	Cafeteria	A4	Martin Conference Room
A8	Auditorium	A5	Health Education Center
		A6	Gift Shop
Floor 1		A	Public Telephones
A	Lobby A/Park A		
B	Link to Hospital Zone B	**Floor 3**	
B	Java City/Atrium	A31	Patient Accommodations
A1	Admissions		
A2	Ambulatory Procedure Ctr.		
A3	Cardiac Cath Lab/EP		

City Center Englewood
Englewood, California

Beauchamp Group

Santa Monica Main Public Library

Santa Monica, California

Beck & Graboski Design Office

Hongkong Land Property Portfolio Signage
Central Hong Kong, China

Calori & Vanden-Eynden / Design Consultants

Zion National Park Wayfinding Program

Springdale, Utah

Biesek Design

Toledo Museum of Art
Toledo, Ohio

Chermayeff & Geismar, Inc.

University Center

Baltimore, Maryland

Cloud Gehshan Associates

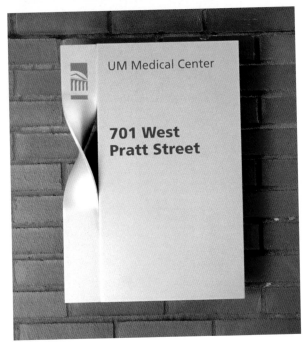

Crate & Barrel World Headquarters
Northbrook, Illinois

Calori & Vanden-Eynden / Design Consultants

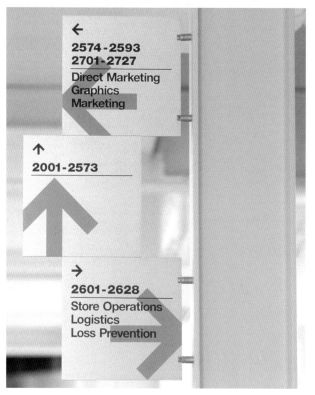

Axcelis Technologies Corporate HQ

Beverly, Massachusetts

Gamble Design LLC

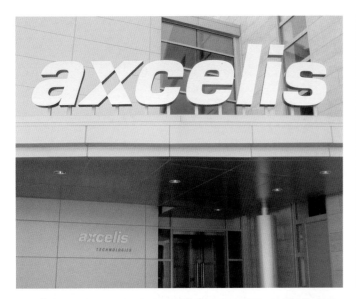

Miami Children's Museum
Miami, Florida

Tom Graboski & Associates, Inc. Design

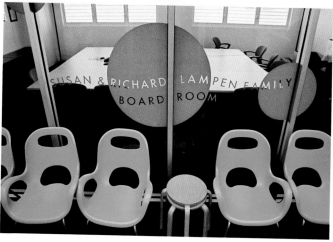

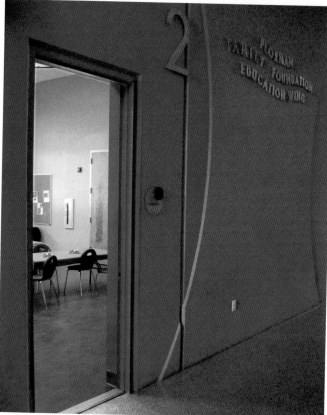

Regional Justice Center
Las Vegas, Nevada

Hunt Design Associates

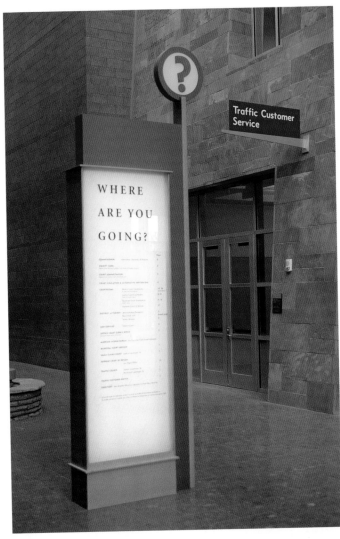

Walk! Philadelphia

Center City District, Philadelphia

Joel Katz Design Associates

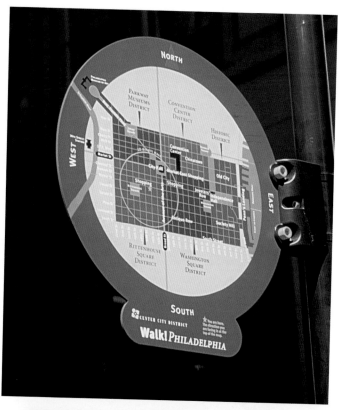

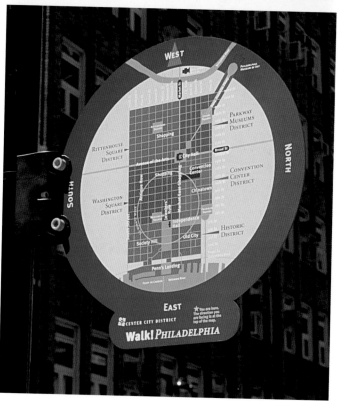

Azia Center Office Tower

Shanghai, China

Calori & Vanden-Eynden / Design Consultants

Kaiser Permanente, Multilingual Signage Program
Santa Clara Medical Center, Medical Office Building, Santa Clara, California

Kate Keating Associates, Inc.

University of Cincinnati, MainStreet District

Cincinnati, Ohio

Kolar Design, Inc./Shortt Design

Toledo Museum of Art

Toledo, Ohio

Chermayeff & Geismar, Inc.

University Center
Baltimore, Maryland

Cloud Gehshan Associates

Law School

Westminster Hall

UM Medical Center

Emergency

Medical School

Dental School

Pharmacy School

VA Medical Center

Light Rail

UniversityCenter

University of Maryland at Baltimore

Louis L. Kaplan Hall

School of Social Work

525 West Redwood Street

UM Medical Center

701 West Pratt Street

Crate & Barrel World Headquarters
Northbrook, Illinois

Calori & Vanden-Eynden / Design Consultants

Axcelis Technologies Corporate HQ
Beverly, Massachusetts

Gamble Design LLC

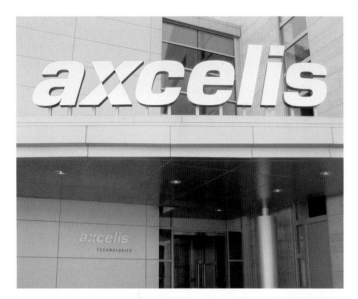

Miami Children's Museum

Miami, Florida

Tom Graboski & Associates, Inc. Design

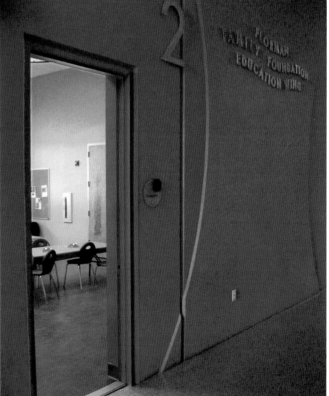

Regional Justice Center

Las Vegas, Nevada

Hunt Design Associates

Walk! Philadelphia

Center City District, Philadelphia

Joel Katz Design Associates

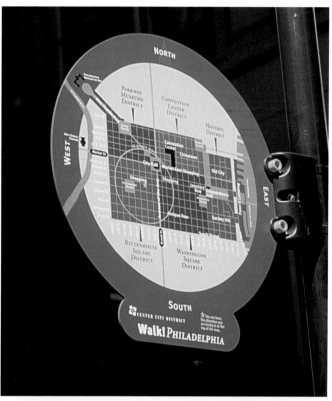

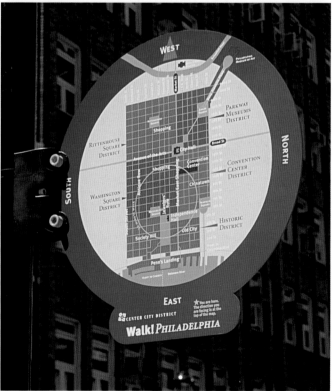

Azia Center Office Tower
Shanghai, China

Calori & Vanden-Eynden / Design Consultants

Jane Voorhees Zimmerli Art Museum

Rutgers University, New Brunswick, New Jersey

Calori & Vanden-Eynden / Design Consultants

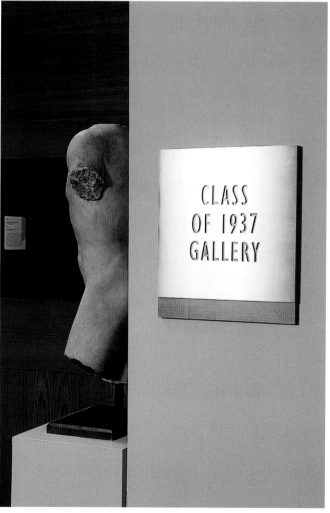

Master Plan/Wayfinding & Signage Design – Terminal D

Dallas/Fort Worth International Airport, Texas

Carol Naughton + Associates, Inc.

Asian Art Museum

San Francisco, California

Debra Nichols Design

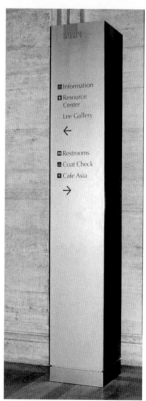

Manhattan Theatre Club at the Biltmore Theater

New York, New York

Poulin + Morris

Manhattan Theatre Club at the Biltmore Theater

Virginia Beach Convention Center
Virginia Beach, Virginia

Calori & Vanden-Eynden / Design Consultants

Roll, Barresi & Associates, Inc.

Universal Studios Wayfinding

Orlando, Florida and Hollywood, California

Selbert Perkins Design Collaborative

Fashion Show Mall

Las Vegas, Nevada

Sussman/Prejza & Company, Inc.

Suzhou International Exposition Centre

Suzhou, China

Calori & Vanden-Eynden / Design Consultants

Banner Good Samaritan Medical Center

Phoenix, Arizona

Thinking Caps

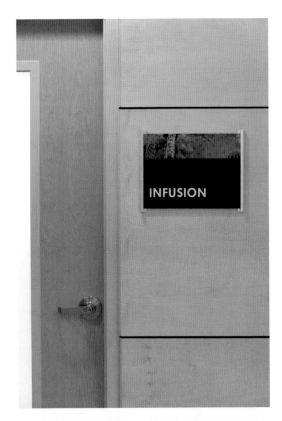

Marion Oliver McCaw Hall

Seattle, Washington

WPA, Inc.

that you, the EG designer, are searching for. In these situations, the color libraries of paint companies offer more options, including metallic, metalflake, iridescent, pearlescent, and other exotic colors. As with the Pantone system, each paint swatch in these libraries is identified by a number and/or name.

Many companies manufacture paint in the United States, but only a few manufacture paint formulated for sign applications, so it's best to start with the color libraries from manufacturers of paints for the sign industry, such as Matthews, Akzo Sikkens, and Wyandotte. If the must-have color is in the library of a nonsign paint company, such as Benjamin Moore or Pratt & Lambert, the EG designer can provide a swatch of the desired color for matching by one of the sign paint manufacturers.

Keep in mind that the gloss level of paint and other sign coatings affects how a given color is perceived. If a paint or coating has a high gloss level, its color will appear deeper and richer than the same color with a matte gloss level. Also keep in mind that the ADA comes into play on paint and other sign coatings and finishes, requiring a nonglare matte or eggshell gloss level. (Coatings, gloss levels, and finishes are discussed further in Chapter 6, "The Hardware System.")

Layout

Thus far we've covered typography, symbols and arrows, color, and other graphic elements, which can be considered the ingredients, so to speak, of the graphic system recipe. Layout is the process part of the recipe, during which the EG designer sizes and arranges these graphic ingredients into formats that determine the visual unity, clarity, and style of the graphic system. Just like cooking, designing layouts is a highly creative process with almost limitless options, just a few of which are explored in this section.

Sign layout expresses the visual character of a sign program's graphic system. Layouts can be bold and flashy or quiet and subtle; they can be contemporary or traditional; they can be clean and straightforward or complex and rich. Accordingly, the visual appearance of the sign graphic system should be considered in conjunction with the appearance of the hardware system, for the appearance of each system affects the other, particularly in terms of size and proportion of sign faces.

Layout cannot take place meaningfully until the sign information content system is finalized—that is, the message content for every sign in the program is known. The message content, along with the size and layout of sign graphics, affect the size of each sign object in a program, thereby ultimately affecting the program's hardware system. Accordingly, one of the key tasks in the layout process is determining the size of the graphics for each sign type. Viewing distance is the chief determinant of typographic size for signage programs, although for certain kinds of signs, typographic size can also be mandated by local codes and the ADA.

Sizing Typography for Viewing Distance

As stated in Chapter 4, effective signage must have adequately sized graphics so users have enough time to read a sign message, understand it, and act on it safely by the time they reach the decision point. Other factors, such as the hierarchical rank of a sign message (primary, secondary, etc.), whether the sign is for pedestrian or vehicular users, sign viewing angle and setback, and more, all interact with viewing distance to determine the size of sign typography.

As a starting point for sizing sign typography, a simple rule of thumb is to use 1″ of character height, as measured on a nonrounded capital character such as an *E*, *H*, or *I* (known as the *cap height*), for every 50′ of viewing distance. According to this formula then, a sign that's to be viewed from a distance of 500′ should theoretically have typography with a 10″ cap height; a sign that's to be viewed from 25′ should theoretically have a 1/2″ cap height—although the ADA mandates a minimum 5/8″ cap height for permanent room identification signs.

I use the word *theoretically* here because this 1:50 rule of thumb is not hard and fast, as no rule of thumb is. And it's not without challengers; in fact, to accommodate a lower-than-normal visual acuity rate in sign users, some authorities advocate a more conservative formula of 1″ of cap height to every 25′ of viewing distance. Another challenger of the 1:50 formula is the ADA, which mandates minimum and maximum cap heights for certain kinds of signs. Local codes also sometimes mandate specific cap heights for certain signs. Message hierarchy also raises a challenge to this formula, in that any primary messages should be larger than secondary messages on a given sign.

A word about cap height is in order here. The use of cap height is key to the graphic system for signage. In signage graphics, capital letter height is used as the measurement standard, instead of typographic point size, which is used for print and Web graphics. Cap height is expressed in inches or fractions thereof, usually in units no smaller than 1/16″. Cap height standards use nonrounded letters because they're more easily measured, and because rounded letters such as *C*, *O*, and *S*, are larger than nonrounded letters, to maintain optical balance in typeface design. Similarly, rounded lowercase letters are also larger than nonrounded ones. Keep in mind that lowercase

5.32 Primary and secondary sign information at Valparaiso University in Valparaiso, Indiana.

5.33 Always measure cap height on squared-off characters, because round characters are larger than the cap height to provide optical balance among different character shapes.

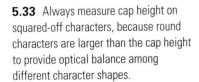

5.33

letters also have descenders, which fall below the baseline of capital letters; and in many typefaces, ascenders which rise above the cap height line.

The dynamics of reading, understanding, and acting on sign information are compounded and more critical in driving situations; consequently, a more complex formula should be used as a starting point for determining vehicular signage cap heights. The formula shown in Figure 5.34 accommodates such dynamics as speed, setback, and other vital factors for vehicular signage.

Certainly, formulas are a useful starting point for determining cap heights, but the only sure way to confirm that typographic sizing is adequate is to test it with mockups and prototypes, optimally under the actual conditions that the signs will be viewed. The degree and formality of such testing varies with each project and design budget, but some form or another of testing and confirming cap heights is highly recommended for every signage project, especially those with a vehicular signage component.

Other Factors Affecting Layouts

Sizing sign typography to viewing distance or to code or ADA mandated sizes is a fundamental aspect of developing sign layouts, but there are other aspects that influence the ultimate design and overall size and proportion of layouts. These include:

- Proportion of symbols and arrows in relation to typography
- Position of symbols and arrows in relation to typography
- Spacing around and between graphic elements
- Layout format proportions

Proportion

There is no one way to proportion symbols and arrows in relation to typography, but suffice it to say that symbols and arrows should be large enough relative to the typography to ensure they are clearly visible.

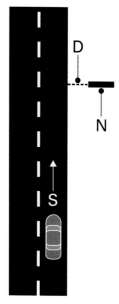

$$\frac{(N+6)S}{100} + \frac{D}{10} = H$$

N: Number of of Messages
S: Speed Limit
D: Setback Distance
H: Height of Letters

5.34 This formula for determining letter height for vehicular signage accommodates the variables of speed, setback, and message quantity.

5.35a, b Whether on an informal or more formalized basis, typographic legibility and sizing should be tested with mockups and prototypes of sign faces.

5.35a

5.35b

Human Factors Researchers Can Improve Environmental Graphic Design Products*

Phil Garvey

What is the most readable font? What symbols are most effective? What arrows and wayfinding systems best guide people to their destination? These are questions environmental graphic designers use their training and experience to answer every day. However, their background does not provide them with the tools to optimize their designs through systematic evaluation, and their closeness to the projects at hand can inadvertently prejudice attempts at impartial in-house assessment. This is where the human factors researcher comes in. Human factors researchers are specialists trained to methodically assess and optimize the effectiveness of the user/environment interface; an interface that begins as sensory input and ends in observable behavior.

Although designers may not be quick to see the need to systematically and independently evaluate their efforts, my own recent experiences as a human factors researcher working with environmental graphic designers in both highway and healthcare environments may

help clarify how these two professions can effectively collaborate to provide clients with the best and most cost-effective product.

While working with the National Park Service, design considerations led Meeker & Associates to recommend the use of an arrow that differed from the standards set by the Federal Highway Administration. To get approval for the use of an alternate arrow, the FHWA required the designers to prove it was at least as good as the standard arrow. The designers turned this task over to the human factors researchers at Penn State. As with most human factors research, the evaluation began with a literature review. That review yielded twelve candidate arrows (see figure) including three used by the FHWA, a chevron, the Montreal Expo arrow, and several crow's foot designs.

An experiment was designed to determine the distance at which the orientation of these arrows could be detected. Full-sized signs using retroreflective materials were viewed by groups of

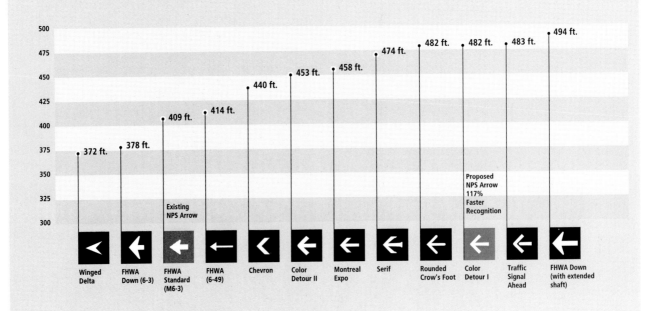

older and younger drivers approaching the arrows in the day and at night from moving vehicles. The results were tabulated and the data subjected to statistical analysis. The conclusion was that the FHWA standard arrow required on National Park Service signs was one of the least legible designs, with the crow's foot arrow recommended by the designers visible 18 percent further away.

In the NPS arrow example, the designers' instincts were correct, but sometimes designers' assumptions do not bear out in practice. This may be the result of an unforeseen age, gender, or cultural bias on the part of the designers, or a lack of familiarity with the environment or end user group to whom the materials are being displayed. Refining communication with the target audience is critical because the implementation (or misimplementation) could have financial- or safety-critical implications.

Although including human factors research in a contract can increase up-front cost, the findings and subsequent refinements can add significant value and longevity to a project and help avoid critical and costly errors and delays, such as in recent instances where the ineffectiveness of untested wayfinding systems has resulted in wholesale system redesign or replacement. These failures are embarrassing for the original

designer, expensive for the client, and harm the field of environmental graphic design in general.

While environmental graphic designers have a set of tools that enables them to creatively address their clients' needs, a critical item missing from their tool belts is a way to systematically, scientifically, and impartially evaluate their designs' effectiveness from the user's perspective. Without adequate methods to determine whether their designs work, not just aesthetically, but also empirically, there will always be failures. While there are rules to guide designers in the effective development of their products just as there are rules that engineers use in the safe construction of highways, in both cases each application is unique and can benefit from empirical, independent evaluation and feedback. When human factors evaluation is included throughout the environmental graphic design process an economical solution is created that helps bridge the disconnects that can exist among a client's desires, human user requirements, and a designer's vision.

Excerpted from The Twelve Percent Solution, first published in SEGD Design, Issue 9, 2005.

Phil Garvey is the principal of the Visual Communication Research Institute (VCRI) in State College, Pennsylvania.

With arrows, which are relatively clear-cut shapes, a common method is to size either the width or height of the arrow to the cap height of the typography. Symbols are more difficult because they can be more visually complex than arrows, and are often too small to be legible when sized to the cap height of the typography, particularly if they are enclosed by a square or circular surround. In such instances, symbols can be sized to a multiple of the cap height: for example, at 1.2 times the cap height, which makes the symbols 20 percent larger than the cap height; or at 1.5 times, which is 50 percent larger. Of course, arrows can be sized to the same proportions as symbols in relation to the typography. Once proportional relationships are established between symbols, arrows, and typography, those relationships should be maintained as consistently as possible for all typographic cap heights displayed on the signs.

5.36 When arrows and symbols are sized to typographic cap height, symbols may be too small to be legible.

5.36

5.37a, b Arrows and symbols sized at 120 and 150 percent of cap height.

5.37a, b

5.38a, b Once established, proportional relationships among graphic elements should be maintained at various sizes.

5.38a, b

Position

As for the proportional relationships of typography, symbols, and arrows, there are several options for the way they are positioned in relation to each other. Two of these options, shown in Figures 5.39 and 5.40 include:

- *Side-by-side positioning* (arrows and symbols positioned in line with typography)
- *Stacked positioning* (arrows and symbols positioned above typography)

As can be seen from the simple examples in Figure 5.41, the proportions of the sign face can vary depending on whether the graphic elements are positioned side by side or stacked.

When arrows and symbols are positioned in line with the typography, there are several options for aligning them horizontally. A commonly used option is to align the horizontal centerlines of the symbols and arrows with the horizontal centerline of the typographic cap height. Similarly, if the arrows and symbols are positioned above or below the typography, their alignment in relation to each other and their distance from the typography need to be established.

5.39

Typography

5.40

5.39 Arrows and symbols positioned in line, or side by side, with typography. In this example, bottoms of arrows and symbols align with the typographic baseline.

5.40 Arrows and symbols positioned above, or *stacked*, with typography. In this example, the vertical space separating them is .5 of the typography's cap height.

To compound the two positioning options just described—and their creative possibilities—for layouts, arrows and symbols can be placed to the left or right of the typography, or be centered with the typography, if the arrows/symbols are positioned above or below the typography. But this is not to say that symbols and arrows are necessarily always paired with each other; often, arrows will be set off from the typography, whereas the symbols will be placed at the end of a line of typography.

Note that it's fairly common to place arrows at the left side of a sign layout regardless of which direction the arrows are pointing, or whether the arrows are positioned in line with or above/below the typography. Considering that we read from left to right, left placement of arrows makes sense, as it fixes the arrows at the beginning of each sign message. It also organizes all the arrows on the left side of the sign layout. Of course, there are also valid reasons to place arrows on the same side of the typography in which the arrow is pointing—for example, placing

← Baggage Claim
↑ Ticketing

← Baggage Claim
↑ Ticketing

5.41a, b

5.41a, b Sign face proportions can vary with side-by-side or stacked positioning of arrow/symbols and typography.

5.42

5.42 Horizontal centerlines of arrows, symbols, and typography aligned.

right-pointing arrows to the right side of the message typography. Again, the possibilities for positioning and aligning typography, symbols, and arrows in sign layouts are endless, but once a positioning scheme is determined, it should generally be employed across the entire range of sign types in a program, to enhance visual consistency. (The color plates show various arrow/typographic alignments.)

Spacing

Spacing around and between graphic elements also affects sign layout proportions and sizes. The terms *figure* and *ground,* which were introduced earlier in this chapter, can be linked to the discussion in Chapter 4; specifically, the figure is the *message footprint,* consisting of the typographic and pictorial graphic elements, and the ground is the background area, or *sign face perimeter,* consisting of *dead space* in which the figure is displayed. The space taken up by the figure graphics is termed the *live space* or *live area,* so a sign face consists of both live and dead space.

Recall from Chapter 4 that the live space consumes significantly less than 100 percent of a sign face's area. The rest of the sign face is taken up by dead space, which includes both typographical spacing and spacing between typography and other graphic elements:

- Margins around the perimeter of the sign face
- Horizontal letter and word spacing within lines of typography
- Horizontal spacing between side-by-side graphic elements, such as gutters between arrows, symbols, and typography
- Vertical spacing between lines of typography
- Vertical spacing between stacked graphic elements, such as spacing between typography and other graphic elements

Dead space is essential for the legibility, clarity, and organized appearance of the sign graphic system, so this section explores each of the dead space elements.

Margins are the dead space around the perimeter of a sign face, and each sign has a top, bottom, left, and right margin. As with most other aspects of layout development, there's no magic rule for determining how large or small margins should be. Needless to say, however, margins should not be so small that the graphics appear too close to the sign perimeter, nor so large that the graphics appear dwarfed by the margins. A good starting place is to look at margins that equal the cap height of the primary message in the layout; for example, 1" margins for typography with a 1" cap height. This relationship can then be enlarged or reduced by multiples of the cap height, such as by 1.2 times cap height for a larger margin or by .8 times cap height for smaller margins. And here's a visual balance tip for horizontally centered layouts: Bottom margins should always be slightly larger than top margins to make them appear equal, as shown in Figure 5.43. This trick is borrowed from picture-framing professionals who cut picture mattes with the bottom matte border slightly larger than the top. It makes sense for arranging type, too, because descenders hang below the typographic baseline.

Horizontal spacing within lines of typography includes letterspacing and word spacing, both of which are essential for good type legibility.

- *Letterspacing*, the space that separates the letters within words, was covered earlier in this chapter.

- *Word spacing* is the space that separates words, and it typically automatically adjusts with the letterspacing, or tracking, that is specified when type is set on computer programs used by EG designers and sign fabricators.

Horizontal spacing is also necessary between side-by-side graphic elements, such as gutters between arrows, symbols, and typography. The term *gutter*, which comes from print graphic design, refers to the space between columns of text on a page. Similarly, in signage graphics, *gutter* can refer to the space between columns of arrows and typography, or the space between columns of arrows and symbols. A good starting point is to use half (.5) the cap height as the unit for gutter spacing, and then adjust it by a greater or lesser multiple, if desired. The same is the case for horizontal spacing of symbols or arrows that are placed at the end of lines of typography. The key to effective horizontal spacing of graphic elements is to space them closely enough so that they appear to belong together and to conserve sign space, but not so tight that the elements appear too crowded.

Typographic line spacing is an important *vertical spacing* element, and can be expressed in two ways:

- As the unit between the baseline of one line of typography to the cap height of the next line of typography (baseline to cap height spacing), which is the open space itself between the lines.

- As the unit between the baseline of one line of typography to the baseline of the next line of typography (baseline to baseline spacing), which is the open space between the lines plus the cap height.

A starting place for determining the amount of vertical line spacing on a baseline-to-cap height basis is to use .5 cap height, which translates to

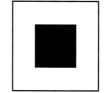

5.43 To achieve visual balance on horizontally centered layouts, make the bottom margin slightly larger than the top margin.

5.44a, b Gutter spacing between arrows, symbols, and typography should not be too tight or too open.

5.45a, b The two ways to indicate typographic line spacing.

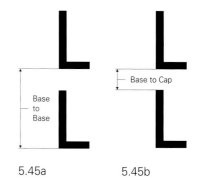

5.44a, b

5.45a   5.45b

1.5 cap height on a baseline-to-baseline basis. This ratio can then be adjusted up or down depending on the typeface being used and other factors. For example, the ratio may have to be increased for typefaces with ascenders that rise above the cap height, or decreased if the typography is set in all capitals.

The line spacing starting-place ratio discussed above is fine for a single message that continues on multiple lines of typography. But another consideration when determining line spacing is how to separate multiple messages, which can each be single or multiple lines, on a given sign layout. Obviously, if all the messages have the same line spacing, it's hard to distinguish one message from another. In such cases, a larger line spacing ratio is needed between messages than within each message.

Vertical spacing between stacked graphic elements, such as between typography and symbols and/or arrows, is also a layout consideration, as when symbols or arrows are placed above or below typography or each other, as shown earlier in Figure 5.40. Again, a good starting point is to use .5 cap height as the open-space ratio between the stacked elements, then adjust it up or down to visually balance the layout.

Layout *format proportions* pertain to the perimeters of the various sign types/faces within a program. The proportions of layout formats ultimately translate into the proportions of sign faces or panels, as expressed in the sign hardware system. Layout format proportions need to account for the maximum quantity of information that is programmed for any given sign type, and the formats can be imposed by site conditions, by the EG designer, or by a combination of both.

An example of a layout format being imposed by site conditions is when low ceiling heights require horizontally formatted overhead signs to fit the

5.46a, b When some messages have multiple lines on multiple message signs, increase line spacing between messages to clearly separate them.

5.46a

5.46b

programmed messages, typically arranged in multiple columns across the sign face. An example of a designer-imposed layout format is when the EG designer decides that all the signs in a program will have a square format. Usually, the layout format proportions for comprehensive sign programs end up being determined by both site conditions and the EG designer. Obviously, the fewer different format proportions a sign program has, the more visually unified the program will be.

Once formats have been established, the EG designer has many ways to place the typography and other graphic elements, both horizontally and vertically, onto the formats.

- Regarding horizontal alignment, the graphic elements can be arranged to align flush left, centered, or flush right.
- Regarding vertical placement, the graphic elements can be arranged at the top, center, or bottom of the sign format.

Figure 5.47 contains a matrix showing these various basic placement options.

Because both single- and multiple-line messages may be programmed for a given sign format, the EG designer also has options for vertical placement of single- and multiple-line messages on the same format. These options include hanging from the top, building from the center, and building from the bottom, as illustrated in Figure 5.48.

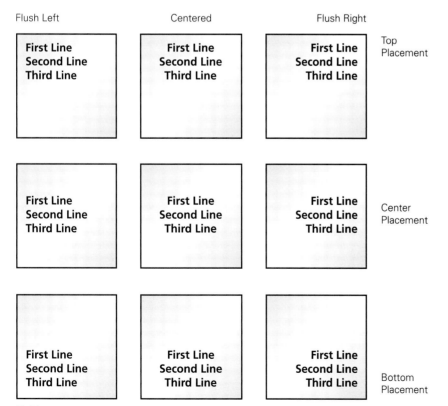

5.47

5.47 Basic alignment and vertical placement options for sign graphics.

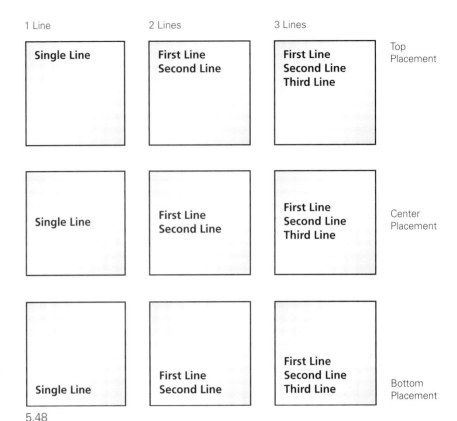

1 Line

2 Lines

3 Lines

| Single Line | First Line
Second Line | First Line
Second Line
Third Line | Top Placement |

| Single Line | First Line
Second Line | First Line
Second Line
Third Line | Center Placement |

| Single Line | First Line
Second Line | First Line
Second Line
Third Line | Bottom Placement |

5.48 Vertical placement and message-building options for single- and multiple-line messages.

5.48

Message Content and Layout

As noted, any variety of messages can appear on a given sign type, which is a critical factor when designing layouts. Since the quantity of message content and the size of the graphics determine the final size and proportional format of a sign type, it is imperative to design layouts for the worst case—meaning the longest—message or set of messages that is to appear on that sign type. Consider a simple example of a theoretical Sign Type A programmed to display a variety of messages, ranging from Women to Electrical Equipment Room—No Storage. If a Sign Type A layout is sized to accommodate only the short message, then longer messages will not fit in the sign format, which can lead to costly design or fabrication changes after the sign package has been finalized.

The importance of designing layouts to accommodate the longest message or messages cannot be overstated. The problem is not fitting less information at a readable or mandated size onto a sign of a given size; the problem is fitting more information than planned for. Remember that a sign can always display less information but that more can't be crammed onto it—at least not at functional or ADA- or code-mandated sizes. This is the single most important reason that it is imperative to develop the sign program's information content system: so that the EG designer can identify the longest messages a layout must accommodate *before* designing the graphic system. To ignore worst-case scenarios in layout development is to invite costly design and/or fabrication changes further on in the design process.

Another important point to keep in mind is that—again, depending on message content—multiple layouts can be designed for a given sign format. For example, a theoretical Sign Type B could display directional information on one unit and identification information on another, and different layouts would typically be required for each of these kinds of messages. And as stated in Chapter 4, the fewer the sign types, the more economical the sign program is to fabricate, and the more unified its appearance. Therefore, it makes sense to display different kinds of information on a given sign type and develop corresponding layouts, rather than to develop a different sign type for each kind of information.

Destination Arrangement on Directional Signs

More often than not, directional signs display multiple destinations, with arrows pointing in several different directions. This raises the question of how to arrange these destinations and the arrows linked to them in the sign layout. There is no standard method for destination arrangement, but there are several options, including the following:

- Arrange by *arrow direction*, whereby all destinations in each given direction are listed together in the layout. But we read from left to right and top to bottom, so the question then arises as to which direction should start the destination listing at the top of the sign layout. Some EG designers start by listing destinations to the left at the top of the sign, as left turns are typically the most difficult to negotiate, and then list directions moving increasingly to the right—for example, listing left destinations first, then destinations straight ahead, then destinations to the right. Other EG designers will list straight-ahead destinations first, as they're in the clearest line of movement. Regardless of the starting point, the directional arrangement order should be consistent for all signs in the program. One advantage of arranging by arrow direction is that it's more visually organized—all destinations in a given direction are listed together rather than being dispersed throughout the listing.

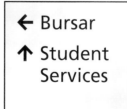

5.49

5.49 Different information content and layouts displayed on the same format and/or sign type promotes visual unity of a sign program.

Another potential advantage is that one arrow in a given direction can serve for multiple destinations, rather than having to pair an arrow with each destination.

- Arrange in *alphabetical order*, whereby destinations are listed alphabetically. The argument for this method is that people look for places by name rather than direction, which is a valid premise. Its disadvantages are that an arrow must be paired with each destination and that directions be interspersed throughout the destination listing— that is, the first destination may be to the right, the second to the left, the third to the right, and the fourth straight ahead.

- Arrange by *proximity*, whereby destinations are listed from the nearest to the farthest. The argument for this method is that destinations should be listed in the order in which people will encounter them, which also has some validity. This method has the same disadvantages as the alphabetical arrangement; in addition, it requires that the proximity to each destination be ascertained from each sign location, to ensure the proper list order on each sign.

- Arrange by *importance*, whereby someone determines which are the prime destinations in an environment, and those destinations are always listed at the top of the layout. This method gets into message ranking and hierarchy, which was discussed in Chapter 4, and it does make some sense in certain settings. It does, however, have the same disadvantages as the alphabetical arrangement method. An additional disadvantage is that it may cause political bickering over which destinations are the top-ranked ones, and this, obviously, can cause project delays.

As noted, there are pros and cons to each of these arrangement methods, and since each project is different the EG designer and client should agree on which method suits the project at hand and then use that method consistently throughout the project. Also note that these methods can be combined to some extent. For example, destinations can be arranged by arrow direction first, and then alphabetically within each directional category, as shown in Figure 5.50.

5.50a, b Messages organized by arrow direction. An arrow can be paired with each destination or serve for multiple destinations in each direction.

5.51 When messages are organized alphabetically an arrow must be paired with each destination. Interspersed arrow directions can be confusing.

```
← Aquarium
← Sports Arena
↑ City Hall
↑ Library
→ Science Center
→ Zoo
```

5.50a

```
← Aquarium
  Sports Arena
↑ City Hall
  Library
→ Science Center
  Zoo
```

5.50b

```
← Aquarium
↑ City Hall
↑ Library
→ Science Center
← Sports Arena
→ Zoo
```

5.51

Overview of Sign Graphic Application Processes

This discussion of the sign graphic system wouldn't be complete without an overview of the many ways in which graphics can be applied to signs, especially because, in addition to layout, graphic application processes greatly affect the appearance of a sign program's graphic system.

Basically, graphics are applied to a sign in one of three ways: flat, raised, or incised. Basic techniques for each are discussed here, but keep in mind that every year many new, proprietary graphic application techniques and materials are developed for the sign industry.

Flat Graphics

Flat graphics are essentially applied to the same plane as the sign surface itself. Four common techniques for applying flat graphics to just about any sign material include:

- *Full-color digital imaging.* This is large-format imprinting, typically by inkjet, on any number of opaque or translucent substrate materials, ranging from cloth to paper to self-adhesive vinyl films, with a photographic range of color and continuous tone. Reproduction quality varies with the resolution of digital output. Other characteristics: fair to excellent durability, depending on substrate and top coatings including UV inhibitors; unlimited color and tonal ranges; and medium to high expense. There are several proprietary products in which the digitally imaged substrate is laminated or embedded in clear plastic resin or fiberglass, for virtually indestructible protection of the graphics.

- *Vinyl decals.* These are self-adhesive, integrally colored, and opaque, translucent, or reflective vinyl film cut by computer into letterforms and

5.52 Full-color digital imaging allows for full tonal ranges on the signage program for the Hollywood & Highland mixed-use project in Los Angeles.

5.53a, b Computer-cut vinyl graphics are widely used in a variety of interior and exterior signage applications, such as for the AIGA Collision Conference in New York City and for the City of Summit, New Jersey.

5.53a

5.53b

5.54

5.55

5.54 Silk-screened graphics on glass doors provide high durability in communal spaces at a New York University dormitory.

5.55 Porcelain enamel provides durable exterior graphics at New York City's Penn South Houses.

other graphic elements. Other characteristics include: excellent reproduction; fair to good durability; limited colors and no tonal ranges; and low expense.

- *Silk-screen inks.* These are thick, opaque, paintlike inks applied with a silk-screen, which is a sophisticated, mechanically or photographically produced stencil. Silk-screening is also used to apply the adhesive to which metal leaf is applied for gilded graphics. Other characteristics include: excellent reproduction; good to excellent durability; unlimited colors; limited tonal ranges; and medium to high expense.

- *Porcelain enamel.* This glass-based coating is typically applied to steel or aluminum by silk-screening and then fired to melt the coating into a hard, smooth, glossy surface. Reproduction quality is generally excellent depending on supplier. Other characteristics include: excellent durability—it's almost indestructible; some limits on colors and tonal ranges; and high expense.

- *Handpainting.* Using this technique, sign paints are applied by hand with a brush, so reproduction quality depends on the skill of the painter. Other characteristics include: fair to good durability; unlimited color and tonal ranges; and low to high expense.

Raised Graphics

Raised graphics are dimensional in that they are raised from the sign's surface. Raised graphic applications are important because, as you'll recall, tactile and Braille letters are required by the ADA for permanent room identification signs. Six common techniques for raised graphics include:

- *Cut solid graphics.* These are solid letterforms or other graphic elements cut from metal, plastic, wood, glass, or stone, and mounted to a sign face or an architectural surface. Cutting devices are typically computer-controlled, and include mechanical routers, waterjets, and lasers; but these graphics can also be produced by a band saw controlled by skilled human hands. Cut solid graphics are suited for smaller, thinner graphic elements, including tactile letters, than fabricated graphics (described next). Other characteristics include: generally excellent reproduction; good to excellent durability, depending on material; and medium to high expense. Also, color availability depends on material or applied paint, and tonal range is possible with the application of digitally imaged self-adhesive vinyl film.

- *Fabricated graphics.* These are hollow graphics, typically letterforms, with faces and sides (*returns*) cut separately and joined together. Commonly used materials are metal and plastic, which can be used singly or in combination, such as an all-metal letter or a letter with metal returns and a plastic face. Fabricated graphics are mounted to a sign face or an architectural surface and are better suited for larger, thicker graphics than cut solid graphics. Other characteristics include: generally excellent reproduction; good to excellent durability; and medium to high expense. Also, color availability depends on materials or applied paints and films, and tonal range is possible with the application of digitally imaged self-adhesive vinyl film. Translucent plastic faces and/or returns can be backlit.

- *Cast metal graphics.* These are solid or semihollow letterforms or plaques such as medallions, for which metal is melted and cast into a mold typically prepared by a craftsperson. Reproduction quality depends on skill of mold maker. Other characteristics include: excellent durability; colors limited based on metal used and/or any paint applied to recessed areas of plaques; no tonal range; and high expense.

5.56 Solid cut glass letters laminated to a glass logo field at ABC Broadcasting's New York City headquarters.

5.57 Monumental fabricated aluminum letters announce Pittsburgh's O'Reilly Theatre.

5.58 Cast metal graphics on a medallion in the paving of Boston's Freedom Trail.

5.57

5.58

5.59

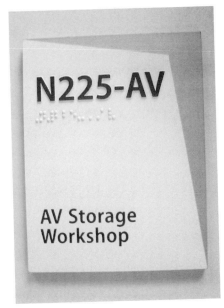

5.60

5.59 Cast plastic resin plaque with tactile & Braille lettering at Philadelphia's Cira Centre office tower.

5.60 Painted photopolymer sign plaque with tactile and Braille room number at the Virginia Beach Convention Center.

5.61 Employee name plaque at Crate & Barrel's World Headquarters has room numbers in stainless steel Braille rasters and cut plastic tactile characters; employee name insert is changeable.

5.61

- *Cast plastic graphics.* For these graphics, liquid plastic resins are cast into letterforms or plaques, with molds made by computer or hand. Cast plastic materials can range from opaque to transparent, and reproduction quality varies with the mold-making process. Other characteristics include: good to excellent durability; color variation based on process or applied paints; no tonal range; and low to medium expense.

- *Photopolymer.* Plaques with raised graphics are made from a photosensitive plastic sheet that forms raised graphics after light exposure and chemical processing. Other characteristics include: good to excellent reproduction quality; good to excellent durability; and low to medium expense. Photopolymer sheet is typically opaque, so colors vary with applied paints, and no tonal range is possible.

- *Rasters.* These are small spheres of metal partially inset into a sign plaque to form Braille letters. Other characteristics include: excellent reproduction quality; excellent durability; colors limited to metals used; tonal range not applicable; and high expense.

Incised Graphics

Incised graphics are dimensional, in that they go into the sign's surface. There are several techniques for incising graphics, and many of them can also be used for raised graphics.

- *Sandblasted graphics* are formed when sand-based grit is blasted with compressed air through a heavy rubber computer-cut stencil mask to carve graphics into the sign surface, which is typically stone or glass, but can also include metal. Reproduction quality depends on the skill of the sandblaster. Other characteristics include: excellent durability; unlimited range of colors to fill the incised graphics; and medium to high expense.

- *Acid etched graphics* are limited to metal and glass, which are covered with an acid-resistant mask in nongraphic areas and then exposed to acid, which eats away the base material in graphic areas. Other characteristics include: excellent reproduction quality; excellent durability; unlimited range of fill colors; and medium to high expense.

- *Engraved or routed graphics* are graphics mechanically cut into the sign surface with power tools, often using lettering templates in cheap, low-tech applications; higher end applications are computer-driven. Routers can cut completely through sheet metal sign surfaces (stencil cutting) for internally illuminated signs. Reproduction quality ranges from very low to excellent, depending on technology used. Other characteristics include: good to excellent durability; color range that varies with technology used; and low to high expense.

5.62

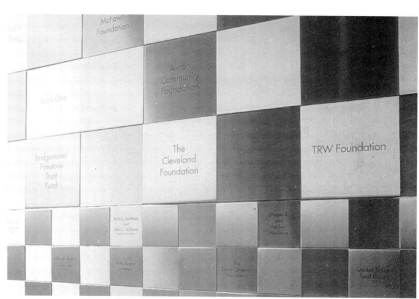

5.63

5.62 Graphics sandblasted into granite donor columns at MidState Medical Center in Meriden, Connecticut.

5.63 Graphics etched and paint-filled in donor wall at Inventure Place, Akron, Ohio.

5.64a, b Router cutting through metal sign faces allows for an open stencil effect (a) at Sarah Lawrence College Heimbold Visual Arts Center, and for backlit graphics (b) at One Raffles Link in Singapore.

5.64a

5.64b

5.65 Graphics hand-carved into cleft slate monument sign.

5.65

- *Hand carving.* Typically, wood or stone is mechanically carved with either hand or power tools. Reproduction quality depends on skill of carver. Other characteristics include: good to excellent durability; unlimited range of fill colors; and medium to high expense.

Chapter Wrap-Up

This chapter has itemized the elemental building blocks of a sign program's graphic system: typography, symbols and arrows, color, and other graphic elements. It then covered the basics of how all these elements are "cooked" together to form a cohesive whole in the layout process. And just as endless variations on recipes make cooking so creative, there are endless variations possible for developing graphic layouts, which frees the EG designer's creative instincts to set the appearance of the sign program's graphic system.

The chapter also reiterated the importance of developing the information content system so that the graphic system can accommodate the worst case (i.e., longest) messages, as well as different kinds of information content. The chapter concluded with basic methods for applying graphics to signs, which, like layout, play a major role in the appearance of the sign program's graphic system. This chapter has also shown how layout affects the size and proportion of signs, which sets the stage for designing the sign program's hardware system, as discussed in the next chapter.

6 The Hardware System

6.1 The sign hardware system.

Sign hardware is the physical embodiment of signage—the environmental objects that display the sign information, as conveyed via the sign graphics.

The hardware system of a sign program is all the physical "stuff" you can actually touch or bump into; it's the tangible, three-dimensional component of a sign program. The hardware system is also the vocabulary of shapes, structures, materials, finishes, mounting, and lighting, as well as the method(s) the EG designer uses to unify all these elements into a family of sign objects.

It is the three-dimensional, sculptural aspect of signage that distinguishes it from other forms of graphic design, an aspect that is more grounded in industrial and architectural design than graphic design. And its intrinsic three-dimensionality is what makes signage such an exciting design challenge. Many people think of signs as basically flat objects that display graphics—which they certainly can be—but as this chapter will show, a sign program's hardware system can be far more visually rich and exciting than a series of flat panels. In my office, we approach the design of a sign program's hardware system by asking a question: Signage is inherently three-dimensional, so how can we exploit that third dimension?

This chapter examines the three-dimensional elements the EG designer manipulates in designing the hardware system of a signage program. It also provides an overview of basic materials, finishes, coatings, and lighting techniques that the EG designer fashions into physical sign objects.

Shape

Shape, or form, is probably the most obvious expression of a sign program's hardware system. The shapes used in a signage program give the program its visual unity and distinctiveness in three-dimensional form. Shapes are virtually limitless for the sign hardware system, and basic shapes can be combined and synthesized into even more distinctive shapes. This section looks at the vocabularies of basic sign shapes the EG designer can manipulate in hardware system design.

Basic Sign Shapes Based on Mounting

Signs do not magically float in space; they must be mounted on or into something else, and what they are mounted to is a major determinant of the intrinsic form a given sign will take. Basically, signs are mounted on horizontal surfaces—such as floors or ceilings—from above or below, or on vertical surfaces—such as walls—from the back or side. This leads to the following four basic types of mounting:

- *Freestanding or ground-mounted*, in which the bottom of the sign is fixed to a horizontal mounting surface, such as a floor.

- *Suspended or ceiling-hung*, in which the top of the sign is fixed to a horizontal mounting surface, such as a ceiling.

- *Projecting or flag-mounted*, in which the side of the sign is fixed perpendicular to a vertical mounting surface, such as a wall.

- *Flush or flat wall-mounted*, in which the back of the sign is fixed parallel to a vertical mounting surface, such as a wall.

The mounting or support structure for each of these types of mounting can be either hidden or expressed, leading to the following overall sign forms listed on the following page and shown in Figure 6.6:

6.2 Freestanding or ground-mounted sign at CityLink shopping mall in Singapore.

6.3 Boat-shaped suspended, or ceiling-hung, sign at Port Imperial Ferry Terminal in Weehawken, New Jersey.

6.4 Projecting, or flag-mounted, sign at Short Pump Town Center in Richmond, Virginia.

6.5 Flush, or flat wall-mounted, sign at the Valentine Riverside Museum in Richmond, Virginia.

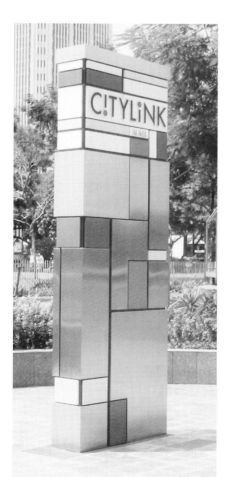

6.2

6.3

6.4

6.5

Freestanding Sign Forms

- Pylon or monolith, in which the entire sign body rises from the ground or floor.

- Lollipop, or "sign on a stick," in which a sign panel on a single post rises from the ground or floor.

- Multiple-posted, in which a sign panel on two or more posts rises from the ground or floor.

Suspended Sign Forms

- Suspended monolith, in which the entire sign body hangs from a ceiling or underhang.

- Suspended pendant, in which a sign panel on a single post hangs from a ceiling or underhang.

- Suspended multiple-posted, in which a sign panel on two or more posts hangs from a ceiling or underhang.

Projecting Sign Forms

- Projecting monolith, in which the entire sign body projects from a wall or other vertical surface.

- Projecting lollipop, in which a sign panel on a single post projects from a wall or other vertical surface.

- Projecting multiple-posted, in which a sign panel on two or more posts projects from a wall or other vertical surface.

Flush-Mounted Sign Forms

- Wall plaque, in which the back of the sign is attached to a wall or other vertical surface, such as a soffit or transom.

Monolithic sign forms typically have hidden, internal support structures, and wall plaques typically don't require expressed, or visible, mounting structures. The support structures are expressed, however, in the other sign forms just outlined.

All of these sign forms, except relatively thin, flush-mounted ones, can be viewed "in the round," providing opportunities for expression of three-dimensional details, as well as providing faces for graphics on more than one side. All nonflush-mounted sign forms can have a minimum of two sides for graphics, if graphics on two or more sides are appropriate and useful.

Given the basic sign forms dictated by mounting factors, sign shapes can be generated based on geometry in elevation, plan, and sectional views, as shown in Figures 6.7 and 6.8.

- *Elevation* views depict the vertical surfaces of an object—front, sides (profiles), and back.

- *Plan* views depict the lateral footprint or perimeter of an object as viewed from the top.

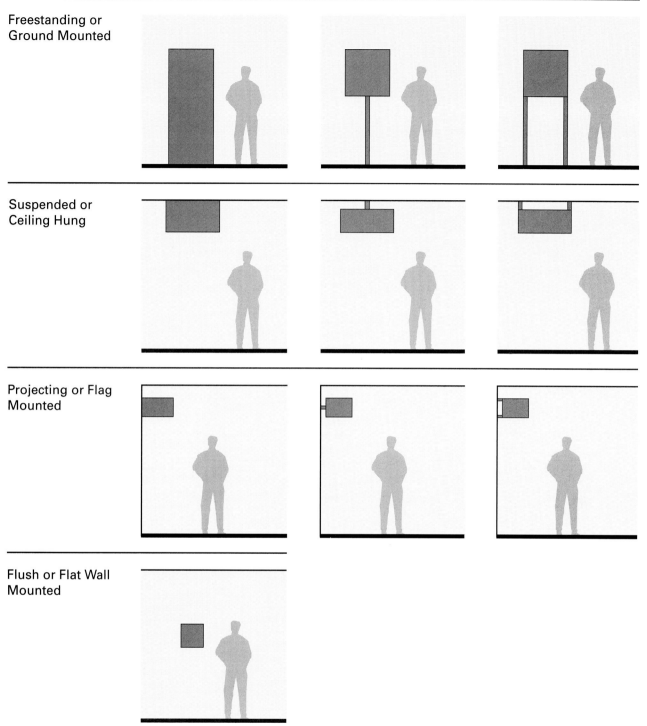

Freestanding or
Ground Mounted

Suspended or
Ceiling Hung

Projecting or Flag
Mounted

Flush or Flat Wall
Mounted

6.6

- *Sectional* views expose the internal parts of an object, depicting slices cut through an object, either lengthwise (longitudinal) or across (traverse), just as a carrot can be cut along its length or across it, with the resulting slices exposing the carrot's structure differently with each direction of cut.

6.6 Sign forms based on mounting type.

The key views of sign shapes are elevation and plan, and they are examined in the following sections.

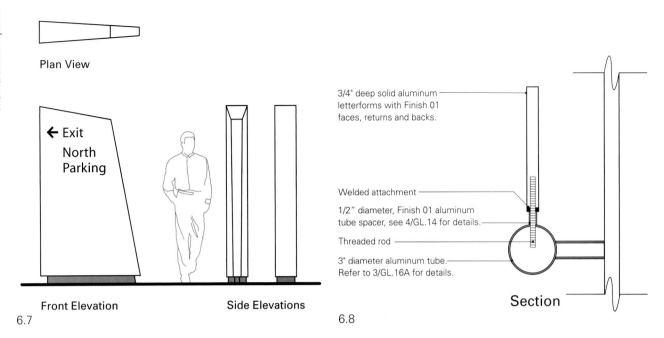

Plan View

← Exit
North
Parking

Front Elevation

Side Elevations

6.7

3/4" deep solid aluminum
letterforms with Finish 01
faces, returns and backs.

Welded attachment

1/2" diameter, Finish 01 aluminum
tube spacer, see 4/GL.14 for details.

Threaded rod

3" diameter aluminum tube.
Refer to 3/GL.16A for details.

Section

6.8

6.7 Plan and elevation views of a freestanding sign.

6.8 A section view through a sign exposes its internal parts.

Vocabulary of Basic Sign Shapes Based on Geometry in Front Elevation

An unlimited number of sign shapes, as viewed straight-on in front elevation, can be generated from elements of the most basic geometric forms: the circle, square, and triangle. Hence, sign shapes in front elevation can be composed of curved, rectilinear, or angled elements, or combinations of these elements. Keep in mind that these shapes can be used for a sign panel on posts, or can be used monolithically. Also keep in mind that graphics are typically most efficiently fitted onto sign shapes that are overall rectilinear in front elevation. See Figure 6.9 for a basic vocabulary of front elevation shapes. These shapes can also be layered over each other to create different plane levels in front elevation.

6.9 Basic vocabulary of sign shapes in front elevation.

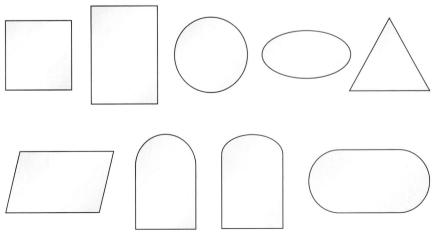

6.9

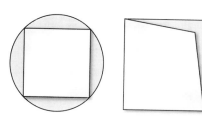

6.10

6.10 Basic sign shapes layered over each other in front elevation create depth and formal interest.

Vocabulary of Basic Sign Shapes Based on Geometry in Plan

The geometry of the top, horizontal view of a sign body or sign panel, although generally more subtly expressive than the front elevation shape, can also provide a limitless number of plan shapes. As with front elevation shapes, plan shapes are composed of curved, rectilinear, and angled elements, as well as combinations of them. Keep in mind that plan shapes can be used for a sign panel on posts, for the posts themselves, and for monolithic sign bodies. Figure 6.11 shows a basic vocabulary of plan shapes. Also keep in mind that some plan shapes, or variations thereof, can be rotated 90 degrees to the vertical and be used for the side elevations or profiles of signs. And to further compound shape generation possibilities, different plan shapes can be combined with different front elevation shapes, as shown in Figure 6.7, in which a wedge-shaped plan view is combined with a trapezoidal front view to create a distinctive sculptural form.

6.11 Basic sign or sign post shapes based on simple geometric shapes in plan.

6.12a, b Curved panels in plan and elevation provide formal unity to the signage program at Inventure Place/The National Inventor's Hall of Fame in Akron, Ohio.

6.11

6.12a

6.12b

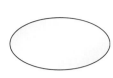

6.13 Sign shapes with contemporary versus traditional connotations.

6.13

Connotations of Form

While 3D sign shape and form do not literally communicate information in a denotative way as sign graphics do, the 3D aspect of signage has powerful stylistic connotations. Three-dimensional sign forms, and the ways the EG designer synthesizes them into sign hardware objects, have stylistic connotations in the same way the shapes of typographic letterforms do. The key, then, to designing a sign program's hardware system is to determine the appropriate 3D formal qualities for the project at hand.

As an example of some of the formal aspects the EG designer mediates in a sign program's hardware system design, consider the myriad styles of that common everyday object we call a chair. Does the chair have a high or low seating height? Is it on four legs, a pedestal, or is it cantilevered? Is it mobile or stationary? Is it all one material, such as wood, or a combination of materials such as steel and leather? Is it upholstered? Is it simple or complex? Is it traditional or contemporary? Similar stylistic questions come into play when designing a sign program's hardware system.

It is beyond the scope of this book to delve into a lengthy examination of the connotations of 3D form, as it is a very complex subject, but it's important to highlight a few very basic pointers on signage hardware system form:

6.14 Exterior signage at the Memphis Public Library is a synthesis of many formal shapes that work together to create a unique stylistic appearance.

- Some front elevation sign shapes are inherently traditional or contemporary. For example, tombstones and horizontal oval shapes have more traditional connotations, whereas more basic shapes such as squares and circles have more contemporary connotations.

- Sign objects are often a synthesis of many formal elements— particularly those signs with exposed fasteners or exposed structures such as posts—and each element has its own formal connotations. How these elements fit with and transition to one another is a key to the stylistic appearance of the sign object.

- Generally, the simpler and sleeker the sign objects, the more contemporary the appearance of the hardware system. Conversely, the more complex and fussy the sign objects, the more traditional the appearance of the hardware system.

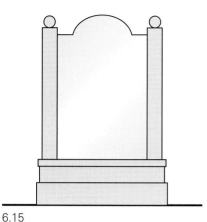 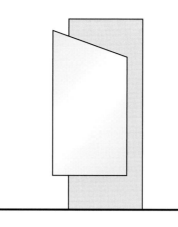

6.15

6.15 Complex, fussy sign shapes tend to be more traditional looking, in contrast to simpler, sleeker shapes, which tend to be more contemporary looking.

- The stylistic characteristics of the graphic system affect the stylistic characteristics of the hardware system, and generally speaking the two should mesh. For example, a crisp, contemporary graphic system is better suited to a contemporary hardware system, and vice versa. Of course, because every project is different, there are some projects in which juxtaposing contemporary graphics with traditional hardware is entirely appropriate, even if difficult to pull off.

- Just as the appearance of the sign graphic system can be quiet and elegant or bold and flashy, so can the appearance of the hardware system. The key is determining which stylistic approach is most appropriate to a given project. For example, clean, simple, almost utilitarian hardware forms may be appropriate for a subway system's signage, but not for a grand hotel's signage. At my office, we discuss whether a sign program's hardware system should fade away or stand out from the project environment.

6.16a Serif typography harmonizes with the rich, traditionally styled hardware system for Smith College in Northampton, Massachusetts.

6.16b Sans serif typography harmonizes with the contemporary styling of the sail-like hardware system for the Virginia Beach Convention Center.

6.16a

6.16b

Unity of Form

It's relatively easy to develop shape or form for a single sign or type of sign, but signage programs are typically composed of several types of signs, which can range from small wall plaques to large freestanding and suspended units and everything in between. In other words, the EG designer must design a whole family of signs for a given project, and this family must be unified in appearance to enhance the sign program's cohesiveness and effectiveness. And just as a human family is composed of individuals, each of whom usually shares some visual similarities that identify them as a related family unit, so too a well-designed sign program is composed of different sign types that share common visual features that identify them as related to each other. You can see examples of projects with unity of form within sign families in the color insert section of this book.

A sign program's graphic system contributes to its two-dimensional unity, and a program's hardware system contributes to its three-dimensional unity, primarily expressed via shape and form. Maintaining unity of 3D form across a broad range of sign mounting conditions and sizes is one of the great design challenges in signage program development, one that really gets the creative juices going. In contrast to architectural design, which typically embraces the design of a singular object—albeit a complex one, a building—design of a signage program's hardware system is more akin to industrial design, in which several different individual objects are often designed as part of a larger line of related products, such as cookware or furniture ensembles.

It's difficult to pin down how an EG designer creates unity of form within a sign family's hardware system, but it typically relies on consistent use of a common or similar 3D detail, or combination of details, throughout all the sign types, regardless of size or mounting condition, in a program. Simple examples of common details and detail combinations include designing all the sign panels in a program to be curved, or designing all the sign panels in a program to be curved and then overlaid on partially exposed flat background panels. Commonalities in mounting structures, such as ground-mounted posts and ceiling-suspension hangers, are details that can also lend formal unity to a sign program's hardware system. See the color insert for examples of formal details that unify sign programs.

EG designers don't need to be slavish in adhering to a common 3D detail or details, but they do need to employ some sort of consistency to make all of the hardware elements of a sign program appear to be related. Continuing with the curved panel example just given, sign panels that are curved in plan may be more appropriate for the signs in the program that have a vertical format, while panels that are curved in side elevation may be more appropriate for the signs in a program that have a horizontal format. The key common detail feature is the curved panels, as shown in

Figure 6.12a and b, not whether they're bowing out on the horizontal or vertical axis.

The EG designer can use sketches, drawings, and simple study models to develop 3D formal unity among all the sign units in the program. It's always useful to look at the entire sign family together and at one scale to see how the units formally relate to one another in the program's range of mounting conditions, as well as in the program's range of sizes.

Sign Mounting Considerations

As stated earlier in this chapter, how signs are mounted is a key determinant of a sign's form, and this section of the chapter explores the factors the EG designer must consider for sign mounting.

Overhead and Eye-Level Mounting Zones

A sign's location, viewing distance, and hierarchy help determine mounting heights and methods. There are two basic zones for placement of sign information and, therefore, for mounting the sign panels that carry that information: an *overhead zone* and an *eye-level zone*.

Generally, for interior environments, signs that convey primary and, sometimes, secondary information are mounted in the overhead zone; signs that convey detailed and/or lower-hierarchy information are mounted at eye level. The reason for this rule of thumb makes sense: Important primary sign information needs to be located high enough so that it's not obstructed by people, vehicles, plants, or other objects in the environment. Less important sign information doesn't need to be—and, in fact, shouldn't be—so prominently placed, and detailed sign information has to be placed at eye level for close study. For example, in an airport, primary directional signs and identification signs such as gate identification numbers are typically mounted overhead, whereas signs conveying less important information, such as office identification, or detailed information, such as the airport orientation map, are placed at eye level.

Of course, many environments, such as museums and hotels, are often more subdued and low-key than those of airports, and in these more subdued environments overhead signs may be completely inappropriate. There are also situations where it's useful to repeat the same information in both the overhead and eye-level zones. A good example of this is a signage program for a retail store in a mall, where an overhead primary identification sign is installed for viewing across the expanse of the mall, and a secondary identification sign is placed at eye-level to enable people walking along the storefronts, and underneath the primary sign, to read the same information.

For interior signs, the zone for displaying eye-level sign information is roughly between 3'-0" and 6'-8" above the finished floor (AFF); the zone for displaying overhead information is anywhere above 6'-6" AFF. Keep in

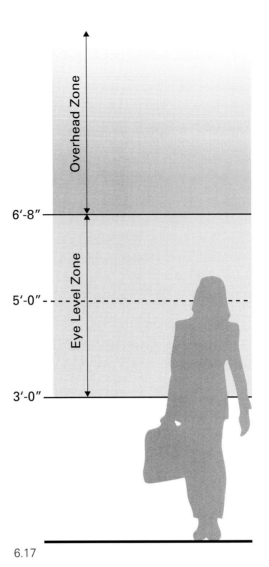

Overhead Zone

6'-8"

Eye Level Zone

5'-0"

3'-0"

6.17 Eye-level and overhead sign viewing/mounting zones. Signs mounted in the eye-level zone are generally for close-up reading; those mounted in the overhead zone are for distance reading.

6.17

mind that if detailed sign information is displayed below 3'-0", many people would have to stoop to read it; and if it's displayed above 6'-8", many people would have to crane their necks to read it. Also keep in mind that overhead information is often displayed on tall, ground-mounted signs, not only on suspended or projecting signs.

In the midst of this discussion of the overhead and eye-level zones, it's important to remember that the ADA requires the horizontal centerline of tactile/Braille permanent room identification signs to be mounted 5'-0" AFF, which is in the eye-level zone. The ADA also requires all overhead ceiling suspended or projecting signs to have a minimum clearance of 80" or 6'-8" AFF.

The concept of overhead and eye-level zones is somewhat different for exterior signage programs. Generally, for pedestrian-oriented exterior signage, these zones are the same as for interior signage. For example, detailed pedestrian information such as neighborhood maps or bus schedules should be placed in the eye-level zone for comfortable reading, and directional information should be placed in the overhead zone so it's above most obstructions in the exterior environment. Wear and vandalism are also considerations for exterior pedestrian signage: The lower sign panels are placed, the more prone they are to being hit by moving objects, covered with graffiti and stickers, or degraded by other kinds of wear and tampering.

Although the eye-level zone is applicable to exterior pedestrian signage, it has little applicability to vehicular-oriented signage, beyond drive-up windows at banks and fast-food purveyors where drivers are not moving and can study detailed information such as a menu. Vehicular sign information, by necessity, must be succinct, for rapid assimilation by drivers moving at speeds up to 70-plus miles per hour. Because of the speed factor, the information on the vast majority of exterior vehicular signs is not, and cannot be, studied in great detail, as can eye-level interior and exterior pedestrian signs.

Generally speaking, when it comes to designing vehicular signage, the slower the speed, the more detailed and lower the sign information can be placed. Moreover, the level of detail of vehicular sign information rarely approaches that which is feasible for pedestrian signage—that is, although vehicular sign information can range from less to more detailed, it can rarely be as detailed as pedestrian signage information. For example, on high-speed roadways such as freeways, primary information must be limited to as few words or lines of text as possible to communicate the message—many, in fact, comprise only one word. At lower speeds, drivers can absorb more information, such as when they approach an intersection with a stop sign or traffic light and slow down long enough to read directional information for several destinations.

Vehicular signage can be literally overhead, in that drivers pass underneath the sign information—for example, signs mounted on overpasses, above garage entrances, and on freestanding sign support structures spanning the roadway. While these *pass-under* signs are fairly common in vehicular signage, more common are *pass-by* vehicular signs, which are mounted adjacent to the roadway and require far less complex support structures than freestanding pass-under signs. Pass-by sign panels are typically mounted lower than pass-under signs, but still need to be high enough to minimize obstruction by vehicles, trees, and other objects in the environment.

Another important factor is that the human eye has a limited range or angle of vision—we do not have 360-degree horizontal vision. And we don't typically rotate our eyes and our heads and necks unless absolutely necessary, such as when backing out of a parking space. Accordingly, signs should be mounted within normal/natural lines of vision when people are looking straight ahead.

6.18 Directional pylons at the Dallas/Fort Worth airport display large graphics in the overhead zone for quick reading at a distance. Smaller, more detailed graphics are displayed in the eye-level zone for close-up reading and study.

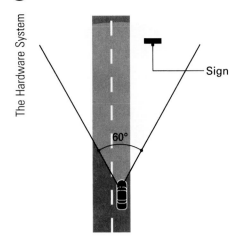

Sign

60°

6.19 Roadway sign mounted within a 60-degree horizontal field of vision.

Horizontally, the angle of vision extends 20 to 30 degrees (40 to 60 degrees total) from the vertical centerline of the eyes when looking straight ahead. Figure 6.19 depicts a sign mounted perpendicular to the line of sight within a 60-degree field of vision. Note, however, that other diagrams may indicate a more dynamic horizontal vision field for people moving in cars, ranging from more than 90 degrees for closer objects and narrowing to 40 degrees for more distant objects.

Vertically, the angle of vision extends 10 to 15 degrees up and down from the horizontal centerline of the eye. Figure 6.20 shows a 10-degree angle up from the centerline. It doesn't show a downward angle because other objects tend to obscure sign information placed below the horizontal centerline, unless the viewer is within relatively close range of the sign. Suffice it to say that signs and sign information generally should not be mounted below 3'-0" above finish floor (AFF) for close-up reading in the eye-level zone, and should not be mounted below 6'-0" for distance reading in the overhead zone.

As just noted, people typically will not rotate their heads to read sign information beyond their horizontal angle of vision; likewise, they generally will not crane their necks to read signs in the overhead zone. Figure 6.20 illustrates how signs mounted in the overhead zone should be primarily for distance reading. It also illustrates how the top height of a sign can increase with viewing distance, as well as how the size of a sign, along with its graphics, should increase with viewing distance.

This information about sign-mounting zones and viewing angles and distances can be useful to EG designers, but it is fungible and therefore should not be considered immutable fact. Sign viewing is a dynamic process with many variables, particularly whether the viewer is moving forward on foot or on wheels. As with many other aspects of EG design, such as typographic size, the designer should conduct some degree of testing, formal or informal, to determine sign-mounting positions suitable for the conditions of the project at hand.

6.20 Signs mounted within a 10-degree vertical field of vision.

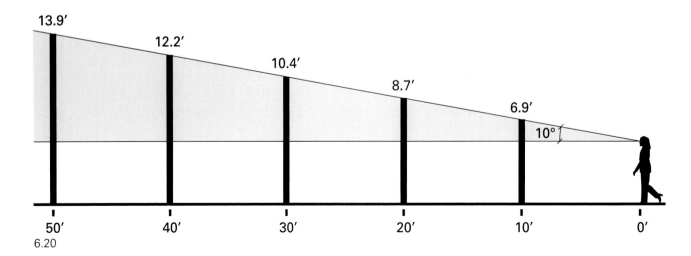

13.9'

12.2'

10.4'

8.7'

6.9'

10°

50'   40'   30'   20'   10'   0'

6.20

Architectural and Site Factors Affecting Mounting

As clearly stated throughout this book, signage programs exist within an environmental context, be it interior, exterior, or both, and the EG designer needs to consider the physical characteristics of the environment within which the signs are to be mounted. Ceiling clearances, wall and corridor widths, obstructions such as columns or trees, and other elements all affect sign mounting decisions. For example, a given building may have ceilings that are too low for ceiling-suspended signs to provide the ADA minimum clearance of 6'-8" AFF, given the maximum sign information content in typography at the ADA minimum cap height of 3". In this case, interior overhead signs are not a design option, so the EG designer must consider other types of mounting, which will in turn affect the formal qualities of the sign hardware system.

Another architectural/site factor is whether the environment provides adequate opportunities to mount signs on existing structures, such as walls, columns, and ceilings for interior signs, or light poles and overpasses for exterior signs. In situations where there are no appropriately located existing structures for sign mounting, such as in the middle of a shopping mall's atrium or an open urban plaza, freestanding signs will be necessary, which naturally has formal consequences for the hardware system. It's also possible that the EG designer may find that freestanding mounting is completely appropriate for certain sign types even when existing structures are available for sign mounting. In an urban signage example, the EG designer may determine that freestanding signs will provide clearer sightlines and experience less visual competition than sign panels mounted on existing structures such as light poles.

Sign mounting must be structurally stable; therefore, it must be coordinated with architectural or site conditions, whether the sign program is for an existing environment or new construction. In new construction, the EG designer can coordinate sign mounting with the project architect, structural engineers, and/or sign fabricator. In existing environments, the EG designer can coordinate sign mountings with the sign fabricator and/or a structural engineer if an architect isn't involved.

Exterior, ground-mounted signs require *footings*, which are concrete legs that penetrate deep into the soil to anchor the sign. The aboveground sign structure can be directly buried into the fresh concrete footer(s) or can be attached at a later time by anchor bolts to the structure laid with the footing(s). In either case, the ground must be dug to lay the footings, which means that utility lines may be breached during the digging. To avoid interfering with local services such as electric, phone, or cable television, the sign fabricator should call for a *markout* of utility lines in the installation locale. Indeed, in many locales digging without a utilities markout is against the law.

As you'll learn later in this chapter, there are myriad ways to join sign parts together and to join signs to their mounting surfaces. But EG designers are not licensed to practice structural engineering or architecture, and should therefore specify that all engineering of sign structures and attachments be performed by professionals in those fields or the sign fabricator.

Sign Size Considerations

Many of the same factors that must be considered regarding sign mounting must also be considered regarding sign size. Certainly, the relationship of viewing angle, viewing distance, and mounting height is a key determinant of the size of any given sign type, as are architectural and site factors, such as a low ceiling or limited wall space. And, as stated in Chapters 4 and 5, sign hierarchy and the quantity of message content are two other key size determinants for any given sign type. So important are they, in fact, that it bears repeating that it is imperative to design for the worst case (longest) message or set of messages programmed for each sign type.

For vehicular signage, road speed and the number of lanes affect the amount of time and the distance that drivers have to react to a sign. These factors, in turn, affect the letter height of a sign message and the total area of the sign panels that display the messages, as shown in Figure 6.21. The information in Figure 6.21 is a starting point only, and as with sign mounting, some degree of testing is necessary to determine the letter heights and panel sizes most suitable for the project at hand.

Recall from Chapters 4 and 5 that local codes may dictate message content and the cap heights of messages for certain interior signs, typically those with life safety messages. Although not all codes mandate a specific size for the actual sign panels on which such messages appear, some do, so it's always important to check the local codes applicable to the project at hand to see if certain panel sizes are mandated. And even when panel sizes for such signs aren't specifically mandated in a code, the message

Vehicular Speed (MPH)	Lane Qty.	Reaction Time (Seconds)	Distance Traveled during Reaction (Feet)	Letter Height (Inches)	Total Area of Sign (Square Feet)	
					Commercial Industrial Sites	Other Sites
15	2	8	176	4	8	6
30			352	7	25	18
45			528	10	50	35
55			704	14	100	70
15	4	10	220	4	8	6
30			440	9	40	28
45			660	13	90	64
55			880	17	150	106
15	6	11	242	5	13	10
30			484	9	140	28
45			726	14	100	70
55			968	19	190	134
55	Freeway	12	1,056	21	230	162

6.21 Table indicating letter heights and panel areas for vehicular signs.

6.21

content and graphic sizes dictated by the code *will* play a role in determining minimum panel sizes. This is also the case with the ADA; although it doesn't require specific panel sizes, its requirements for the sizes of various sign graphics affect the minimum size of the panel on which they're displayed.

Chapter 4 explained how local sign ordinances may restrict the size of exterior signs, usually expressed in terms of square footage. Other sign ordinance restrictions may include other aspects of the hardware system for exterior signs, such as height, form or shape, materials, illumination, and others.

Overall Size

Thus far this section has focused on the size of sign panels, the part of a sign that displays messages, as opposed to the overall size of a sign, including its mounting structures. In the case of flush wall-mounted signs, where the back of the sign panel is mounted directly to a wall, there is no visible ancillary structure to support the sign panel, so the overall size of this kind of sign is the sign panel itself. In the case of freestanding, suspended, and projecting signs, however, there is some sort of support structure for the sign panel, and this structure contributes to the overall size of the sign. As noted earlier in this chapter, the support structure may be exposed, as in the single vertical post of a lollipop sign, or may be hidden, as in a monolithic pylon.

This discussion of the overall size of a sign is germane to local sign ordinances as they may restrict two aspects of size: actual height from the ground to the top of the sign (*height restriction*) and the square footage of the sign (*area restriction*). Refer back to Chapter 4 for more on local exterior sign ordinances.

Depth

Another important sign hardware size consideration is depth. We can't forget that signs, even flush-mounted wall plaques, are three-dimensional objects and that depth is the added third dimension! The depth of a sign can range from negligible—essentially two-dimensional or planar—to deeper than its length or width. Factors that contribute to determining depth include:

- The depth required of mounting structures to adequately secure the sign.

- Informational requirements: Signs with messages on one or two sides can be relatively thin, but signs that have information on three or more sides need to be deeper, to provide an adequate message area on each sign face.

- ADA limitations on depth of objects, including signs, projecting from walls. The ADA also limits the overhang of freestanding objects, including signs, mounted on posts or pylons.

- The visual effect sought by the EG designer.

Proportion and Scale

Proportion and scale are related to size in the sign hardware system. The rule of thumb for proportion is to trust your gut; that is, if a freestanding sign looks too thin depth-wise to stand up, it probably won't unless it has major foundational support. Conversely, excess depth can make signs appear too bulky. Accordingly, it's important to study the front and side views of all the sign types in a program to achieve three-dimensional proportional harmony. Always consult with a sign fabricator or engineer if you have any questions about structural matters.

The EG designer can also manipulate the scale of the sign hardware system in relation to the program's environment. The scale of the various sign types can be just right for their surroundings, or the scale of certain or all the sign types in a program can be enlarged to create a bigger, more dramatic visual impact. In certain environments, smaller scaled signs may be appropriate to create a sense of subdued elegance; but they should never be so small that they cannot be easily read at the intended viewing distance or that they violate any ADA or code requirements for typographic or panel sizes.

A final word about size in the sign hardware system: The fewer sign sizes there are in a program, the more visually unified the program will be. Keep in mind that a sign of a given size can display variable quantities of informational content, from a little to a lot—although never so much as to cause information overload—depending on how the various kinds of sign messages are laid out in the graphic system.

Sign Lighting Overview

Just as lighting adds interest and drama to stage productions, lighting can add interest and drama, as well as visibility, to signage. Lighting components are physical objects, making sign illumination part of the sign hardware system. Basically, there are three options for lighting signs: externally, internally, or no lighting. This section presents a basic overview of sign lighting techniques in relation to each of these sign illumination options.

Decisions on whether to light and how to light some or all the sign types in a program depend on many factors, among them whether a sign is in an interior or exterior environment, ambient light levels within the sign program's environment, a sign's hierarchical rank (primary, secondary, or tertiary) within the program, cost considerations, local sign ordinances, ADA recommendations for sign lighting, the desired visual effect, and others. In addition, new technologies and products for lighting signs are always being developed, so the EG designer may want to engage a lighting consultant, electrical engineer, or sign fabricator for more technical information on sign illumination.

For both external and internal illumination, electrical power must be brought to the sign location, which is a cost factor that requires coordination between the EG designer and the project architect or electrical engineer, as well as between the sign fabricator and other construction trades. Ongoing electrical consumption is another cost factor. Sign illumination may be on around the clock, or be controlled with an automatic timer to save energy. The latter is the case in particular for exterior signs or interior signs in high-daylight environments. Maintenance is also a consideration, as most illuminated signs must be checked periodically to replace burned out lamps and to ensure that other electrical components are in good condition.

Due to these cost and maintenance factors, lower-hierarchy signs within a program, such as room identification plaques in a hotel, are rarely illuminated. Keep in mind, however, that the ADA recommends—not requires—that sign surfaces be uniformly illuminated within a range of 100 to 300 lux (10 to 30 foot-candles). Additionally, the ADA recommends that signs "be located such that the illumination level on the surface of the sign is not significantly exceeded by the ambient light or visible bright lighting source behind or in front of the sign." Note that the ambient light level at any given sign location may be adequate to meet these ADA recommendations without requiring any sign-specific lighting sources. Also keep in mind that local sign ordinances may place limitations on the illumination of exterior signs, including glare from any lighting sources.

In signage programs for new construction, the earlier the EG designer can identify the locations of illuminated signs, the easier it will be for the project's engineers to coordinate sending power to those locations without change orders or ripping out finished surfaces to lay electrical conduit. Even if it's still undecided as to whether a given sign type may be illuminated, it's wise to have power run to the appropriate sign locations so that the power is there when or if needed. Of course, the EG designer should be judicious and not have power run to hundreds of sign locations where it's unlikely to ever be needed.

At the minimum, the EG designer should specify the following:

- That externally and internally illuminated signs be fabricated so that they are evenly illuminated with no so-called hot or cold spots.
- That all electrical components be Underwriters Laboratory (UL) approved and in conformance with any applicable safety or energy codes.
- That all electrical engineering for a sign program be performed by other parties with the proper credentials, such as an electrical engineer or a sign fabricator.

External Illumination

The term *external illumination* refers to lighting that is outside of a sign but specifically dedicated to and aimed at the sign for purposes of illuminating it. This definition does not include *ambient lighting*, which is lighting dedicated to other purposes in the sign environment, such as general room or street lighting. External lighting reflects off a sign's surface and is achieved with

6.22

6.22 Flush, ground-mounted floodlights wash over the externally illuminated verde marble monument sign at the International Trade Center in Mt. Olive, New Jersey.

6.23 External light from car headlights illuminates retroreflective vinyl graphics, which don't require light fixtures or electrical power.

floodlights or spotlights directed onto either the entire sign face or just the sign graphics. External illumination is more commonly used for signs in exterior environments than interior environments, although it can make for very dramatic effects in interior settings.

External light sources include incandescent, fluorescent, halogen, mercury or sodium vapor, and other kinds of lamps. Although all these sources emit what is generally considered *white light*, the color temperature of the light varies with the source, and the color temperature of the light source can tinge the color of the sign itself. For example, sodium vapor lighting has an orangey cast and mercury vapor has a bluish cast; even common tubular fluorescent lamps are available in various color temperatures, ranging from cool to warm. The fixtures housing external light sources can be mounted below or above the sign, and can vary from sleek and minimalist to highly noticeable, so the look of the lamp fixtures must always be considered in external sign illumination.

One external sign illumination technique that doesn't require electrical power is specially engineered reflective vinyl films that capture, intensify, and reflect back light from car headlights. These retroreflective vinyl films are available in white, black, and a limited range of bright colors. They can be used for reflective sign graphics, reflective sign backgrounds, or both. But a word of caution here: Never use reflective black film on reflective white film or vice versa, because both reflect back white light, resulting in disappearing graphics! Retroreflective vinyl films are typically used for traffic control and roadway directional signs at sites where there is little or no ambient lighting at night.

Internal Illumination

Internal illumination refers to light that is transmitted from within a sign. It is commonly used for signs in both exterior and interior environments; as such, internally illuminated signs can take several forms, the most common being a rectangular sign box with a translucent plastic face on which the graphics and background are completely backlit by fluorescent lamps. This form is typified in signs for big-box stores, gas stations, and other commercial establishments. Some internally illuminated sign boxes have just the graphics backlit on opaque backgrounds, which is less commercial in appearance, while others have just the backgrounds backlit with opaque graphics.

Typically, the light source in an internally illuminated sign is completely hidden, although sometimes the glowing light source itself is the sign, as in those made of exposed neon or other luminous tubing. Some internally illuminated signs aren't even rectangular boxes; instead, they're individually fabricated letters that can be lit in three ways: with light coming through the face of each letter, with light coming through the face and returns (sides) of each letter, or with light spilling out around the returns of an opaque letter in a halo or silhouette effect. Another form of internal illumination is edge lighting, where the edge of a transparent glass or plastic sheet is placed on a light source, and the light is conducted through the transparent sheet to illuminate graphics etched or sandblasted into it.

There are many light sources for internal sign illumination, with new forms and technologies being developed and refined on a regular basis. That said, straight tubular fluorescent lamps are the workhorses used to backlight most sign boxes, although there are also special fluorescent lamp shapes, such as U-shapes, available for sign box illumination. Custom-bent neon-type lamps are the traditional method for backlighting individually fabricated letters, although light emitting diodes (LEDs) are rapidly becoming a viable lighting source for individual letters.

6.24 A directory in a Hong Kong retail atrium uses two kinds of internal illumination effects: the opaque stainless steel header panel, where only the graphics are backlit, and the map panel, where the background and graphics of the map insert are backlit.

6.25 This internally illuminated sign at a New York University dormitory combines backlit graphics on an opaque disk background with halo lighting spilling out around the disk to silhouette it.

6.26 An internally illuminated sign at the Rock and Roll Hall of Fame and Museum in Cleveland, Ohio, where the glowing neon tubing light source is formed into letters.

6.25

6.26

6.27

6.28

6.27 The internally illuminated individual letters at the Pacific Design Center in Los Angeles have opaque metal faces overlaid on letters with backlit acrylic faces and opaque metal returns.

6.28 Internal illumination by silhouette lighting forms a halo of lights around opaque, fabricated aluminum symbols in the exhibit halls of the Virginia Beach Convention Center.

Single-socket compact fluorescent lamps are also proving to be useful for internal sign illumination.

All internally illuminated signs must be thicker than other types of signs, to accommodate lamps and their mounts, the space required between the lamps and the sign face, wiring, and other electrical components such as ballasts and transformers. Providing access to the interior of sign boxes, for servicing lamps and electrical equipment, is also an important consideration when designing internally illuminated signs. The EG designer should take care to specify that all internally illuminated signs be fabricated to prevent leakage of light at seams and joints, and with adequate venting to dissipate any heat that can build up within the sign. Additionally, the EG designer should specify that all illumination is even, with no hot or cold spots.

Nonillumination

Nonillumination of signs is a perfectly viable option for signs in exterior or interior environments with high enough ambient light levels (whether from artificial or natural sources) for signs to be seen and read without dedicated sign lighting. Entire sign programs have been developed with no illumination at all for many environments, and function perfectly well.

Nonillumination also makes sense if the site doesn't operate at night or if it doesn't want to convey an overly commercial look. Nonillumination is, obviously, the least expensive option, requiring no electrical installation or incurring no ongoing energy-consumption costs.

Sign Materials Overview

Sign materials are just that—raw materials, such as pallets of aluminum sheets or steel I-beams. It's the EG designer's creative mind and the sign fabricator's skills that give materials form and life as three-dimensional sign objects. And that is one of the truly magical aspects of EG design.

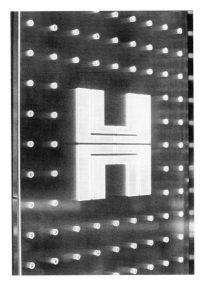

6.29 Internal illumination by edge lighting on a pedestrian bridge in Hong Kong, where the light source placed on the edge of clear acrylic sheet illuminates the graphics engraved into it.

Materials are the essence of a sign program's hardware system—they are the very stuff from which signs are fabricated. As such, they have a significant bearing on the visual appearance of the sign hardware system. The EG designer has a virtually endless range of materials from which to compose a sign program's hardware system, and fascinating new materials are introduced on a regular basis. An entire book could be written on sign materials, so by necessity this section highlights only the basic materials that can be used in the sign hardware system.

Some sign materials are used as purely *structural* components, either expressed or hidden, while others are used as exposed *finish* components, such as sign faces, plaques, and cladding over internal structures. And some sign materials, such as wood and aluminum, are used as both structural and finish components.

Materials as Your Muse

The guideline here is: Let the materials be your muse. Certain sign materials that are inherently attractive are rarely covered up with paints or other opaque coatings, although they may require a clear coating for protection. Other sign materials are covered up with opaque coatings because they need to be a specific color, they need to be protected from the elements, or they're inherently unattractive. Most materials can take a variety of finishes— smooth, rough, grained, and so on—that either come from the material's manufacturer or are added in the sign fabricator's shop. (More on this later, in the "Overview of Coatings and Finishes Applied to Signs" section.)

Each basic type of sign material has inherent qualities, such as the transparency of glass, the flexibility of fabric, or the shininess of metal, and each of these qualities can and should be exploited by the EG designer. Plastics are perhaps the ultimate material chameleon, in that they can mimic glass, metals, or even wood and stone. Plastics also have inherent qualities that are valuable unto themselves, such as ease of formability, break resistance, and their relatively light weight.

Unity of Materials

Unity of materials is just as important to the visual coherence of a sign program's hardware system as unity of form. As with sign form, the point is to use a unified materials palette to create a family resemblance among all the various types of signs within the program. This doesn't mean that all the materials within the program's palette need to be used on each and every sign type, but that perhaps one or two materials are featured in all the sign types in the program. (See the color insert for examples of sign programs with unified materials.)

Materials and Processes

Materials for exposed sign finish components are available in a variety of forms, most commonly in flat sheets, plates, or slabs of various

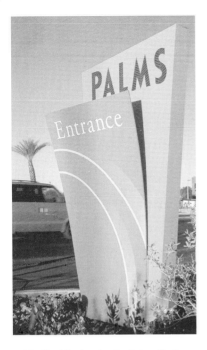

6.30 On this sign for the Palms Casino in Las Vegas, Nevada, a metal panel is rolled into a graceful curve.

thicknesses, and can be processed in various ways, depending on the specific kind of material. All flat finish materials can be cut into various shapes or drilled with holes by various processes. Aside from cutting and drilling, workability diverges with the inherent physical properties of each basic material. For example, sheets of metal can be bent at an acute angle or rolled into a curve relatively easily, but stone can't be bent or rolled because it's brittle and will break. In another example, plastic is the only sign material that can be readily vacuum-formed into a specific shape by heating the plastic sheet and drawing it down over the shape with a vacuum pump; after the plastic cools, it retains the shape.

It is apparent from just these two examples that there are myriad workshop processes for even basic sign materials, so a comprehensive discussion of them is beyond the scope of this book. There's no doubt, however, that EG design is facilitated by a basic knowledge of the techniques by which various sign materials can be processed in a shop, and there are several sources for gaining that knowledge.

The SEGD Web site provides a message board for its members, where both professional (designers) and industry (fabricators and manufacturers) members share information about sign materials and fabrication processes, among other topics. In addition, most SEGD industry members are willing to meet with EG designers to discuss materials and production techniques for a given project, and are often willing to conduct shop tours for EG designers, which can be very illuminating to both newcomers and seasoned professionals in the field. Additionally, SEGD industry members hold a trade exposition at the SEGD's annual conference, which is a wonderful source of information on materials and fabrication processes, including several that are cutting-edge. The SEGD also has an extensive glossary of signage terms available to its membership, which contains valuable information on sign materials and fabrication processes. EG designers can also access technical information at www.signweb.com, which is geared toward sign fabricators.

Materials for sign structural components, whether expressed or hidden, are available in a variety of forms. Wood structural components are typically solid, and available in several cross-sectional shapes, such as square, rectangular, round, and sometimes fancy shapes, such as fluted columns or turned spindles. Metal structural components are typically hollow or open extrusions or forgings. Many of these shapes are used for general construction industry applications and are available in a variety of basic cross-sectional shapes, such as round, square, and rectangular tubing, as well as L-shaped angles, C-shaped channels, and the classic I-beam. There are also manufacturers of extruded aluminum support components with more varied sectional shapes geared specifically to signage applications.

Size Does Matter

It's important to keep in mind that both finish and structural signage materials are manufactured in certain standard sizes, as this will have consequences for the appearance of a sign program's hardware system. Not only can material size be a design constraint, but so can the size of equipment for working, finishing, or applying graphics to the material. Size is generally not a problem with the smaller sign types within a program, but it can become a major challenge when working with the larger sign types, where seams and joints can become a design factor.

Seams and joints can generally be minimized or hidden on opaque or painted-over materials such as metal, wood, and opaque plastics, but they cannot be hidden on fabrics or transparent materials such as glass or clear plastics. When faced with material or processing size constraints, the EG designer will often press the "reveal" technique into service, which is a neat design trick that actually exposes and plays up a seam or a joint. This can often look better than trying to hide a joint that can't be hidden successfully.

Basic Sign Materials

While reading about the basic sign materials described in this section keep in mind that there are many proprietary products with their own unique qualities and properties within these broad categories of sign materials. Additionally, there are many products that are composites of these materials, capitalizing on properties of each constituent material to create a new set of properties—for example, an aluminum-plastic "sandwich" that's as flat as a solid sheet of aluminum of the same thickness but with substantially reduced weight. And, of course, new sign materials are constantly under development.

Sources for information on materials and products used in signage include manufacturers' and suppliers' catalogs, design and architecture magazines, and companies that provide compendia of manufacturers, such as Sweets and the Thomas Register. Most of these sources, as well as others (e.g., www.materialconnexion.com), can be found on the Internet, which has become invaluable for conducting materials research. Also note that EG designers should always obtain samples of materials they're considering for use and that most materials manufacturers are happy to provide samples to designers. Most EGD offices maintain a library of materials information, ranging from catalogs and swatch boards to samples and mock-ups.

A word about green design and materials: It is beyond the scope of this book to examine the environmental factors relating to materials and processes for a sign program's hardware system or for application of sign graphics. Suffice it to say that EG designers should always consider the environmental impact—from sourcing, to manufacture and processing, to delivery, to disposal and recycling—of the materials and processes they specify. Good, solid design that's not overly trendy—and therefore not quickly dated—also contributes to environmental sustainability.

6.31 Strategically placed reveals in the background panel enhance the main identification sign for the Lycée Français de New York.

Environmental Graphics and LEED*
Nadav Malin

By now most designers have encountered, or at least heard about, the Leadership in Energy and Environmental Design (LEED) Rating System from the United States Green Building Council. But the opportunities for environmental graphic designers to contribute to LEED certification of projects—and to benefit from its market pull—are just beginning to be explored.

How does environmental graphic design fit into the LEED system? Ideally, LEED—and green building design in general—is driving architects and developers to think more holistically about their design process. The systems integration needed for a cost-effective green project is not feasible in a linear design process, requiring instead an integrated design approach that brings all disciplines together in a collaborative process. This collaborative approach should help bring all consultants, including environmental graphic designers, to the table earlier in the design process, when they can help inform basic layout and circulation decisions.

More specifically, there are several credits in LEED that are likely to be affected directly by the work of environmental graphic designers.

Light Pollution

Not only does light pollution deprive everyone of a view of the stars, it also disrupts the migration patterns and reproductive behavior of many birds, animals, and insects. To achieve the light-pollution point in LEED, there can be no uplighting that escapes into the sky; any uplighting must be intercepted by an object. Thus, any lighted outdoor signage would have to be downlit, internally illuminated, or uplit using a very tightly controlled fixture.

Indoor Emissions from Materials

Several points in the "Indoor Environmental Quality" section of LEED can be achieved by avoiding the use of certain products that might contribute to indoor pollution. There are limits on the amount of volatile organic compounds (VOCs) that can be released from paints, coatings, adhesives, and sealants, for example. To ensure that your work doesn't undermine the project's ability to earn these points, verify that any of these materials that are applied on-site meet the VOC requirements, and do as much painting and sealing as possible off-site in a properly controlled and ventilated setting.

Also in this category is a point for avoiding composite wood products made with urea formaldehyde binders. If your project is seeking to achieve this point, then conventional particleboard, medium-density fiberboard (MDF), and hardboard are all off limits. A few companies make wood-fiber panel products using a polyurethane binder instead of urea-formaldehyde. (In fact, museums have been a primary market for these alternative panel products due to their interest in avoiding the deleterious effect of formaldehyde on artwork or other fragile items, either in a collection or on display.) Several other companies make panels from agricultural fibers, such as rice straw or wheat straw, that are comparable to MDF. These so-called ag-fiber panels are all made with polyurethane binders.

Green Materials

LEED's "Materials & Resources" section includes five credits, with a total of seven points, for the use of materials that have certain green characteristics. Most of these points are achieved based on the percentage of all materials in the building that these green products represent. For example, one point is achieved if at least 5 percent of all products used in a project are made from rapidly renewable materials such as cork, bamboo, or linseed oil. These calculations are done based on the dollar value of the products. Other credits in this section encourage the use of salvaged materials, recycled-content materials, and materials that are produced locally.

LEED deals with wood a little differently from how it addresses other materials. To get the certified wood point in LEED, at least 50 percent of all wood products used must be certified green in accordance with the standards of the Forest Stewardship Council.

Outreach and Education

There is no credit in the current versions of LEED that specifically rewards outreach and education efforts, but many projects have used LEED's Innovation Points option to get credit for such activities. This represents a major opportunity for environmental graphic designers to develop interpretive signage and exhibits that clue visitors into the green features of the facility.

These requirements apply whenever the work of the graphic designer is within the scope of services delivered by the architect (or whoever is applying for the LEED certification). If your work as an environmental graphic designer is performed under a separate contract, apart from

the basic scope of services, it may be exempt from meeting the LEED requirements. But in that case it also cannot contribute to LEED credits.

Resources

There are several sources that designers can use to find and learn about green materials:

- *GreenSpec Directory* from BuildingGreen, Inc. includes listings of products that have been screened for environmental pedigree by the editors of *Environmental Building News*. This directory carries no advertising, so the listings are not influenced by potential revenue from suppliers. *GreenSpec* is available in a paperbound volume or online as part of the BuildingGreen Suite at www.BuildingGreen.com This latter tool allows users to browse listings (in addition to articles and case studies) by LEED credit.

- *Environmental Design & Construction* magazine also produces an annual green products resource guide, which is available at www.edcmag.com.

- The GreenSage Web site (www.greensage.com) provides access to green materials.

- Listings of materials that have been certified as low in emission of indoor pollutants are available from the Greenguard Environmental Institute (www.greenguard.org).

Nadav Malin is vice president of BuildingGreen, Inc., editor of Environmental Building News, *and co-editor of the* GreenSpec *product directory.*

*Reprinted from SEGD Design number 07 (2005), with permission.

Metals

Metals, in both structural and sheet forms, are among the most highly utilized sign materials. Additionally, certain metals can be melted and cast into complex forms, including hardware components such as sign bases and as medallions and plaques.

All metals have good to excellent structural properties, although they all oxidize or corrode to a greater or lesser extent. Metals can take a range of surface finishes, from a mirror polish to a coarse-brushed grain. Metals can also be painted, although stainless steel, bronze, and brass are so attractive in their natural state they rarely are. Typical metals used for signage include:

- *Aluminum.* Used for sign faces, plaques, cladding, trim, and lightweight to medium-weight structures, as well as for castings. Considered one of the "white" metals, aluminum is a lighter shade of gray than stainless steel. Other characteristics include: good appearance; good durability; light weight; and medium to high expense. Aluminum also typically benefits from clear or opaque protective coatings, although such coatings are not necessarily required.

- *Carbon steel.* This metal is typically used for concealed medium-weight to heavyweight sign structures, not for appearance. Other characteristics include: high durability; heavy weight; and medium to high expense. Carbon steel also requires rust-inhibiting paints or coatings.

- *Stainless steel.* Stainless steel is typically used for sign faces, plaques, cladding, and trim (it's generally too expensive for structures). Another of the "white" metals, stainless steel is a darker shade of gray than aluminum. Other characteristics include: excellent appearance (it's rarely painted); excellent durability; heavy weight; and high expense. Because it does not rust, or rusts minimally, (hence the name "stainless") protective coatings are not usually required.

6.32 Contrast of mirror-polished bronze and brush-finish stainless steel letters is exploited in the main identification sign for Manhattan's 420 Fifth Avenue.

6.33 Sides of stainless steel pylon are rolled into a scroll for this dedicatory sign in New York City.

6.32

6.33

- *Bronze, brass, and copper.* These copper alloys (also called the "yellow" or "red" metals) are typically used for sign faces, plaques, trim, and castings. Like stainless steel, they're too expensive for structures. Other characteristics include: excellent appearance; good to excellent durability; heavy weight; and high expense. These alloys also require a protective coating—although often they're intentionally oxidized to a rich brown or green patina before coating.

Plastics

Plastics have a number of unique properties that can be exploited for signage, such as transparency, formability, break resistance, and relatively low weight compared to other sign materials. As such, plastics are another commonly used sign material, although they're used primarily for exposed-finish components, not structural components. And because certain plastics allow light to pass through them, they are almost always used for internally illuminated sign faces. Plastics and plastic resins are also moldable by various processes into an infinite variety of shapes, an invaluable feature in signage design and production. Plastics in sheet form are most commonly used in signage, although plastic resin liquids and pellets can also be cast into various sculptural forms.

The two primary sign plastics are *acrylic* and *polycarbonate* (commonly called *polycarb*), both of which have the glasslike properties of transparency and translucency; but, unlike glass, they don't chip and shatter. In fact, polycarbonate is the clear, bulletproof material used to shield bank tellers and presidential limousines.

There are some technical differences between acrylic and polycarbonate, but they are both used for sign faces, plaques, cladding, and trim. Due to their capability to be transparent or translucent, they are widely used for the faces of internally illuminated sign boxes and letters. They're also widely used for vacuum-formed sign faces that have graphics in relief, as well as for clear protective lenses on signs such as directories and menu boards.

6.34 The federal star feature of this cast metal base distinctively brands all the signs in Washington, DC's citywide signage program. The north arrow cast into the base orients visitors to the city's confusing street plan.

6.35

6.35 Clear acrylic sign panel with edge-lit graphics on back side and cut copper letters on front side floats in front of a serving station at a New York City corporate dining facility.

Acrylic sheet, in particular, is available in a fairly wide range of colors and textures, from completely transparent to completely opaque, and both acrylic and polycarbonate can be painted to a custom color. There are several manufacturers of acrylic and polycarbonate sheet, each with its own trade name and line of colors, textures, and other features. Grades with UV inhibitors should be used for exterior signage, as both acrylic and polycarb tend to yellow with exposure to the sun. Both feature a good appearance, medium to high durability, light to medium weight, and medium to high expense. Most plastics, including acrylics and polycarbonates, do not require any applied protective coatings, but they do tend to scratch more readily than other sign materials.

Other plastics used in signage include styrenes, vinyls, phenolics, and photopolymers, all of which have their own unique properties. There are several manufacturers of signage materials (which typically come in sheet form, some of which are flexible) made from these types of plastics. Many are sold under trade names and utilize proprietary manufacturing techniques that result in unique products, such as expanded polyvinyl chloride (PVC) sheet that's half the weight of solid PVC sheet, but is very strong for sign panel use. Other specialized plastics used for signage include metallized or holographic films and sheets; photosensitive plastic

6.36 Plastic sheet is available in a wide variety of textures and forms, including laminations and embedments.

6.36

6.37

6.38

sheets, which yield raised tactile and Braille graphics when exposed to light and chemically processed; and plastic resin sheets embedded with all kinds of decorative materials or glass fibers for strength.

The list of proprietary plastic products that can be used for signage is virtually unlimited, and new products are constantly being introduced. A word of warning, though: Some of these plastic products look downright cheap and tacky, whereas others are very attractive.

Glass

Glass was invented centuries before plastics, and because of its inherent transparency, glass has long been used as a signage material, particularly as clear protective lenses on sign cabinets such as directories. Glass has also long been used for edge-lighting applications and as the tubing that encases neon and other luminous gases used for signage. Glass sheet is used for sign panels, lenses, and plaques, typically in transparent form with the familiar slightly greenish tint; a completely colorless low-iron content glass sheet is also available, but at greater expense. Additionally, glass sheet is available in a wide variety of colors, levels of transparency or opacity, and surface textures, typically from specialized art glass suppliers.

Glass sheet is very hard and scratchproof, but with a great enough impact, it will shatter or chip. For this reason, glass is often tempered or laminated or both. Tempered glass sheet is treated after manufacture so that it will crumble into rectangular clumps rather than shatter into sharp shards on impact. Tempered glass, however, cannot be cut, drilled, sandblasted, or otherwise mechanically processed without breaking, so any tooling or graphic application processes must be performed before a glass sign is tempered.

Laminated glass can be tempered or not, and consists of two or more sheets of glass that are permanently laminated together with a clear plastic

6.37 Photopolymer is a plastic sheet commonly used for ADA-compliant raised tactile and Braille graphics, as shown on this room identification sign, which also has a changeable message window at Valparaiso University in Valparaiso, Indiana.

6.38 Cast plastic resin sign at Philadelphia's Cira Centre office tower.

6.39 Three laminated glass panels form the tenant signage pylon for Philadelphia's Cira Centre office tower. The middle panel has a translucent lamination interlayer.

6.40

6.41

6.40 Monumental 1 meter high artisan-cast glass letters evoke icy coolness at the One Raffles Quay office complex in tropical Singapore.

6.41 Etched glass wall plaque at Pittsburgh's O'Reilly Theater has raised tactile and Braille characters on a frosted background.

interlayer that holds the glass fragments together if the laminated sheet is impacted. The lamination interlayer is quite strong; in fact, the most common application of laminated glass is in car windshields, which seldom deform even if riddled with cracks from an impact. Large freestanding glass signs can be self-supporting if made from several sheets of glass that are laminated together, although laminated edges should be protected from the elements on exterior signs. Also, many glass suppliers can manipulate the color, texture, and opacity of the lamination interlayer.

Glass sign panels typically need a support structure, which is usually visible due to the transparency of glass. Supports can include a continuous frame that surrounds the sign perimeter, or individual supports at strategic points, although opaque glass panels can be supported by hidden structures. Frameless glass signs should always have *eased edges*, which are very slightly beveled at a 45-degree angle to prevent chipping and ease the sharpness of 90-degree cuts.

Other characteristics of glass include: excellent appearance; good to excellent durability; heavy weight; and medium to high expense. It does not require protective coatings, but it must be cleaned periodically to maintain transparency.

Wood

As sign materials, wood and wood products are less commonly used today than they were a few decades ago, having been replaced to a great extent by new materials on the plastics front. Nevertheless, wood and products made from wood, such as particleboard, are still used for some signage, including sign faces and plaques, as well as for lightweight structures.

6.42

6.43

Wood products come in both structural and sheet forms, from cheap pine two-by-fours and plywood to fancy lathe-turned posts and exotic solid hardwood or veneered panels. All wood products can be painted or clear-coated, and can take a range of surface textures, from smooth to highly textured. Typically, the more lowly and unattractive the wood product, such as medium-density fiberboard (MDF), the more likely it is to be used simply as substrate panel, to be covered up with paint and graphics. On the other hand, richly grained hardwood can be exploited for its attractive appearance in signage design, as it is in fine furniture and cabinetry. In many cases, surfaces of lower-quality wood products are laminated with a veneer, which is a thin layer of high-quality wood, often with unusual graining.

Other characteristics of wood products range from poor to excellent appearance; low to high durability; light to medium weight; and low to high expense. Wood products, particularly in exterior applications, must be protected with opaque paint or clear sealer.

Fabrics

Fabric is a sign material that has the unique property of flexibility; consequently, it is typically used for exterior signage applications such as awnings, billboards, banners, and flags. In the case of awnings and billboards, the fabric is stretched over a rigid frame; fabric banners and flags are freer to move with the wind, so they can lend animation and a festive quality to a site.

Typical sign fabrics are made of natural fibers, such as cotton, or synthetic fibers, and can be opaque, translucent, or open-mesh. Certain sign fabrics

6.42 Blue-stained curly maple wood veneer letters are inlaid flush with curly maple veneer in the donor recognition wall at the O'Reilly Theater in Pittsburgh.

6.43 Wood sign panels overlaid with stencil-cut aluminum graphic panels at Rutgers University's Zimmerli Art Museum in New Brunswick, New Jersey.

6.44

6.45

6.44 Banners move with the wind, lending animation and festivity to a site—here, to the streets of Ardmore, Pennsylvania, a Philadelphia suburb.

6.45 Fabric banners for this multiple-building medical facility create a sense of place along a busy Manhattan streetscape.

are available under trade names in a fairly wide range of colors, including some metallics. Translucent vinyl-coated sign fabrics are commonly used for internally illuminated awnings and sign faces, and opaque vinyl-coated sign fabrics are used for billboards and other large outdoor signs. A reinforcement netting is often woven into these vinyl-coated fabrics, which can be visually objectionable when viewed at close range.

Obviously, sign fabrics cannot be used structurally, and all fabric signs have limited life spans. When necessary they should be coated with UV inhibitors to reduce degradation from sun exposure. Most fabric signs have a good to excellent appearance and low to medium durability; they are lightweight, and their expense is low to medium. Keep in mind, however, that fabrication and installation of structures to hold fabric signs involve additional expense.

Masonry

Masonry is a somewhat uncommon material for signage, but thanks to its inherent monumentality, it can be used to great effect. Masonry materials for signage include stone, brick, and precast concrete varieties that are typically used in architectural applications. Masonry can be used for sign faces and plaques, and masonry signs can be either solid and self-supporting or supported by an internal steel structure.

Stone, the most prestigious of the masonry materials, includes marble, granite, slate, limestone, sandstone, and others; and many textural and

6.46

6.47

6.46 This masonry sign monument, cut from a single 15-ton piece of bluestone has a natural cleft finish and hand-carved graphics. Dramatic external lighting accentuates the sign's presence against the downtown lights of Richmond, Virginia.

6.47 Logotype in cut limestone at ABC Broadcasting's New York City headquarters complex.

color varieties of each of these types of stone are also available. Stone can be used for both exterior and interior signage, although many marble varieties are too soft for exterior use. Stone surface textures can vary, from a mirror polish to a rough natural texture, depending on the type of stone used. Like glass, exposed edges of certain types of stone may require easing to reduce chipping and sharpness. Other characteristics of masonry sign materials are: a very good to excellent appearance; very high durability; very high weight; and high to very high expense.

Adhesives and Fasteners

Adhesives and fasteners are literally the nuts and bolts and glue and tape that hold signage hardware units together and signage hardware units to their mounting surfaces. Adhesives used for sign hardware are far more sophisticated than ordinary household glues and tapes, and include liquids, gels, and tapes that can establish extremely powerful bonds between surfaces of sign components without physically penetrating the components. In fact, some of the adhesives used in the sign industry come from the aircraft industry, where they're used to bond aircraft skins to airframes. Indeed some adhesives are considered to create *chemical welds*. Adhesives are typically used to join finish sign materials to each other or to structural components, as well as to secure signs to their mounting surfaces.

Fasteners include nuts, bolts, screws, clips, and other devices typically made of metal that penetrate sign components to form strong mechanical connections within sign units, and between sign units and their mounting structures or surfaces. Mechanical connections are very strong and are usually necessary for securing sign structures together, for securing sign

6.48 A monumental 28' high sign of precast concrete with smooth and rough texture zones marks an entrance to this large office and industrial park in Mt. Olive, New Jersey.

bodies to their structures, and, in the case of heavier sign units, for securing sign units to mounting surfaces. Unlike adhesives, which form an effectively permanent bond, mechanical fasteners have the advantage of being removable, which allows access to the interiors of sign units for servicing, such as to replace burned-out lamps or to update directory listings.

Fasteners are manufactured from a variety of metals, including stainless steel, galvanized steel, aluminum, brass, and chrome-plated brass. When attractiveness and corrosion resistance are considerations, stainless steel fasteners are often employed. But because fasteners often join dissimilar metals, such as aluminum and stainless steel, they and the metals they join must be protected against corrosion that results from a weak galvanic or electrical reaction that occurs when such metals come in contact with one another.

Many mechanical fasteners and connections are not terribly attractive in appearance, but often they can be concealed—sometimes with ease, sometimes with difficulty, depending on the application. But there are times when there's no choice but to leave the fasteners exposed to view. In such situations, the EG designer may choose to minimize the appearance of the exposed fasteners by hiding them in a reveal or painting them the same color as the sign panel; alternatively, the designer may choose to accentuate the appearance of the exposed fasteners, thereby making them a design asset rather than a liability. Fortunately, there are several types of fasteners that are quite attractive and thereby suitable for exploitation as a design feature.

Some designed objects, such as the Eiffel Tower, revel in their exposed mechanics. Others, such as the Statue of Liberty, also engineered by Gustav Eiffel, intentionally hide their nuts and bolts. The choice boils down to what is the appropriate aesthetic for the project at hand. Examples of signs and sign programs with purposefully exposed fasteners can be found throughout this book.

Welding is another form of mechanical connection, in which two pieces of the same metal are essentially melted together along a joint by heat or electricity. Welding forms very strong connections and is often used for connecting hidden structural components. Welding can also join together finish sign components, when the raised bead formed by the welding process is ground smooth.

Regarding sign mounting, lighter sign units such as wall plaques can be readily secured to mounting surfaces with just adhesives, typically double-sided foam tape, which is often used in conjunction with silicone gel adhesive. Adhesive mounting is often combined with mechanical fasteners, such as when a foam tape/silicone bond is augmented with mechanical fasteners for extra mounting support, a combination known as *screw and glue*. And mounting pins for individual cut or fabricated letters, or for heavier sign plaques, are often secured with adhesives or mechanical parts into pockets drilled into a wall. Large and/or heavy sign units often require connection into a building's underlying structural system, which can be inches—or sometimes feet—beyond a ceiling or wall surface.

In addition to those just mentioned, there are several methods and products for securing signs together or to their mounting surfaces. These methods and products often provide connections that make it possible to remove sign panels or other components; they range from magnetized sheeting to hook-and-loop fasteners, commonly known as Velcro, a trademarked product.

Electronic Message Display Devices

Electronic message display devices draw the human eye like a flame draws a moth. These glowing, often animated devices are digitally controlled screens that display changeable and updatable sign messages, such as the flight information display systems (FIDS) at airports that list the airline, flight number, gate number, and arrival or departure time, and status of inbound and outbound flights. Other applications of electronic or dynamic displays include interactive building and campus directories, time and temperature displays, track-side train arrival information, scoreboards, stock tickers, marquees, and electronic message centers that post events or sales taking place at a venue or retailer. The possibilities for use of electronic variable message displays are endless, as is the need for changeable, updatable information. To meet this demand, new applications for dynamic displays are being developed daily.

It isn't the point of this book to go into technical detail about electronic display devices, as it's a complex, evolving subject, with new devices and improvements to existing devices becoming available almost daily. That said, at the time of this writing, two of the most common dynamic display devices are light-emitting diode (LED) matrices and liquid crystal display (LCD) screens. With LED and LCD devices, the sign message or image is displayed on the device itself. There are also developing technologies that can project digital information and images onto other, remote surfaces, such as walls and floors.

When evaluating the use of LED and LCD display components for a sign program, the EG designer should be aware of the following important hardware system design considerations for these devices:

- Size and proportional limitations of active display area, display panel housing, and any other associated components

- Resolution and viewing angle limitations

- Brightness of viewing environment

- Need for electrical and datacom feeds

- Venting, heating, cooling, and weather protection constraints

6.49a

6.49b

6.49a, b Monocolor electronic LED display devices provide real-time train arrival and departure information at gates and platforms at stations along Amtrak's Northeast Corridor, from Boston to Washington, DC.

Other considerations for LED, LCD, and other dynamic display devices, which are typically beyond the skills base of most EG designers, are control and content. Electronic display devices are basically empty canvases, waiting to be filled with informational and/or image content. How that content is delivered to the display devices is the control issue. What that content is composed of is the content issue.

All dynamic display devices are computer-controlled to a greater or lesser extent. The display devices can be tied into a larger computer or communications network maintained by the client, can be on their own dedicated network, or can be individually controlled. The point is, each installation is different, hence requires information systems (IS) experts to create or tailor control software to each specific display application.

6.50 This full-color electronic LED board can be programmed to display images, animations, and multiple lines of text in various sizes and styles to announce coming events.

Content for dynamic display devices can range from simple generic text messages to sharp typeface and graphics rendition to full streaming video. Even nonvideo, still content can be animated with flashes, crawls, dissolves, wipes, zooms, and other simple techniques. Although EG designers don't often have the opportunity to become involved with the production of content for dynamic display devices, the appearance and quality of that content should be a concern because, more often than not, both are lacking. At my office we always advise our clients to consider carefully the content that will be displayed, who will generate that content, how that content will be arranged and presented, who will update and manage the content over time, and other similar concerns.

The best sources for information about dynamic display devices are their manufacturers, as they will tend to have the most up-to-date technical information about their products. Many manufacturers can also provide control systems, including computer hardware and software, engineered for their devices and the client's needs, along with training for the end users on the client side. Some manufacturers even offer turnkey systems, which include cabinetry for the display devices, content development and management, all controlling systems and equipment, and end-user training.

Stock Sign Hardware Systems

There are several manufacturers of proprietary "stock" sign hardware systems in several different styles—some quite attractive—for both interior and exterior use. Each of these stock systems, typically patented, offers a unique hardware system, often with specially interlocking and/or changeable parts. Most stock systems are kits of hardware parts that can be configured in many different ways by the EG designer. Manufacturers of stock systems also offer a range of techniques for applying graphics to their hardware systems, including ADA-compliant tactile and Braille graphics, which also provides creative opportunities to the EG designer.

Although this book is geared toward custom-designed sign programs, including the hardware system, I mention stock hardware systems because they can sometimes play a useful role in sign programs that are primarily custom-designed. A strategy of adopting stylistically compatible stock systems, or components of them, can make good sense for certain sign types within a custom-designed program. Such situations include when ease of changeability, maintenance, and cost savings are critical factors.

Stock systems have both pros and cons. Pros include:

- *Ease of changeability and maintenance.* This feature is particularly useful for building or mall directories that feature several strips listing tenant names, which change on an ongoing basis. Many stock directory manufacturers offer convenient strip reorder services that provide new strips that match the originals in size, color, and material, as well as in typeface, type size, and type position. This ease of changeability is also useful for employee name and other signs requiring regular updating. Additionally, many stock manufacturers offer software and templates so that end users of their products can laser-print their own new inserts in-house. Other sign components are also easily replaced.

- *Design cost savings.* Because the hardware system is already designed in a stock system, EG designers don't need to spend as much time as they would on custom design of the hardware aspect of a sign program. Note, however, that even with stock systems, the EG designer still must spend time researching the various available systems, evaluating

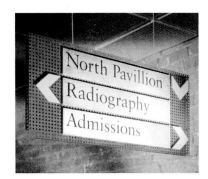

6.51 This stock sign hardware system, designed by EG designer Roger Whitehouse, features the ease of changeability common to most of these systems.

6.52 This stock sign hardware system features curved aluminum sign panel extrusions with flat aluminum caps. In this example, the custom-designed graphics are composed of a plastic insert with raised tactile and Braille lettering.

and selecting one, and configuring and specifying it for the project at hand. Of course, the EG designer must also develop the graphic system for a stock hardware system, which is important to keep in mind because a unique graphic system can serve to customize even a stock hardware system.

- *Manufacturing cost savings.* These should accrue due to the fact that sign fabricators don't have to completely reinvent the wheel when using stock systems. However, many stock systems still need to be worked, by cutting, painting, assembling, applying graphics, and so on, in the manufacturer's or fabricator's shop, to make a finished sign. This can lower the manufacturing cost savings of a stock system over a custom-designed, custom-built one.

Cons of stock hardware systems include the following:

- *Stylistic limitations.* Because each stock hardware system is predesigned, each has its own three-dimensional appearance, which often doesn't lend itself to much manipulation by the EG designer, thereby locking the designer into a given style that is undistinguishable from that of another project using the same system.

- *Size limitations.* These tend to be more of a problem with exterior stock systems than interior ones, because exterior systems often are not large enough to carry typographic sizes adequate for good readability by drivers, unless they're used in lower-speed environments such as service drives and parking areas. Even interior stock systems may not be available in sizes or proportions that suit the necessary message content or viewing conditions.

- *Quality.* Some stock systems have materials that look downright cheap, and/or have parts that fit together badly. In this regard, be aware that the photos in stock system catalogs can be deceiving, so the EG designer should always obtain actual samples of any stock systems under evaluation to assess their quality and suitability for the project at hand.

Most stock systems are available "to the trade," meaning that they can be purchased by custom sign fabricators for use in larger overall sign programs that are primarily custom. A few stock systems, however, are still available only directly from the system manufacturer, which makes them difficult for the EG designer to incorporate into a larger program involving custom fabrication, as this situation requires two different sources for the program's signs: the stock system manufacturer and the custom sign fabricator.

Sign Materials and Codes

From the preceding discussion of sign materials, it would seem an endless palette of materials is available for the EG designer to manipulate on a formal basis. It's important to know, however, that the use of certain sign materials may be prescribed by both local sign ordinances and building codes. For example, a local sign ordinance for a historical district may require that all exterior signs be made of painted, carved wood, or at least have the appearance of being made of such materials, to maintain the district's historical quality. Sign ordinances for other districts may favor the use of fabric banners, or masonry signs, or metal signs accented with neon; or there may be no restrictions on sign materials. Sign ordinances also may prohibit certain materials, such as metal sign boxes with internally illuminated plastic faces, or electronic message display devices.

Building codes can also prescribe certain sign materials, usually for life safety reasons. These codes typically concern flammability and durability of sign materials, as well as the integrity of structural and electrical systems.

Overview of Coatings and Finishes Applied to Signs

Just as there is a wide array of materials used for a signage program's hardware system, there is a wide range of coatings and finishes that provide decorative or protective surface treatments for sign materials. As in the materials section of this chapter, this section provides an overview of basic coatings and finishes for basic sign materials. And, as with materials, samples and swatches of coatings and finishes under consideration should be obtained whenever possible.

The meaning of the term *coating* is fairly clear: It's a dissimilar substance, such as paint, that's applied to the surface of another material, thereby creating a new final, outer surface. The term *finish*, however, can be more confusing because it's often used to refer to two slightly different things. On one hand, it can refer to the gloss level of an applied coating, such as matte finish paint; on the other hand, it can refer to a surface texture created on a material, such as brushed finish aluminum. In both senses, the word *finish* refers to surface treatments, but the former meaning involves a substance applied to the material, while the latter involves the material itself. To minimize this confusion, this chapter will use *gloss level* instead of *finish* when referring to coatings. Note that the ADA recommends an eggshell, or low gloss level, on sign surfaces.

Coatings

Coatings for sign hardware components include paints and clear coatings, powder coatings, porcelain enamel, patinas and oxide coatings, and vinyl or other plastic films. Each of these basic coating categories is described in more detail here.

Paints and Clear Coatings

Paints and clear coatings, often referred to as *liquid* or *organic coatings*, are probably the most common and well-known coatings for signs.

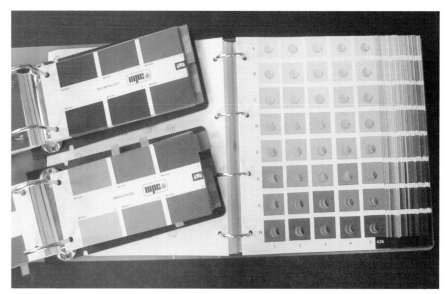

6.53

6.53 Paint swatch books from two sign paint manufacturers.

Extremely versatile, paints and clear coatings can be applied to virtually any material on the planet, and can easily conform to complex three-dimensional shapes. Not your ordinary roller-applied latex wall paint, sign paints are specifically formulated to withstand the ravages of continuous exposure to the elements—sun, rain, ice, snow, and sand—just as automotive paints are.

Manufacturers of sign paints offer a wide range of colors, including metallics and pearlescents, and gloss levels, from high gloss to dead matte. Each sign paint manufacturer offers its own range of colors, and most sign paint systems can provide custom matching of colors from another color system, providing the EG designer with a virtually unlimited palette of colors from which to choose.

Sign paints typically require a primer or base coat that's applied directly to the sign material before application of the topcoat, which contains the selected color. Sign paints are usually applied by spray gun to achieve a smooth, even surface, and are baked in a large oven after application to "cure" the paint, which dries and hardens it.

In addition to opaque sign paints, there are also liquid clear coatings, which typically perform a protective function while allowing the base material to show through, as clear polyurethane varnish protects a wood floor while allowing the beauty of the wood's grain to show. In signage, clear coats are commonly used to prevent the darkening and discoloring that oxidation causes on the "yellow" and "red" metals, such as brass or copper. Aluminum is also often clear-coated to reduce oxidation, although this is not strictly required since oxidation doesn't substantially affect the appearance or strength of aluminum. In addition to their use on unpainted materials, clear coats are often applied over painted sign materials, just as they are on many of today's automotive body components. As with opaque paints, clear coats are available in a wide range of gloss levels.

Powder Coatings

Powder coatings, like paints, provide an opaque coating over sign materials, and are generally considered more durable than paint coatings. Also like paints, powder coatings can easily conform to complex shapes. But unlike liquid paints, powder coatings are finely ground, electrically charged particles that are sprayed dry onto the sign material; the particles are held in place by an electrostatic charge until the coated material is heated in a curing oven to fuse the particles together into a uniform coating. Due to the relatively high heat involved in powder coat curing, it was originally used only on metals, but technological developments are making it increasingly possible to use powder coats on plastic and wood materials.

Powder coating is a newer process than liquid coating, so it's not as widely used as other coatings in the sign or other industries, but it is gaining ground and becoming more widely available as a coating option. However, because it's not as widely used as liquid coating, color palettes for powder coating are generally more limited than those of paints, but custom colors can be developed. Powder coats can also be metallic or clear, and can range from high to low gloss. Additionally, powder coat textures can range from smooth to wrinkled to rough.

Porcelain Enamel

Porcelain enamel is an extremely durable coating in which finely ground glass particles are applied to a metal base (typically, aluminum or steel in the sign industry) and heated to a very high temperature to fuse the particles into a smooth glass coating, which is noticeably thicker and richer than most other coatings used in the sign industry. Porcelain enameling has ancient roots in both Eastern and Western cultures, as can be seen on jewelry and other decorative objects, such as intricate Chinese cloisonné vases and lavish French Fabergé eggs.

In signs with porcelain enamel coatings, the graphics are typically fused into the coating, rather than being applied later by a different process, resulting in very durable, surface-integrated graphics. For this reason, porcelain enameling is an ideal coating for signs in high-wear environments such as subway stations and exterior exhibits. In fact, the porcelain enamel signs of the London Underground are so emblematic of that system that miniature enameled signs are sold as souvenirs of London.

Recent developments in signage applications of porcelain enameling allow graphics with a high degree of resolution and tonal range, as well as wider color ranges—although exact color matching isn't always possible.

Porcelain enamel coatings can range from transparent to opaque, but opaque colors are typically used for signage. The gloss level of porcelain coatings can range from high to low. Porcelain enamel coatings are generally used on flat sign panels, as these coatings don't readily conform to complex three-dimensional shapes. Few sign fabricators have porcelain-enameling equipment, so most porcelain work is subcontracted to specialty suppliers.

Patinas and Oxide Coatings

Patinas and oxide coatings occur only on metals and are the result of corrosion, a chemical reaction between metals and elements, such as oxygen or sulfur, in the environment. The term *patina* refers to the coatings that form on the yellow and red metals, such as bronze, brass, and copper. When exposed to weather, these metals will naturally turn brown, and then greenish, just as a copper penny does over time. This process can be hastened, and the resulting colors somewhat controlled, by the application of different chemicals to the copper alloy metals, and then sealing the surface to prevent further oxidation. Verdigris, a green or greenish-blue coating, such as that on the Statue of Liberty, is a common patina, as is a dark brown patina.

Anodizing is a process by which the oxide layer that naturally forms on the surface of aluminum is thickened by an electrochemical process, forming a very hard, integral, almost glasslike surface coating. The resulting aluminum oxide coating is effectively clear, although slightly cloudy, making clear anodized aluminum slightly less shiny than unanodized aluminum. Anodized aluminum can be colored in bright or subtle tones using various dyes, and recently developed processes allow full-color, photographic-quality graphics to be integral to a clear anodized coating.

Aluminum sheet can be anodized by the sheet manufacturer, or aluminum components can be anodized on a batch basis after assembly. Most sign fabricators don't have anodizing facilities so they either use preanodized sheets or send aluminum sign components to an outside anodizing supplier.

Rust is an oxide layer that develops on the surface of all iron and steel, except for stainless steel. Unlike the aluminum oxide coating that strengthens the surface of anodized aluminum, the iron oxide or rust that forms on steel typically weakens it and detracts from its appearance. For this reason, steel used in signage is almost always painted to prevent rust. That said, an iron oxide coating can lend a certain rustic appearance, and Cor-Ten and other weathering steels are specifically manufactured to oxidize to a reddish brown naturally over time in exterior environments without losing their strength and without extensive surface flaking.

All patinas and oxide coatings conform to complex shapes, particularly if applied under controlled versus natural conditions. Gloss levels vary with the base material, process and any additional topcoating used over the oxidized coating.

Plastic and Vinyl Films

Plastic and vinyl films are thin, flexible self-adhesive sheets that can be applied to a range of sign materials. There are clear protective films, including antigraffiti films, that are applied to materials with or without other coatings, as well as translucent and opaque films in a fairly limited range of integral colors. Other plastic films simulate metal, wood, and stone surfaces with varying degrees of success—some are very realistic, others aren't. High resolutions and unlimited colors and tonal ranges are available when white vinyl films are digitally imaged with graphics.

Vinyl and plastic films with a high gloss level are widely available, and some films have semigloss or matte surfaces. The self-adhesive films used in signage are suitable for application to primarily flat surfaces, as they typically don't conform to complex shapes.

Finishes

In an effort to reduce the confusion between the terms *finishes* and *coatings*, as used in this book, the term *finishes* refers to textures created directly on the surfaces of certain sign materials. Finish textures can be imparted to the material's surface either during the material manufacturing process or after manufacturing, typically in the sign fabricator's shop after the sign material has been worked or assembled by the shop personnel.

Most postmanufacturing-imparted finishes are created by mechanical devices using abrasives such as belt sanders and sandblasting guns, although some are created by chemical etching. The texture of mechanical finishes varies with the texture of the abrasive used—the smaller the abrasive particles, the smoother the finish, and vice versa. Although there is a wide range of both manufacturing-imparted and postmanufacturing-imparted finishes, this section will focus on the basic finishes for most of the essential sign materials.

Metal Finishes

Metal finishes can range from a completely smooth, mirrorlike polish to coarser textures consisting of scratches to the metal surface. One of the most common examples of the latter is a grained, directional texture, often called a *brushed* or *satin* finish. Another type of scratched finish is a nondirectional, or random, finish, in which the scratches have no discernable grain direction.

Other mechanical finishes for metals include sandblasting and bead blasting, which produce a uniform blanket of pits rather than scratches in the metal surface, giving the surface a more frosted look than scratch finishes. Metal surfaces are also sometimes acid-etched, which creates a finely frosted surface. Some metals are available with unique

6.54

6.55

6.54 Random-finished aluminum sign plaques provide interest and hide scratches at this dormitory in New York City.

6.55 Mirror-polished beveled edges of this sign plaque contrast with the satin finished face.

manufacturing-imparted finishes, such as embossed textures; but in the sign industry, most metal finishes are imparted in the sign fabricator's shop.

Plastic Finishes

Plastic finishes are typically imparted in the manufacturing process and are rarely altered in the sign fabricator's shop. The most common factory-imparted finish for acrylic and polycarbonate sheet is a completely smooth, mirrorlike polish, although some frosted and other textured finishes are available for these commonly used sign plastics. Other plastics used in the sign industry have factory-imparted finishes that range from completely mirrorlike smooth to pebbled to directionally grained.

Glass Finishes

Glass finishes can be imparted by the glass manufacturer or a glass supplier; the most common is the typical completely smooth polish. A wide range of glass surface textures and patterns can be created in the manufacturing process, while others are imparted by mechanical or chemical processes after manufacturing. Chemical etching and sandblasting are used to create frosted-glass finishes, with chemical etching producing a finer frosted texture than sandblasting. Mechanically produced scratch finishes are not typical for glass.

Stone Finishes

Stone finishes are typically created by the stone quarry or stone supplier. Stone finishes range from completely smooth, mirrorlike polishes to rough-hewn textures. Honed stone finishes are produced mechanically and are smooth, but nonreflective, effectively like a frosted finish on glass or metal. Thermal stone finishes are more roughly textured, created by heating the stone surface, causing it to break along the crystalline structures inherent to certain granular stones such as granite. Cleft finishes are also rough-textured, imparted along natural layers inherent to certain sedimentary stones such as slate.

Chapter Wrap-Up

This chapter has explored the many facets of designing the three-dimensional hardware objects of a sign program. This examination included development of sign shape or form, mounting, and size, as well as an overview of the basic lighting techniques, materials, coatings, and finishes the EG designer manipulates in the design of a sign program's hardware system.

The hardware system, because it is the three-dimensional embodiment of signage, is often considered the most complex design challenge, but it is that inherent complexity that also makes it the richest for creative manipulation. The hardware system is where signs come to life as physical objects in the built environment, and this chapter provided the EG designer with a sampling of the basic tips and tools for creating those objects. There's a whole world of forms, materials, processes, and techniques for the EG designer to exploit in developing a sign program's hardware system, so go out there and have fun exploring!

Project Credits

Unless indicated below, all photos were provided by the author. Project-related photos, except Figure 5.9a, represent the design work of the author's office, Calori & Vanden-Eynden / Design Consultants Ltd. (C&VE), or of the offices listed below.

Figure 5.28 courtesy of Gamble Design LLC
Figure 5.29 courtesy of Whitehouse & Company
Figure 5.31b courtesy of Roll, Barresi & Associates, Inc.
Figure 5.31c courtesy of Hunt Design Associates
Figure 5.32 courtesy of Carol Naughton + Associates, Inc.
Figure 5.35b courtesy of Phil Garvey
Figure 5.52 courtesy of Sussman/Prejza & Company, Inc.
Figure 5.55 courtesy of Poulin + Morris
Figure 5.58 courtesy of Roll, Barresi & Associates, Inc.
Figure 5.64a courtesy of Poulin + Morris
Figure 6.4 courtesy of Huie Design, Inc.
Figure 6.14 courtesy of Lorenc + Yoo Design
Figure 6.16a courtesy of Roll, Barresi & Associates, Inc.
Figure 6.18 courtesy of Carol Naughton + Associates, Inc.
Figure 6.26 courtesy of Calori & Vanden-Eynden / Design Consultants and
    Alexander Isley Inc.
Figure 6.27 courtesy of Selbert Perkins Design Collaborative
Figure 6.30 courtesy of Sussman/Prejza & Company, Inc.
Figure 6.31 courtesy of Poulin + Morris
Figure 6.37 courtesy of Carol Naughton + Associates, Inc.
Figure 6.44 courtesy of Cloud Gehshan Associates
Figure 6.51 courtesy of Whitehouse & Company

Color Insert
Color page 2 courtesy of AGS
Color page 3 courtesy of Beauchamp Group
Color page 4 courtesy of Beck & Graboski Design Office
Color page 6 courtesy of Biesek Design
Color page 7 courtesy of Chermayeff & Geismar, Inc.
Color page 8 courtesy of Cloud Gehshan Associates
Color page 10 courtesy of Gamble Design LLC
Color page 11 courtesy of Tom Graboski & Associates, Inc. Design
Color page 12 courtesy of Hunt Design Associates
Color page 13 ©Center City District, Philadelphia; design by Joel Katz
    Design Associates.
Color page 15 courtesy of Kate Keating Associates, Inc
Color page 16 courtesy of Kolar Design, Inc./Shortt Design
Color page 18 courtesy of Lebowitz|Gould|Design, Inc.
Color page 19 courtesy of Lorenc + Yoo Design
Color page 20 courtesy of Mayer/Reed
Color page 22 courtesy of Carol Naughton + Associates, Inc.
Color page 23 courtesy of Debra Nichols Design
Color page 24 courtesy of Poulin + Morris
Color page 26 courtesy of Roll, Barresi & Associates, Inc.
Color page 27 courtesy of Selbert Perkins Design Collaborative
Color page 28 courtesy of Sussman/Prejza & Company, Inc.
Color page 30 courtesy of Thinking Caps
Color page 31 courtesy of WPA, Inc.
Color page 32 courtesy of Lance Wyman Ltd. and Whitehouse & Company

Bibliography

Arthur, Paul, and Romedi Passini. *Wayfinding: People, Signs, and Architecture.* New York: McGraw-Hill Book Co., 1992.

Ashby, Michael, and Kara Johnson. *Materials and Design: The Art and Science of Material Selection in Product Design.* Oxford: Butterworth-Heinemann, 1999.

Berger, Craig. *Wayfinding: Designing and Implementing Graphic Navigational Systems.* Mies, Switzerland: RotoVision SA, 2005.

Beylerian, George, Andrew Dent, and Anita Moryadas (eds). *Material ConneXion: The Global Resource of New and Innovative Materials for Architects, Artists and Designers.* Hoboken, N.J.: John Wiley and Sons, 2005.

Carter, Rob, Ben Day, and Philip Meggs. *Typographic Design: Form and Communication.* 4th edition. Hoboken, N.J.: John Wiley and Sons, 2006.

Chermayeff, Ivan, Thomas Geismar, and Steff Geissbuhler, *designing:.* New York: Graphis Inc., 2003.

Ching, Francis D. K. *Architectural Graphics.* 4th edition. New York: John Wiley and Sons, 2003.

Craig, James, Irene Korol Scala, and William Bevington. *Designing with Type: The Essential Guide to Typography.* 5th edition. New York: Watson-Guptill Publications, 2006.

Deibler Finke, Gail. *City Signs: Innovative Urban Graphics.* New York: Madison Square Press: Distributed in the U.S. and Canada by Van Nostrand Reinhold, 1994.

———.*Urban Identities.* New York: Madison Square Press, 1998.

———. Edited by Leslie Galley Dilworth. *You Are Here: Graphics that Direct, Explain & Entertain.* New York: Watson-Guptill Publications, 1998.

Elam, Kimberly. *Grid Systems: Principles of Organizing Type.* New York: Princeton Architectural Press, 2004.

Erhart, Joseph. *Guidelines for Airport Signing and Graphics: Terminals and Landside*, 2nd ed., Celebration, FL: Apple Designs, Inc, 1994. Also available on CD from Apple Designs at www.appledesigns.net/guidelines.htm.

Follis, John, and Dave Hammer. *Architectural Signing and Graphics.* New York: Whitney Library of Design, 1979.

Griffin, Kenneth W. *Building Type Basics for Transit Facilities.* Hoboken, N.J.: John Wiley and Sons, 2004.

Hora, Mies. *Official Signs & Icons 2.* Stony Point, N.Y.: Ultimate Symbol Inc., 2005.

Hunt, Wayne. (ed.) *Designing & Planning Environmental Graphics.* New York: Madison Square Press, 1994.

——— *Environmental Graphics: Projects & Process.* New York: Madison Square Press, 2003.

———. *Urban Entertainment Graphics: Theme Parks & Entertainment Environments.* New York: Madison Square Press: Van Nostrand Reinhold, 1997.

Itten, Johannes. *The Elements of Color.* New York: Van Nostrand Reinhold, 1970.

Kunz, Willi. *Typography: Macro- and Microaesthetic.* Sulgen, Switzerland: Verlag Niggli AG, 2004.

Koberg, Don, and Jim Bagnall. *The Universal Traveler: A Soft-Systems Guide to Creativity, Problem-Solving, and the Process of Reaching Goals.* Menlo Park, Calif.: Crisp Learning, 2003.

Lesko, Jim. *Industrial Design: Materials and Manufacturing.* New York: John Wiley and Sons, 1999.

Lupton, Ellen. *Thinking with Type: A Critical Guide for Designers, Writers, Editors, & Students.* New York: Princeton Architectural Press, 2004.

Lynch, Kevin. *The Image of the City.* Cambridge, Mass.: The MIT Press, 1960.

McLendon, Charles B., and Mick Blackstone. *Signage: Graphic Communications in the Built World.* New York: McGraw-Hill, 1982.

Meggs, Philip, and Alston W. Purvis. *Meggs' History of Graphic Design.* 4th edition. Hoboken, N.J.: John Wiley and Sons, 2006.

Mollerup, Per. *Wayshowing: A Guide to Environmental Signage Principles & Practices.* Baden, Switzerland: Lars Muller, 2006.

Ramsey, Charles George, and John Ray Jr. Hoke (eds). *Architectural Graphic Standards, Tenth Edition.* New York: John Wiley and Sons, 2000.

Tilley, Alvin R., and Henry Dreyfuss Associates. *The Measure of Man and Woman: Human Factors in Design.* New York: John Wiley and Sons, 2001.

Trulove, James Grayson. *This Way: Signage Design for Public Spaces.* Gloucester, Mass.: Rockport Publishers, Inc., 2000.

White, Alexander W. *The Elements of Graphic Design: Space, Unity, Page Architecture, and Type.* New York: Allworth Press, 2002.

Index